The South Staffordshire Railway

Volume One

Dudley-Walsall-Lichfield-Burton
(including the Black Country Branches)

by
Bob Yate

British Library Cataloguing in Publication Data
A Record for this book is available from the British Library
ISBN 978 0 85361 700 6

Typeset by Oakwood Graphics.
Repro by PKmediaworks, Cranborne, Dorset.
Printed by Cambrian Printers, Aberystwyth, Ceredigion.

To Sandra

LNWR '7F' class 0-8-0 No. 49411 standing in platform 3 at Walsall station on 11th June, 1960. The extent that the platform awnings covered the entire length of the platforms can be appreciated in this view.   *Alec Swain/Transport Treasury*

Front cover: A Fowler '4F' class 0-6-0 taking the Brownhills line at Ryecroft Junction with a lengthy haul of empty coal wagons, almost certainly bound for Norton Junction yard on a frosty day in 1962.   *R. Selvey*

Rear cover, top: Bescot's pride and joy was this double chimney Stanier 'Black Five' 4-6-0 No. 44766, seen here leaving the former MR carriage sidings at Pleck and about to pass beneath the Corporation Street road bridge. It was working the empty stock for an excursion into Walsall station, probably in 1963.   *R. Selvey*

Rear cover, bottom: An unidentified class '31' Brush A1A-A1A seen banking a steel train away from Great Bridge towards Dudley.   *K. Hodgkins*

Published by The Oakwood Press (Usk), P.O. Box 13, Usk, Mon., NP15 1YS.
E-mail: sales@oakwoodpress.co.uk
Website: www.oakwoodpress.co.uk

Contents

Introduction

At the time of the inception of the South Staffordshire Railway (SSR), rail traffic across Birmingham was seriously impeded by the restrictive nature of the route arrangements around Curzon Street and Lawley Street stations. This new railway was intended as a through route for traffic to and from Southern England and South Wales to Northern England, that would bypass this bottleneck. Its route northwards from the Oxford, Worcester & Wolverhampton Railway (OWWR) at Dudley, would provide links to the Great Western Railway (GWR) at Wednesbury (then under construction) and the London & North Western Railway (LNWR) at Bescot and Lichfield, reaching the Midland Railway (MR) at Wichnor Junction, with running powers onwards to Burton.

However, the intention was not entirely achieved. In the first place, the sprawling industrialization of the West Midlands area that the line traversed proved to yield so much traffic, that its capacity was fully taken up in servicing these needs. Secondly, the amount of through freight traffic was only ever minimal, mostly because the early routes were soon revised to virtually eliminate the bottleneck. Through passenger traffic over the SSR never materialized. Nonetheless, this line was successful with the more modest nature of its traffic, which with the development of the Cannock Chase coalfield reached enormous proportions in the first half of the 20th century. Local passenger traffic grew to acceptable levels, but was destined to be eventually withdrawn from the South Staffordshire Railway main line and its branches. The exception was the Walsall to Birmingham commuter service, which however, mostly used the LNWR lines.

The promoters, owners and lessees of the line had numerous other local business interests which not only complemented the railway, but provided employment and betterment of the local populace. The individuals involved earned the respect and gratitude of the local communities, although such is the nature of mankind that this has not been entirely remembered in any lasting form.

The mostly local traffic drew on a number of interesting operating procedures, as well as a wide variety of locomotives from those of the original SSR, through a miscellany of LNWR and MR types and onwards through the standard London, Midland & Scottish Railway (LMS) and British Railways (BR) types, well into the modern diesel era.

Eventually, the middle portion from Walsall to Anglesea Sidings (Brownhills) was closed entirely in 1984, and onwards to Lichfield City in 2001. The southern half of the route, from Dudley to Bescot was closed entirely in 1993, although its future as part of the Midland Metro system appears to be secure.

In this volume, we shall look at the construction and development of the main line, as well as the small branches to Dudley Port, the Darlaston Loop, and the Princes End branch, plus those mineral lines extending eastwards. A second volume will follow, which will examine the line from Walsall through Cannock to Rugeley, together with the numerous mineral lines that made up the railway complex serving the Cannock Chase coalfield.

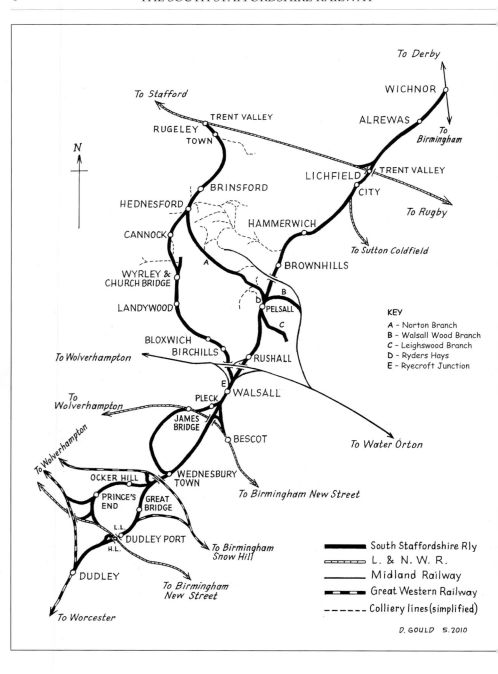

KEY

A – Norton Branch
B – Walsall Wood Branch
C – Leighswood Branch
D – Ryders Hays
E – Ryecroft Junction

South Staffordshire Rly
L. & N. W. R.
Midland Railway
Great Western Railway
Colliery lines (simplified)

D. GOULD 5.2010

Abbreviations

The following abbreviations are used throughout the text:

BCN	Birmingham Canal Navigation
BoT	Board of Trade
BR	British Railways (later British Rail)
BWDR	Birmingham, Wolverhampton & Dudley Railway
CCWR	Cannock Chase & Wolverhampton Railway
dmu	Diesel multiple unit
emu	Electric multiple unit
EWS	English, Welsh & Scottish Railways
GJR	Grand Junction Railway
GWR	Great Western Railway
HST	High speed train
L&BR	London & Birmingham Railway
LMR	London Midland Region of BR
LMS	London, Midland & Scottish Railway
LNWR	London & North Western Railway
MBR	Manchester & Birmingham Railway
MR	Midland Railway
NSR	North Staffordshire Railway
OWWR	Oxford, Worcester & Wolverhampton Railway
SSJR	South Staffordshire Junction Railway
SSR	South Staffordshire Railway
TVMGJR	Trent Valley, Midlands & Grand Junction Railway
TVR	Trent Valley Railway
WMR	West Midland Railway
WR	Western Region of BR
WWR	Wolverhampton & Walsall Railway

The company seal for the South Staffordshire Railway.

Courtesy National Railway Museum

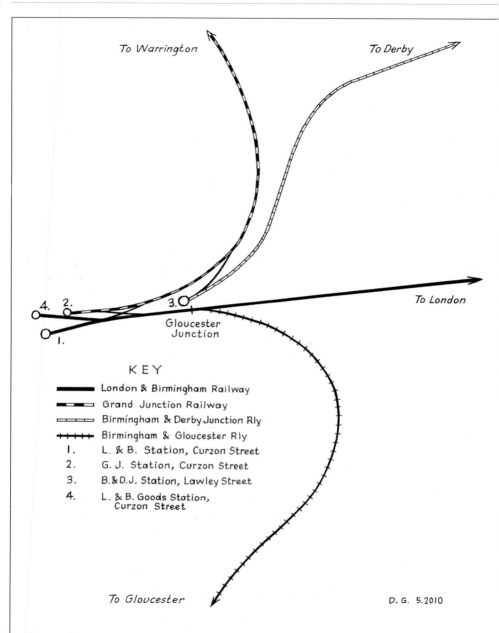

KEY

━━━━	London & Birmingham Railway
━─━□	Grand Junction Railway
▭▭▭	Birmingham & Derby Junction Rly
┼┼┼┼┼	Birmingham & Gloucester Rly
1.	L. & B. Station, Curzon Street
2.	G. J. Station, Curzon Street
3.	B. & D. J. Station, Lawley Street
4.	L. & B. Goods Station, Curzon Street

To Warrington

To Derby

To London

4. 2. 3.
1.

Gloucester
Junction

To Gloucester

D. G. 5.2010

Birmingham approaches in 1845. An indication of how all lines led to the terminus stations at Curzon Street, thus requiring reversals for through traffic.

Chapter One

The Formation and Organization
of the Company

Background

At the time of the first dawn of our railway, most of the railway routes ran on a north-west or north-east to south-east axis (as indicated in the accompanying map), so that there had been little interest in a potential route flowing north to south-west. In any case, the lines opened at this time were still discovering their traffic potentials and their limitations. Primary amongst the limitations was the congestion of traffic around Curzon Street and Lawley Street stations in Birmingham. Finding a solution was to tax the ingenuity of the relevant companies to the utmost, until finally the outcome was the opening of New Street station in 1854.

Indeed, prior to this time, the only incursion into what was later to become South Staffordshire Railway territory was a branch line included in Chapter Nine of the Grand Junction Railway Act (Vict. 5 & 6) of 12th June, 1835, that was to run from Wednesbury to Walsall. However, this was never built, possibly because the Grand Junction Railway (GJR) saw itself as primarily a passenger railway and did not foresee this as a valuable feeder line.

Dudley was seen as an attractive target by several other promoters, but their intentions all reached this town from the south, and it was left to the Oxford, Worcester and Wolverhampton Railway to reach the town. Although incorporated on 4th August, 1845, it did not reach Dudley until 1851, a year after the SSR had commenced passenger operation. Relations between the two companies (and their successors) were generally satisfactory over the years, but there were inevitably disagreements, mostly over traffic matters, and we shall look at these later.

The Midland Railway had been formed in 1844, and also had its sights set on Walsall and Dudley, but was initially quite happy to have the SSR join its system at Wichnor Junction, in exchange for running powers over this line to the two towns. The MR was wise enough to realise that reaching these towns was sufficiently valuable to justify backing the new line financially, as we shall see.

Similarly, the GJR eventually realised that not only did the new line not interfere with its traffic, but could prove to be a positive benefit, worthy of its financial backing. This move had the secondary purpose of limiting the MR influence in the area. Earlier, the GJR had been backing the OWWR when an independent line, as it wanted its own line to London, separate from the London & Birmingham Railway (L&BR) with whom it did not enjoy the best relations. Matters changed completely with the formation of the LNWR (*see below*), and the Great Western Railway involvement with the OWWR. So by combining with the MR on the SSR project, it was hoped that they would be able to contain the advancement of the GWR broad gauge into the West Midlands. This they achieved, in that the OWWR broad gauge lines never reached beyond

Evesham. However, the subsequent GWR backing (and eventual purchase) of the Birmingham, Wolverhampton & Dudley Railway (BWDR) meant that the broad gauge did reach Wolverhampton from Birmingham, but that their branch to Dudley was destined to become standard gauge.

The year 1846 was the height of the 'Railway Mania', and saw the formation of the London and North Western Railway on 16th July by the amalgamation of the GJR, the L&BR, and the Manchester & Birmingham Railway (MBR). On 3rd August, the BWDR was incorporated, the construction of New Street station was authorized, and the enabling Act for the South Staffordshire Junction Railway (SSJR) was passed (Vict. 9 & 10, cap. 300) - this being the first name adopted for the company. There had been little opposition to the Act when presented at Parliament, which comes as no real surprise considering its backers.

Coincidentally with the promotion of the SSJR, a separate company, the Trent Valley, Midlands & Grand Junction Railway (TVMGJR) was also being promoted in 1845 to construct a 16½ mile line from Walsall to Wichnor, with a triangular junction at Lichfield to the Trent Valley Railway (which was under construction and to be worked by the GJR, L&BR and MBR). The subscribers were:

> The Honourable Colonel Anson
> Edmund Peel
> Joshua Proctor Westhead
> Henry Newbery
> James Durham
> Henry Tootal
> James Walkinshaw
> The Honourable Captain Carnegie
> Robert Scott
> John Ellis

This company had an authorized share capital of £420,000 made up from 35,000 shares of £12 each, and received its enabling Act on the same day, 3rd August, 1846 (Vict. 9 & 10, cap. 316).

Formation of the Company

The Provisional Committee of the SSJR was formed from the original promoters, and procured the Bill to be passed through Parliament for the authorization and incorporation of the company and the construction of a line from a junction with the OWWR at Dudley to Walsall (Albert Street) where it made an end-on junction with the TVMGJR, plus a branch from Walsall to the GJR at Bescot. At a meeting at 38 Parliament Street, Westminster on 2nd July, 1845 the initial agreements made previously on 23rd February, and 13th June, 1845 with the TVMGJR for their subsequent amalgamation were appended in Committee to the Bill, although these agreements were later to be amended, cancelled and then reintroduced, as we shall see.

The first meeting of the members of the SSJR was held on 10th July, 1845 at the George Hotel, in Walsall. Initially 105 persons had applied for 5,020 shares, but the final list of members totalled some 85 persons, all of whom comprised the rather extensive Provisional Committee, but in reality may be considered as the first subscribers to the railway. This committeee was headed by Charles Smith Forster as Chairman. Subsequently, in the period up to 4th November, 1845, a further 30 were added, and eight withdrew. A Committee of Management was elected at the first meeting, from which any three could form a quorum, and comprised:

Richard Croft Chawner, Wall, Lichfield (Chairman)
Charles Smith Forster, Hampstead Hall, near Wall, Lichfield
Lord Hatherton, Teddesley Park, Staffordshire
Captain Dyott, Freeford Hall, Lichfield
The Honourable Edward Richard Littleton, Hatherton Hall, Staffordshire
plus Messrs. Henry Hill, Charles Forster Cotterill, John Perks, John Bright, Arthur Adams and John Mott

A Traffic Committee was also elected at this time, comprising the same five first-named gentlemen as above, plus Messrs William Matthews, Charles Forster Cotterill, William Harrison, Henry Crane and John Brearley. The capital of the company was proposed at £500,000 in £25 shares (although this was later altered to £525,000), with a deposit being payable of £1 7s. 6d. per share on application.

A formal proposal for amalgamation with the TVMGJR was proposed on 14th July, 1845, but it was noted at a further Provisional Committee meeting only 10 days later that the amalgamation could not proceed because of legal difficulties. This same meeting approved the making available of 5,000 shares to the GJR. The meeting also noted that Joseph Locke had turned down the offer of Engineer for the line, and it was agreed that an offer would be made for this post to Isambard Kingdom Brunel. This came to nothing as Brunel replied that he was too busy with other lines to be able to take up the appointment, but Locke subsequently offered to act as Consulting Engineer. This was recorded at a Management Committee meeting held at the Swan Hotel in Lichfield on 7th August, 1845, and just over a week later, on 15th August, the TVMGJR again turned down the offer of amalgamation. On 21st August, another meeting, this time held at the company offices in Bradford Street, Walsall, agreed to make 1,000 shares available to the OWWR. Shortly after, on 6th September, the committee was informed that the TVMGJR was now ready to merge. On 3rd August, 1846 the enabling Acts for both companies were passed, as mentioned above. Section 72 of the SSJR Act gave powers for amalgamation with the TVMGJR, and Section 51 of their Act gave powers to amalgamate with the SSJR. The merger went ahead with commendable speed, and was effective from 6th October, on which date the newly enlarged company also changed its name to the somewhat shorter 'South Staffordshire Railway Company', dropping the word 'Junction' used previously.

The first meeting of the new company took place on the same day, 6th October, 1846, at the company offices in Bradford Street, Walsall. The Directors were elected (not surprisingly from both previous companies, and also representing the LNWR and MR interests, as well as independent shareholders) as follows:

Charles Forster	Edward Richard Littleton	Colonel Anson
Edward Butler	Robert Scott	Captain Dyott
Richard Chawner	Henry Tootal	Richard Greene
Thomas Booth	Joseph Hornby	Philip Williams
Peter Potter	George Holyoake	Isaac Badger
Henry Newbery	Joseph Walker	Samuel Beale
Henry Myatt	Sir E.A. Scott	Lord Hatherton

At a meeting of the Land & Works Committee on 13th October, authority was given to survey the line to Cannock - but further reference to this line will be deferred until Volume Two of this work.

The share capital of the new company was fixed at £945,000, being £525,000 from the former SSJR and £420,000 from the TVMGJR, approved at a Directors Meeting on 25th January, 1847. The LNWR eventually subscribed £131,000 to the new company.

Further Acts were required to confirm the amalgamation of the two companies, and these were both passed on 9th July, 1847 (Vict. 10 & 11, cap. 189 for the SSJR, and Vict. 10 & 11, cap. 194 for the TVMGJR), which also confirmed the new company name. The SSJR Act also permitted the construction of additional lines from Walsall to Cannock, as well as the Wyrley and Norton branches - although these latter two were not built under the auspices of the SSR. This same Act permitted running powers over the MR from Wichnor Junction into Burton.

It is appropriate at this point to introduce some of the early officers and managers of the company. Charles Forster had been elected as Chairman of the Board of Directors and Richard Chawner as Secretary at the first Board Meeting mentioned above, and at the same time John Robinson McClean (often spelt as M'Clean) was appointed as Engineer and later, a Mr Lee was confirmed as Resident Engineer. John Douglas Payne was appointed as General Manager, having come from the Birmingham & Gloucester Railway, which was formed in 1836. He will be remembered for his part in the notorious 'Battle of the Gauges' at Gloucester, which was staged to give the Gauge Commissioners a shocking display of confusion arising from the transhipment of goods and passengers between trains of differing gauges, thus ensuring their sympathy for the standardization of the rail gauge. John N. Brown was appointed as goods manager, with his office being located at Great Bridge, as this was most convenient for the many major customers with their ironworks and foundries in this vicinity. John Brown had also been with John Payne at Gloucester, and when in 1855 John Payne resigned, John Brown took over as General Manager, although combining this with his continuing role as goods manager. He eventually died on 21st January, 1895 quite suddenly, aged 74 years. By this time his local reputation had enabled him to become Chairman of the Birmingham District & Counties Bank, as well as holding Directorships with the Gloucester Railway Carriage & Wagon Company Ltd, the Patent Shaft & Axletree Company Ltd, and the South Staffordshire Waterworks Company Ltd.

George Potter Neele will be remembered for his major work *Railway Reminiscences* (originally published in 1904 by McCorquodale), and much information from this important book relating to the early operation of the SSR has been used in the compilation of this volume. His association with the SSR began when he applied for the position of General Manager in 1849, which was eventually awarded to John Payne. Fortunately, he was offered, and accepted the post of chief clerk which he filled until the lease of the line was taken over by the LNWR in 1861, after which he enjoyed a remarkable career with the LNWR, finishing as superintendent of the line. The Locomotive Department was headed by George Wells, who had served his time at the L&BR locomotive workshops at Wolverton. He was replaced in 1851 by Henry Brogden, who was the son of George Brogden, an associate of John McClean, and whom we shall meet again in Chapter Four. Henry's brother Alexander was also appointed around this time to examine the running costs of the company, and eventually became the MP for Wednesbury. Coincidentally with these appointments, McClean's brother-in-law, J.R. Newsam became the accountant, and was considered to be the typical 'courtly Irish gentleman', becoming popular in Walsall and enhancing the influence of the Masonic Lodge in that town.

The appointment of friends and relatives into positions of trust must not necessarily be seen as simply that of nepotism, for it should be remembered that these were relatively early days in the management of railways, and the individual railways grew at such a ferocious pace that they became some of the largest businesses in the country very quickly. It was clearly desirable to ensure that the persons placed as managers were those who had proved themselves in similar positions on other railways. However, such persons were in short supply, and the railways employing them would do everything to keep their best personnel. The next best criteria was that of persons who were personally known to have the qualities sought for the positions, and this is what often occurred, although this doesn't mean that a certain amount of favouritism was never practised !

Horatio Bennett became the Company Secretary, having been one of the leading lawyers of Walsall, in which position he also represented the company as its solicitor. Mr Edward Adams of Westminster, was commissioned as the company's Architect, principally in charge of the design of the stations, goods depots and other structures. He was an old Queen Mary's Grammar School boy, and had designed the new Queen Mary's School in Lichfield Street, Walsall which was built in a very similar style to the new Walsall station erected in 1849.

Following the takeover of the lease in 1861 (*see Chapter Four*), the LNWR appointed some of its own men into the more senior positions. William Baker became Engineer, replacing McClean who had surrendered the lease, and Charles Caukwell became General Manager, succeeding John Brown. Finally, Richard Moon (Chairman of the LNWR) became Chairman of the SSR until it was vested in the LNWR as from 15th July, 1867.

Gradient Profile of the SSR Main Line

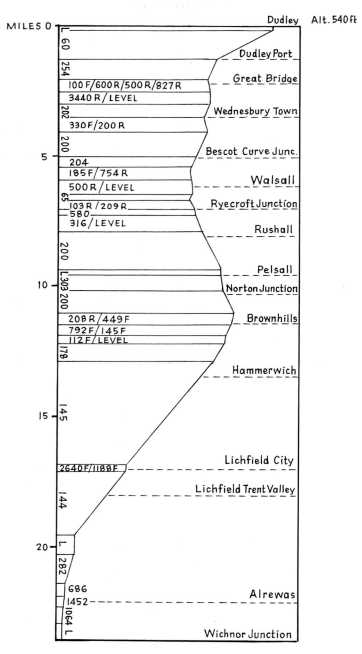

For the sake of clarity, minor gradient changes of less than ¼ mile have been omitted.

Chapter Two

Construction and Opening of the Main Line

Planning

The original Act of 3rd August, 1846 gave the SSJR authority to construct the line from Walsall to Dudley, plus spurs from Pleck to the GJR (LNWR) at James Bridge, and the Bescot curve again joining the GJR (LNWR). Also included was a branch line from Rushall to lime pits at Linley (or Lindley) which was never built. The TVMGJR Act had given powers for the line from an end-on junction with the SSJR at Walsall (Albert Street) to the MR at Wichnor, with a spur to join the Trent Valley Railway (TVR) at Lichfield. The SSR had surveyed its own route from Walsall to Lichfield, running via Rushall, Walsall Wood, Ogley Hay and Wall. However, the TVMGJR route, surveyed by Robert Stephenson, via Rushall, Pelsall, Brownhills and Hammerwich was chosen.

Matters began to move quite quickly after the amalgamation, and at a meeting of the Land & Works Committee on 10th October, 1846 it was decided that Contract No. 1 would be for the section from Walsall to Bescot and would be put out to tender. On 9th November, 1846 a further meeting noted that the entire line from the GJR at Bescot to Walsall had been staked out. Furthermore, branches from Walsall to Cannock, as well as the Norton and Wyrley branches had been surveyed, although authority for the construction of these lines had not yet been sought, let alone granted. McClean reported to the committee that he believed the line to Cannock should be continued northwards to join the TVR at Rugeley. The minutes of this meeting do not record the response, which was presumably negative, but McClean's foresight in raising this issue at this time can be considered as remarkable.

A measure of the satisfaction with which the Directors viewed the work of John McClean (acting through his own business of McClean & Stileman, of Birmingham) is that at a Board Meeting on 27th July, 1847 it was agreed that he would be paid at the rate of £350 per mile 'for engineering'.

At the same meeting, the Board of Directors reported that the Bill approving the amalgamation had included the necessary powers for the additional lines and that had been passed (Vict. 10 & 11, cap. 189) on 9th July. However, the powers for the extra lines were allowed to lapse, and were not renewed for some seven years, when an Act was passed on 2nd June, 1854 (Vict. 17, cap. 53) which authorized the Cannock and Norton branches. The branch to Wyrley was finally included in the SSR Act of 23rd July, 1855 (Vict. 18 & 19, cap. 175) which also included the lines from Wednesbury to Darlaston, Wednesbury to Tipton and the Walsall Wood (Leighswood) branch. The delay is attributed to a general lack of confidence in the immediate business future at this time, which lasted until 1849, and was only really boosted by the Great Exhibition of 1851.

Having detailed the various legal requirements for each of the lines, we can now examine the construction and opening of each of the lines.

Walsall to Bescot

Tenders for the construction of the 1 mile 62 chain line were received in December 1846 from Coker & Fitzpatrick, Brassey & Company, Frost & Bate, Simmons & Ritson, and James & John Frost. The tender from Coker & Fitzpatrick (which was recorded as being valid until 31st December) was accepted. Although details of the unsuccessful bids have not survived that of Coker & Fitzpatrick is summarized as follows:

	£	s.	d.
Earthworks	2,822	10	6
Permanent Way	1,958	19	6
Culverts	234	13	4
Fencing, bridges	1,042	10	0
Other	327	0	0
Contingency	100	0	0
Total	6,485	13	4

The 'Other' category included £300 to cover maintenance of the line for 12 months from completion.

However, the Board of Directors were informed on 1st January, 1847 that Mr Coker's name had been withdrawn from the tender, and replaced by a Mr Richard Mullon, whose sureties were James Park of Sedgley Park and John Harnett of Bloomsbury. Less than three weeks later, on 19th January, the Directors were informed that Mr Mullon had now declined, and he had been replaced by William Jew (sometimes referred to as William Tew). The change of partners for Mr Fitzpatrick was now settled.

Earlier, on 15th December, 1846 the Directors awarded the contract for 1,000 tons of rails to Bagnall's of Wednesbury at £9 18s. 6d. per ton, and 250 tons of chairs at £6 18s. 6d. per ton. In January, 1847 eleven tenders were received for sleepers, and the contract was given on 25th January, 1847 to Harrison & Singleton.

The minutes of the company's meetings contain little on the progress of the works for this short line, so these were presumably completed without difficulty. The Secretary of the company requested approval to open the railway in a letter to the Board of Trade, enclosing the Engineer's certificate, on 14th October, 1847. Subsequently, Captain Wynne inspected the line and reported that the line contained no bridges, other than one viaduct over the River Tame constructed of five 20 ft timber spans, each with brick abutments. The culverts were built using blue Staffordshire brick. There were six level crossings - one over a turnpike road, one over a footpath and four on occupation roads. The turnpike level crossing was fitted with a gate that shut across the road, and next to it was a lodge for the watchman. It should be mentioned here that most early railways were constructed with level crossings rather than bridges, not necessarily as a cost-cutting measure, but because level crossings were perfectly adequate for the amount of traffic on both railways and roads at that time. Rails installed were of 72 lb. per yard, and the chairs used were either 19 lb. or 24 lb. each. Switches (points) were of the Fox & Miller patent at the junction with the LNWR, and a semaphore signal was erected there as protection. A turntable had been installed at Walsall. Captain Wynne's approval was granted, and the date of opening of the line was fixed for Monday 1st November, 1847.

Two accounts of the opening of the line are worthy of reproduction here. Firstly, from the *Wolverhampton Chronicle* of Wednesday 3rd November, 1847:

SOUTH STAFFORDSHIRE RAILWAY

The Birmingham and Walsall branch of this railway was opened on Monday morning last. The first train, consisting of nine carriages, arrived from Birmingham at the Walsall station at twenty-five minutes past nine, and was greeted by some thousands of spectators and the slamming of the bells at St. Matthew's church. The time occupied in the turning of the engine and tender, affixing them to the rear of the train, and receiving the passengers (seventy-five in number), occupied fifteen minutes, when the train returned to Birmingham, where it arrived in twenty-three minutes. Between two and three o' clock in the afternoon, and seven and eight in the evening, the same process took place, the number of passengers increasing each time. The trains will run from Birmingham to Walsall, and return, three times every day, except Sunday, when they will be restricted to two journeys, one in the morning and one in the evening. The station at Bridgeman-place, Walsall, is pleasantly situated, being adjacent to the race course, from which the trains may be observed for some distance; and there is no intervening object between the line and the houses in Bradford–street, from which the trains may be seen the whole length of the meadows, and the line from Birmingham to Walsall being chiefly on the level, renders the journey particularly pleasing to passengers. The benefits accruing from the opening of this branch of the South Staffordshire Railway must be perceptible, as in cases of urgency parties residing in Birmingham and Walsall may be brought together in a much shorter period that they hitherto could be; and, as provision is made for allowing passengers to carry a considerable weight of luggage (expressed in the time bill), it must be highly advantageous to persons trading between the two towns.

Secondly, the *Staffordshire Advertiser* of Saturday 6th November, 1847:

SOUTH STAFFORDSHIRE RAILWAY
OPENING OF THE LINE FROM BESCOT TO WALSALL

This portion of the line, which connects the town of Walsall with the London and North Western Railway at Bescot Bridge, was opened with much spirit on Monday last, the line having been previously examined and favourably reported upon by the Government Inspector, Captain Symonds [*sic*]. The first train from Birmingham was dispatched at 8 h 45 m, and contained an immense number of passengers, including several of the Directors of the line, who expressed themselves fully satisfied with the regular and easy motion. Crowds of persons assembled at different points of the branch line, to catch a glimpse of the train. During the day, three trains ran each way, carrying no less than three hundred passengers.

After arranging matters satisfactorily, the Directors dined together at the George Hotel, where a sumptuous entertainment was provided, and invitations given to the principal inhabitants of the district.

Not specifically mentioned in either account is that the first trains used LNWR locomotives and carriages, as the SSR rolling stock had not yet been delivered. The second account is interesting in that it describes the Inspector as being Captain Symonds, whereas the SSR records, including correspondence, give him as being Captain Wynne. For once, the newspaper reports spared readers the usual lengthy description of the guests attending the event, and details of the speeches (normally very self congratulatory) that were given before, during and after such dinners.

Until the opening of the line, the nearest railway station, opened by the GJR and by this time operated by the LNWR was at Bescot, and from its opening in 1837 was named 'Bescot Bridge'. It was renamed 'Walsall' around 1842, but reverted to 'Bescot Bridge' with the opening of the SSR. Passengers wanting to travel to Walsall hitherto had to rely on a coach service from this station to the George Hotel in the centre of Walsall. As the station was positioned north of the junction with the SSR, the coach service continued for those passengers travelling from the north, until the station was closed in 1850. An LNWR service of two daily trains from here to Birmingham had previously been provided, at a cost of 1s. 6d. for third class and 2s. 0d. for 1st class. The original station was replaced by one further south serving both lines, and being known simply as 'Bescot', which was eventually renamed 'Bescot Stadium ' in 1991. Meanwhile the original station had not been demolished, and was reopened on 1st February, 1881 as 'Wood Green (Old Bescot)', finally closing for good on 5th May, 1941.

The new SSR station in Walsall was sited on the southern side of Bridgeman Place, and was only ever intended as a temporary station. There are no descriptions of this station, but it must have been a rather unprepossessing structure. Because its replacement was not available for another two years, the local people expressed their feelings that Walsall was being treated 'as an out of the way place'.

Concluding the account of the opening of this first line, it is interesting to note that at a Board Meeting on 1st March, 1849 it was reported that 'electric telegraph had been established between Walsall and the LNWR at Bescot'. This was presumably in advance of this method of communication being adopted along the remainder of the routes.

Walsall to Wichnor

The line from Walsall to Wichnor Junction was 16 miles and 77½ chains (just a fraction under 17 miles, as originally measured). Tenders were invited, but details of those submitted have not survived, although we do know that the contract (Contract No. 3) for this entire section was awarded at a meeting of the Board of Directors on 17th May, 1847 to Thomas Earle.

Matters soon got under way, and the sometimes lengthy procedure of obtaining the necessary land proceeded reasonable well. It is worth noting in this regard that shares to the value of £100 were made available to the Earl of Bradford so as to facilitate the exchange of land in Walsall area, and a Directors Report of 13th March, 1848 commented that all the required land had been purchased. It also recorded that the contractor had shifted 345,000 cubic yards of earth, had laid 4,800 bricks, and was currently employing 766 men and 111 horses. It was anticipated that the line would be finished by November, a forecast that proved more than a little optimistic. A subsequent Directors Report, on 8th July, 1848 recorded the approval to erect a temporary 'locomotive station' at Walsall, and one at Alrewas - these were possibly for the purposes of the contractors, although no locomotives have been discovered to have been used by the contractors. Possibly, it was decided that these temporary structures would suffice until a realistic idea could be determined of the exact requirements.

On 11th September, 1848 McClean reported that only four bridges and some light embankments remained to be completed. Evidently, the Summer weather had been favourable, allowing work to proceed as planned. The Winter months slowed down the work somewhat, but Captain G. Wynne inspected the line on 1st March, 1849 and recorded that there were 12 level crossings with gates and keepers' lodges, but that the junction with the MR at Wichnor had not yet been put in, with about 200 yards of approach track to be laid. Nonetheless, he approved the line from Walsall to Lichfield, totalling 10 miles and 50 chains (just over 10½ miles), but deferred the remainder until the junction was complete.

This was soon accomplished, and on 4th April he inspected the remainder of the line, including the junction, noting that there were two signals on the MR protecting the junction, and that auxiliary signals were placed 400 yards from these. His letter the following day gave approval for the remainder of the line, which opened four days later. Illustrating just how anxious the company were to open the new line without further delay, the following advertisement appeared in the *Staffordshire Advertiser* on Saturday 7th April, 1849:

SOUTH STAFFORDSHIRE RAILWAY
OPENING OF A FURTHER PORTION OF THE LINE

On and after Monday, April 9th, this line will be OPENED FROM WALSALL TO LICHFIELD, ALREWAS and BURTON, where it joins the Leicester and Swannington, North Staffordshire, and Midland Railways, by which a great saving of mileage to railway communication will be gained by the South Staffordshire Railway.

Time Tables may be obtained at all stations on the line.

Omnibuses from the Red Cow Coach Office, Wolverhampton (through Willenhall) meet the trains at Walsall Station.

J.D. Payne   General Manager
Walsall   April 2nd, 1849

The following extract from the *Wolverhampton Chronicle* of Wednesday 11th April, 1849 gives a very full account of the opening day on the 9th April, and most is reproduced here, as it also provides a useful description of parts of the line at that time:

OPENING OF THE SOUTH STAFFORDSHIRE RAILWAY

Monday last witnessed a main step towards the completion of this undertaking in the opening of the line for the conveyance of passengers and parcels from Walsall to Lichfield and Alrewas, and thence to Burton-upon-Trent, shortly before reaching which, by a junction with the Birmingham and Derby railway, it is brought into communication with the leading lines to the northern and eastern parts of the kingdom. As many of our readers are aware, a partial opening of the line, that is from Walsall to Birmingham, took place some time ago. By the opening of this present portion of the railway the undertaking may be considered almost complete, the branch line from Walsall by Wednesbury and Tipton to Dudley (where the line will come into the Oxford, Worcester, and Wolverhampton railway) alone remaining to be constructed, in order to open a communication as nearly as possible direct from Worcester and Bristol to Hull, and thus connecting by railway the

Early engraving of the first Lichfield Trent Valley station, opened by the LNWR in August 1849.
Courtesy Lichfield Archives

Early engraving of the first Lichfield City station, opened by the SSR in April 1849.
Courtesy Lichfield Archives

THE RAILWAY STATION LICHFIELD

Bristol Channel with the Humber and the North Sea. In the course of the line junctions also take place directly with the London and North Western, the Trent Valley, and Leicester and Swannington railways, and immediately with the North Staffordshire and Midland Counties, and other lines ; an advantage resulting from its peculiar and almost central position among the railways we have noticed.

The opening of the portion of the line we have more particularly noticed was announced by advertisements and other means, and an impression prevailed that the starting of the first train from Walsall to Lichfield and Burton would be marked by some public meeting at that place. Nothing of the kind, however, had been arranged, and the first train departed at about twenty minutes past eight o'clock in the morning, without any other particular demonstration of the event than the gathering of a small number of spectators on the bridge over the railway near to the town. The next train, which left at thirty-five minutes past nine o'clock, was similarly witnessed. The Directors, it was stated, held a meeting at Birmingham at about midday, from whence they went in a special train of first class carriages to Walsall, and proceeded on to Lichfield and Burton, where they arrived shortly before one o'clock. On their return to Lichfield, which took place about three o'clock, they were met at the station, which was gaily decorated with flags, by the Mayor and Corporation of the city, who had gone thither for the purpose in procession, preceded by the town crier in his scarlet costume, and the macebearers, bearing the unusually massive silver gilt maces presented to the corporation by King Charles the Second, and his brother King James. A very considerable number of spectators, taking into account the unfavourable state of the weather, had assembled at the station and in its neighbourhood, and accompanied by the Directors and the Mayor and Corporation into the town, the arrival of the train conveying the Directors from Burton and the entry of the procession into the town being greeted by repeated and joyous peals from the beautifully toned bells of St Mary's church, whose lively sounds, it may be hoped, gave a presage of the advantages likely to accrue to the ancient and celebrated city of Lichfield from the celebration of which the day's proceedings took place. A sumptuous dinner at the George Hotel, and a ball at the Town Hall in the evening, also marked the occurrence.

The direction of the line of railway and its connexions we have already mentioned ; yet, by way of episode, although it is unmarked by any peculiarity of construction, and no other than the ordinary difficulties attending such undertakings have had to be overcome, some sketch of its principal features and adjuncts may not be altogether uninteresting.

The station at Walsall is situated slightly to the westward of the town, and within about two hundred yards of one of the principal streets - Digbeth - leading to the Market-place, the approach being made by a new street (Railway-street) running almost parallel with Bradford-street, which overlooks a portion of the railway. The station itself is a neat structure in the Elizabethan style having a recessed portico towards the street, which gives entrance to the different offices in the building. A wide and suitable terrace or walk fronts the building towards the railway, and upon open it the doors of the Directors', manager's, and other offices, while opposite to it is an ample wooden platform, for the accommodation of passengers coming from Burton or Lichfield or going towards Birmingham. Travellers going eastward get into the carriages from the terrace or walk. Large shedding on the farther side of the platform is appropriated to the reception of carriages and engines when not in use ; and adverting to the carriages we have to notice that they are peculiarly handsome and commodious in their construction. The first class carriages bear on their panels the coats of arms of the borough of Walsall, supported by a representation (on a shield) of Dudley Castle on the left, and the device of the city of Lichfield on the dexter side of the bearing. The centre compartment of each carriage is appropriated to first class passengers, those paying second class fares occupying the separate compartments, between which the first class compartment is situate. The third class carriages are close, and also divided into compartments, and, compared with most of the carriages of that class, are unusually comfortable vehicles.

A somewhat deep cutting (for a short distance under the town) brings the train on its departure for Lichfield to the eastern side of the town, whence the line passes, on a considerable embankment, over the black and swampy soil of Pelsall, where a small station is erected. In its progress it soon enters upon Cannock Chase, and fine views of that extensive tract of open country to the northward are occasionally afforded. Leaving Brownhills and Hammerwich to the left, and having three times crossed the Wyrley and Essington Canal, the line emerges from the several cuttings required in its passage across the Chase, upon a considerable embankment, which affords a fine view of the surrounding country, having Lichfield and its beautiful Cathedral slightly to the left, and the celebrated eminence of Borrowcop Hill on the right. Between these the line crosses St. John-street by means of a handsome Gothic arch, embattled, and reaches the Lichfield station, which is situate on a piece of land well known in the neighbourhood as Levett's Field. The approach from the city is by means of a new road, which nearly fronts the entrance into the city from Birmingham, adjoining to St John's Hospital. The station at Lichfield is similar in style and somewhat similar in construction (though on a larger scale) to that at Walsall. From Lichfield the line, passing through a deep cutting of hard red sandstone, a little to the southward of St Michael's Church, crosses the road to Burton and the Trent Valley Railway, and reaches Alrewas, where a curved branch northward effects a junction with the Trent Valley line. Shortly after the waters of the Trent are crossed by means of a long and handsome viaduct, south of Wichnor Bridge, while a little further southward a similar structure affords a roadway for the Leicester and Swannington line, and brings it into communication with the Birmingham and Derby Junction rails. From this point the line of the South Staffordshire Railway is almost on a perfect level, but yet affording an extensive prospect bounded, however, by the almost semi-circular sweep of the distant hills of Derbyshire in the foreground, and ranging on the left to the foliaged masses of Needwood Forest, and to the comparatively barren height of Tutbury, marking the course of the swift flowing Dove, while to the south the extensive plantations and pastures of Leicestershire exhibit their luxuriant verdure.

The extent of the line from Walsall to its junction with the Birmingham and Derby Railway is about seventeen miles, and owing to the weight of the rails, upwards of seventy pounds to the yard, and the excellent execution of the earthwork and the exact level of the joints of the rails, which reflect the highest credit upon the contractors, Messrs Earle, Combe, and Harby, and the subcontractors generally, the motion of the train throughout was particularly smooth and easy, even at the highest speed. The engines too, of which we may here notice, there are six - (those for the passenger trains named Walsall, Lichfield, Wednesbury, and Dudley, and those for goods and luggage trains Birmingham and Wolverhampton) - are of the most improved construction, having patent wheels and axletrees, and were built by Messrs Fairburn and Son, of Manchester, under the direction of Messrs Maclean [sic] and Stileman, engineers to the line, and of Mr. E. Marsden, mechanical engineer ; and to the two last named gentlemen we have to express our thanks for the information they afforded, and the accommodation given throughout our inspection of the undertaking.

The remainder of this lengthy report detailed the speeches and toasts given at the dinner at the George Hotel, Lichfield. It is worthy of note that the following persons are recorded as amongst those attending:

Earl Talbot, Viscount Ingestre, Viscount Lewisham, Viscount Anson, Captain Dyott, C.S. Forster, W. Mott, Thomas Hodson, Thomas Johnson, Philip Williams, R. Greene, R.C. Chawner T.G. Lomax, plus the Sheriff of Lichfield (Major Majendie) , the Mayor of Lichfield (J.F. Dyott), and most of the Aldermen and Town Councillors.

Following the dinner, a public ball was held at the Guildhall in Walsall, to continue the celebrations. The hall was recorded in the *Staffordshire Advertiser* of Saturday 14th April, 1849 as having been gaily decorated for the occasion, and that around 150 guests continued dancing until the early hours of the morning.

One matter of note is the reference in both the advertisement and the newspaper report to the Leicester & Swannington Railway, which actually did not reach Burton, nor was it ever linked to the Birmingham to Derby line, *south of Wichnor Junction*. The MR, however, did extend it to reach Burton at Branston Junction, about five miles *north of Wichnor* on 1st August, 1849. So this latter comment is particularly puzzling.

Intermediate stations were opened at this time at Rushall, Pelsall, Brownhills, Hammerwich, Lichfield City, Lichfield Trent Valley Junction, Alrewas and Wichnor, although some sources give August 1849 (some four months later) as the date of opening for Lichfield Trent Valley Junction. However, at least some were evidently incomplete, as a Directors Report dated 5th September, 1849 stated 'stations and sidings are nearly completed, with exception of the junctions with the Trent Valley Railway line, where better accommodation is required for the exchange of passengers with the LNWR'. This state of affairs is borne out by the fact that the stations at Rushall, Brownhills and Hammerwich were not actually included in the timetables until June 1849. It would seem that the arrangements at Hammerwich were soon found to be unsatisfactory, as the platforms were extended in August 1858 at a cost of £28.

The original temporary station in Bridgeman Place, Walsall closed with the opening of the line to Wichnor, and the splendid new station mentioned in the newspaper report above, opened a short distance further north, in Station Street. It appears that the locomotive department was expected to continue with the use of the temporary facilities provided earlier, and it was not until 5th June, 1857 that a contract was approved by the Board of Directors for the construction of an engine shed at Walsall by a Mr Branson, for the amount of £1,050.

At the other end of the line, a three-road locomotive shed was erected in 1854 at Wichnor Junction, in the fork of the junction. The total cost was given as £1,782 18s. 4d. By 1866, the shed had an allocation of 14 engines, comprising nine for branch line goods, two for main line goods, two for shunting, and one for passenger duties. The shed eventually closed in 1896, and the engines were transferred to the LNWR shed at Horninglow in Burton. The structure survived for a number of years before being demolished.

A further station was opened at Ryder's Hays in April, 1856, but lasted less than two years, closing on 1st February, 1858. Several years later, the original TVR station at Lichfield and the SSR Lichfield Trent Valley Junction stations were closed as from 3rd July, 1871. These two stations were remote from each other, and a new, combined station was constructed south of each of the original stations to be known as Lichfield Trent Valley, High Level (for the SSR route) and Low Level (for the TVR route), opening on this date.

Walsall to Dudley

A contract for the construction of this section was approved at the same meeting of the Board of Directors on 17th May, 1847 that had awarded that for the Walsall to Wichnor section. This time, the contract (No. 2) for the 5¼ mile line was given to Messrs Hoof & Hill. No record is available for the value of the contract, nor of any other tenders received. Hoof & Hill also worked on the northern section of the Birmingham, Wolverhampton & Stour Valley Railway (Wolverhampton to Birmingham New Street) that was completed in 1852. There are no positive records of the contractors using locomotives on either of these two contracts, but this appears likely as they held an auction of surplus equipment at their yard in Horseley Fields, Wolverhampton on 18th June, 1852 which included one locomotive. This was *Wellington*, an outside cylinder 0-4-2 built by Tayleur & Company of the Vulcan Foundry, Newton-le-Willows around 1836. It had been originally supplied to the Bolton & Leigh Railway as their No. 39, but eventually found its way to John Hargreaves Jnr, a carrier of Bolton, who sold it to the MR, who retained the name, but changed the number to their 295 in July 1840. It subsequent history is not known.

A Directors Report dated 13th March, 1848 mentions that work on this section had been less rapid than the work on the other section. It appears that work on other railways in the area, which connected to this line, had created difficulties. This can only have referred to the BWDR then simultaneously under construction. This should not really have occurred, for as we shall see, McClean was the Engineer for both railways !

The Land & Works Committee issued a contract for the supply of 35,000 sleepers at a price of 3s. 9d. each, awarded again to Harris & Singleton, on 29th June, 1848. A report from McClean dated 11th September, 1848 stated that 'between Dudley and Walsall works are now progressing vigorously'. This rate of progress appears to have been maintained, as the following entry just a year later from a Directors Report dated 13th September, 1849 confirms:

> On the remaining part of the line between Great Bridge and Bescot the contractors are carrying on the works with the greatest possible despatch, and we have every reason to expect, should the weather continue favourable, that the portion of the railway between Dudley and Bescot, which completed [sic] the main line will be opened for traffic early in November next.

The apparent delay in construction of the section from Great Bridge to Bescot was due to appalling weather experienced at the time, plus difficulties in the purchase of land from Edward Elwell near to Bescot. Furthermore, subsidence arising from the many abandoned shallow mines, known locally as 'crowning-in' had created difficulties in stabilizing the land beneath the line. This problem would continue to cause difficulties in subsequent years, as we shall see in Chapter Seven.

One of the casualties resulting from the construction of the line was the firm of J. Hartland, who had operated the Eagle Furnaces at Great Bridge from at least 1823. Their works were demolished to make way for the new trackbed.

Section 20 of the 1846 BWDR Act, passed on the same day as the SSR enabling Act, provided that construction of this section by the SSR must be completed to

Dudley within three years of the date of the Act. Failure to do so would entitle the BWDR to complete the line from Great Bridge to Dudley. If the SSR reached Dudley first, the BWDR would have running powers over the section from just south of Great Bridge to Dudley, but if the BWDR finished the line, the SSR would have these running powers. Although the SSR was able to run a token service on 1st November, 1849 this was some three months later than the legally required deadline. However, this mattered little as McClean was the Engineer for both the SSR and the BWDR, so was unlikely to insist on the terms of the 1846 Acts being strictly enforced ! Nonetheless this service was deemed enough to have satisfied the requirements of the 1846 Acts. A report in the *Wolverhampton Chronicle* dated 7th November, 1849 optimistically expected the full opening of the line before the end of 1849:

SOUTH STAFFORDSHIRE RAILWAY

On Thursday, November the 1st, this line of railway was traversed by an engine and train of carriages between Walsall and Dudley, previous to its inspection by the Government. The banks and slopes along the line were thronged with spectators to witness the first invasion of their smoky district. On arriving at Dudley, an excellent collation was provided by the engineers of the line, Messrs M'Lean [sic] and Stileman, at which about forty ladies and gentlemen sat down. There can now be no doubt that the whole of the line will be opened for traffic before the close of the present year, which will give the necessary facilities for travelling between the towns of Dudley, Wednesbury, Walsall, and Birmingham. Although the route, as between Dudley and Birmingham, will be somewhat circuitous, the time occupied in travelling will not exceed thirty minutes.

Captain G. Wynne first inspected the line on 30th November, 1849 and commented on the many worked out quarries and mines adjacent to the line, which might give rise to subsidence. He was more critical of the standard of some of the work: 'Permanent way is laid throughout, but generally in a rough state and many parts are insufficiently ballasted. Station arrangements with regard to platforms and signals were incomplete'. He went on to mention that one culvert had not had the centres removed. One bridge at 2 miles 17 chains was in a dangerous state as one abutment was out of line caused by a weakness in the embankment, and he required it to be taken down and rebuilt. Further changes to the plans were noted where the radius of certain lines had been reduced. He was unable to pass the line for opening to passenger traffic.

The line opened for regular goods workings on 1st March, 1850, and on 10th April Captain Wynne returned to re-inspect the line. He found that the signals and platforms were now complete, and that the offending bridge had been rebuilt. There had been no further settlement of grounds, but he recommended vigilance on this matter, and later events were indeed to prove the wisdom of his caution. His letter the following day approved the line for opening to passengers. Curiously, there no immediate rush to open, and this may have had something to with the station at Dudley, which was of a temporary nature, and although not necessarily causing any concern to the safety of the line, would not recommend itself to future passengers if not altogether acceptable. In any event, this was another matter that would bedevil the railway at Dudley for some time. Another matter was that Captain Wynne's letter did not specifically refer to the new east to south curve at Bescot, so that the company were not sure whether this had been approved or not. Their letter to the Board of Trade on 20th April requested clarification, which was presumably promptly forthcoming, although this has not survived.

The line opened for passenger traffic on Wednesday 1st May, 1850 and was reported at length in the *Wolverhampton Chronicle* of 8th May. The following are abstracts of the more relevant parts of the report:

SOUTH STAFFORDSHIRE RAILWAY
OPENING OF THE DUDLEY BRANCH

On Wednesday last this line was opened for the conveyance of passengers, parcels, and goods to Dudley, thus giving a direct communication by railway between Birmingham, Wednesbury, Great Bridge, Tipton, Dudley, Walsall, Lichfield, and Burton ; and by means of omnibuses and coaches running in connection with the line, accommodation is afforded to the inhabitants of Brierley Hill, Stourbridge, Kidderminster, Bewdley, Stourport, Leominster, Ludlow, &c. The line, as our readers are aware, has for some time been opened from Burton to Lichfield, Walsall, and Birmingham, but, considering the vast population and the mining wealth of the district through which it runs, the most important portion of the line was opened to the public on Wednesday. We have on former occasions given a description of the line and the country through which it runs between Alrewas and Bescot Junction ; and as it respects the remaining portion of the line, from Bescot to Dudley, we may observe generally , that the line is not remarkable for tunnels or deep cuttings. Notwithstanding the absence of any apparently heavy works, the formation of the line must have been attended with serious difficulties, and the utmost skill and attention must have been exercised by the engineers and subcontractors, owing to the numerous collieries over which the line passes. At Bescot the junction of the Dudley portion and the other part of the line is accomplished by means of a decline and a curve, the latter greater than any we remember to have before witnessed. In honour of the opening, all the stations along the line were gaily and tastefully decorated with evergreens, &c and great numbers of flags and banners, with appropriate devices were hung out on every available point and the locomotive engines were in their holiday attire. The first trains started about half-past eight o'clock, and throughout the day large crowds lined almost every bridge and embankment, testifying by their hearty plaudits the pleasure such an event had universally excited. As train after train swept past the great ironworks that lie so thickly between Wednesbury, Great Bridge and Dudley Port, the grim forms of the men were seen issuing forth to welcome the mighty Promethean spirit whose iron sinews they had perhaps helped to fashion. The great incident of the day, however, took place at Dudley, about four in the afternoon. The inhabitants had been requested to accompany the Directors in procession from the station to the town, and at the hour mentioned there could not have fewer than twenty thousand persons gathered together from Dudley and the immediate district. For several hundred yards on both sides of the line, and from the station to the centre of the town (a distance of nearly half a mile), a compact body of spectators was assembled. On the platform were the most respectable of the inhabitants, with many gentlemen connected with the iron trade, and the boys of the Grammar School were marshalled in front, under the Rev. A. K. Thompson, head master, and the Rev. J. F. Fairhead, second master. The Directors and their friends came from Walsall to Dudley by special train, and as may be anticipated, they were welcomed most enthusiastically by the immense concourse. As soon as they had reached the platform, Master Thomas Auden, one of the senior boys of the Grammar School, advanced towards C.S. Forster, Esq, Chairman of the Board of Directors, and read a Latin address.

A translation of this address was given , but is not repeated here.

Mr Forster received the address in a very courteous and kindly manner, and promised the whole school a gratuitous trip during next week to Lichfield, or anywhere else the boys might choose, and expressed a hope that the headmaster would give them a holiday for the purpose. He alluded to the forthcoming illumination of the caverns, and trusted the boys would also have an opportunity of witnessing those wonderful excavations.

The address was received with much cheering, and the Head Master briefly stated that he very cheerfully responded to give the boys a holiday, and trusted that it would be in his power on a future occasion to give a holiday to boys equally well deserving as those he had under his care.

A procession of the Directors and other gentlemen was then formed – headed by the Mayor of Dudley, Thomas Fereday, Esq. with the chairman and deputy-chairman of the company, preceded by the grammar school boys, and the Dudley brass band and proceeded to the Hotel, order being very efficiently maintained by Superintendent Jewkes and a body of police.

THE DINNER

At five o'clock a large body of gentlemen, numbering nearly 120, sat down to dinner at the Hotel. The assembly room was suitably decorated for the occasion with evergreens and inscriptions, namely 'God save the Queen', 'Prosperity to the South Staffordshire Railway', and 'Prosperity to the Iron Trade'. The tables were profusely decorated with the delicacies of the season, and in addition to the ordinary wine supplied by the landlord (Mr. Smith), the company were indebted to the liberality of Mr. Hill, the contractor, for an unlimited quantity of champagne.

The persons attending the dinner included the following notables:

T. Fereday (Mayor of Dudley), C.S. Forster (Chairman, SSR), R.C. Chawner (Vice Chairman, SSR), R. Smith, Captain Dyott, Edward Buller, P. Williams, Samuel Beale (deputy chairman of the MR), Harvey Wyatt, J.B. Payne, Thomas Johnson, A. Adams, S. Haines - all Directors; J.R. M'Clean and F.C. Stileman - engineers; H. Barnett - secretary; J.D. Payne - general manager; Messrs Hoof and Hill - contractors.

The report continued at length with details of the speeches and toasts made during the dinner, but curiously omitted to name the hotel where the dinner was served.

The intermediate stations of Wednesbury, Great Bridge, and Dudley Port (Low Level) were opened on the same day, but the station at Dudley, as mentioned earlier was only of a temporary nature. It was located to the north of the Tipton Road in Dudley, and next to the SSR goods depot. A further station was eventually erected south of this site, but was inconveniently positioned, as it was some 50 yards away from the OWWR station, although that did not open until 20th December, 1852. Further developments at Dudley are examined in Chapter Six.

This section of line also included the Bescot Curve, linking the Bescot to Walsall line to the Dudley to Walsall line, and thus completing a triangular junction that permitted through working between Bescot and Dudley. Thus the through trains from Birmingham to Dudley used this route until shortly after the opening of New Street station and the 'Sedgeley Loop' in 1854. Thereafter, the steeply-graded curve continued to see use for goods trains to and from Bescot yard to the Dudley line.

Chapter Three

The Branches

Sedgeley Junction to Dudley Port High Level: 'The Sedgeley Loop'

Authority for the short line from the SSR main line from what was to become Sedgeley Junction to Dudley Port High Level was incorporated in the SSR Act of 24th July, 1851 (Vict. 14 & 15, cap. 94). This gave the SSR running powers into the LNWR High Level station, and gave the LNWR reciprocal running powers from there through to Dudley. The passing of the Act was reported to the Board of Directors at their meeting on 20th August, 1851.

A Directors Report of 18th February, 1852 included the tenders received for the construction of the line, somewhat confusingly referred to as the 'Tipton branch', as follows:

	£	s.	d.
Frost & Bate	6,706	10	8
J. Morley	5,752	18	8
Hiram Cooper	4,400	0	0
Thomas & Jacob Nowell	4,100	0	0
David Wylie	4,100	0	0
Hezekiah Brook	3,763	17	8
Francis Piggott	3,501	2	8
Henry Hemberman	3,340	0	0

The contract was awarded to Francis Piggott of Rugeley, for completion in just four months, and with a penalty of £50 per week if the time was exceeded. Shortly after, on 20th March, 1852 a Directors Meeting required McClean to prepare a report on this line, although there is no record of his response. This may have had some bearing on the start of the works, as there was a delay in the commencement of the construction, possibly due to difficulties in purchasing the required land. Consequently, the line was not available for inspection until September 1853, and it seems likely that the penalties were not enforced, although no mention is made in the surviving records.

The junction on the SSR line was always spelt as 'Sedgeley', even though the correct spelling for the town of this name is and was 'Sedgley'. The layout at the junction with the Stour Valley line became somewhat problematical for the inspecting officer, Captain D. Galton. In a letter dated 14th September, 1853, he described the line as being carried over a road by cast-iron girders, and over the Birmingham Canal (which ran alongside and parallel to the LNWR Stour Valley line) by wrought-iron tubular girders. The line was double track from Sedgeley Junction, but became single when adjacent to the LNWR High Level station, giving the SSR one platform face at the station, which had opened on 1st July, 1852. There was insufficient room between the LNWR line and the canal to install double track and the necessary two platform faces. As the line continued at the eastern end of the station, it once again became double to the point where it made a junction with the LNWR line. Captain Galton therefore agreed to open the section from Dudley to Dudley Port station, but was unhappy about the arrangement of the junction with the LNWR line, and approval for the section from the platform to this junction was therefore delayed for one month.

Services from Dudley to Dudley Port High Level only, and using the single platform line had commenced by 14th October, 1853. There were no intermediate stations erected on the short line, which was initially operated on the permissive block system, at least until 1854.

The inspector visited the site again on 19th October, 1853 and found that the arrangements were still the same. Traffic from Dudley to Dudley Port was recorded as being of a great volume, and he maintained that the single line section should be doubled to permit through working.

After a further visit, Captain Galton refused (in a letter dated 17th November) to allow the single line section to the junction to be allowed to open for passenger traffic, as he believed that through working from Kidderminster and Stourbridge to Birmingham would commence if he did. He was convinced of the danger of working trains from opposite directions into the single line platform section, and would not be moved from this position.

Further correspondence followed, and McClean suggested that the junction with the LNWR be moved to the other (western end) of the platform, as there was simply no room to put in a section of double track at the platform. In a letter dated 16th December, 1853 Captain Galton agreed to this option, provided that through trains did not enter the single line section. This meant that all through trains would have to use the main (LNWR) platform faces, and thus take up valuable track capacity - but there was no other alternative. Terminating trains would still be permitted to use the single line section and platform face, provided that they came to a stop before reaching the single line section, and that the station master's approval was given for them to proceed. One result is that the length of the line has subsequently been quoted as 38 or 43 chains by different sources, which is the length to the new junction, whereas the original 58 chains is believed to be to the original junction. This remodelling also presented the opportunity to install two double-ended sidings on the up side (Dudley direction) only, which were latterly used mainly for carriage storage. Access to these sidings was controlled by an Annett's key from Sedgeley Junction box.

Thus the line finally came into use for through trains as from Monday 2nd January, 1854. The following announcement appeared in the *Wolverhampton Chronicle* of 28th December, 1853:

STOUR VALLEY AND SOUTH STAFFORDSHIRE RAILWAYS
The loop line enabling trains to run direct between Birmingham and Dudley, without change of carriages, will be opened on Monday next. The distance will be performed in twenty-five minutes, at the present fares, and eight additional trains will run daily. A very great increase of accommodation to the public will, in consequence, be afforded.

No newspaper reports have been traced subsequent to the opening, which was very likely a low key affair anyway, but in any case there had been a very heavy snowfall the previous weekend, and the newspaper coverage was mostly concerned with the after effects of the snowstorm.

Stanier 'Jubilee' class 4-6-0 No. 45638 *Zanzibar* pulls out of Dudley Port High Level in July 1949 with an express for Manchester. On the right a Webb 2-4-2T waits in the branch platform with the shuttle for Dudley, a trip it will make several times each day. The station building on the up platform, on the left, was evidently being renewed at this time.   *M. Whitehouse Collection*

The Webb LNWR 2-4-2Ts were the mainstay of the shuttles between Dudley and Dudley Port for decades. Here, we see the last one in service, around 1949, still declaring its LMS ownership, but bearing its new BR number. Although still attached to its two-coach autotrain, it has taken a break from passenger duties to perform some shunting at the Palethorpes' loading platform at Sedgeley Junction. The guard or shunter is hanging out of the last door calling on the driver as he backs up the siding.   *D. Wilson*

Although through trains were introduced from Birmingham New Street to Kidderminster during 1854, they were required to use the main line platforms, until the required track modifications were made. As a result, several ran via Walsall (see Chapter Seven). Only from 1st March, 1856 were these services able to use the branch platform at Dudley Port, but the complications of operation from Dudley to Kidderminster, coupled with the reluctance of the GWR to participate in their operation, meant that the service was short lived. After all, the GWR already had its own service operating from Snow Hill station to Kidderminster, and saw no reason to help its competitor. Consequently, the service was discontinued beyond Dudley in 1867, with the through New Street to Dudley services totalling two in each direction on weekdays and none on Sundays in 1874, rising to seven each way in 1882, then declining to three each way in 1905. This new service between New Street and Dudley took only 35 minutes, compared to 50 travelling via Walsall. In April 1910 there were four trains to Dudley (although one started from Monument Lane) on weekdays, with five on Saturdays, but still none on Sundays. In the opposite direction, there were four from Dudley on weekdays and five on Saturdays. However, the service was discontinued during World War I, but restarted afterwards with just one each way on weekdays and Saturdays in July 1922. The service was curtailed once more, this time for duration of World War II, but never recommenced.

In the meantime, the connecting service for the short four or five minute run from Dudley to Dudley Port prospered, in which form it continued for many years, earning the soubriquet of 'The Dudley Dasher' - although this name was also applied to the Walsall to Dudley trains. The following table shows the changing pattern of services on this route over the years:

| | Dudley-Dudley Port | | Dudley Port-Dudley | |
Year	Weekdays	Sundays	Weekdays	Sundays
1883	25	6	23	6
1885	32	9	33	9
1898	38	9	39	9
1910	49	11	41	11
1911	51	11	43	11
1914	53	12	49	13
1915	60	17	60	17
1922	54	14	54	14
1953	7	6	7	6
1964	1	0	1	0

At its peak, the weekday services provided trains at intervals of around 15 to 20 minutes throughout much of the day. 1964 was, of course, the final year of services.

As no turntable facilities were provided at Dudley Port, tank engines were probably used from the very start. Locomotives used on the early trains would presumably have included the McConnell 0-4-2WTs, although confirmation of the precise motive power would be welcomed. Soon after their introduction, the Webb 4 ft 6 in. 2-4-2T and 5 ft 6 in. 2-4-2Ts appeared on this duty, the latter class right up to the 1950s. These were permanently attached as push-pull units,

Track relaying work going on at Dudley Port High Level in the 1950s, with possibly the rebuilding of one of the retaining walls adjacent to the canal. The steam crane has been borrowed from Bescot motive power depot for the purpose. The closeness of the canal to the line used by the Dudley shuttles can be appreciated. *K. Hodgkins*

Renewal work on the Birmingham Canal Navigation bridge over the SSR at Dudley Port was started in July 1957. Work is in progress here on the 10th, with the canal drained, and the new concrete bridge for the canal on the right, waiting to be slid into position. This was done over one weekend in August, and traffic resumed shortly afterwards on both the canal and the SSR. In the background, an Ivatt 2-6-2T is waiting in the High Level station with an autotrain for Dudley. *K. Hodgkins Collection*

designated by the LNWR and LMS as 'motor trains', and obviating the need to run-round, which would have otherwise entailed occupation of the main line at Dudley Port, and this would have been decidedly unpopular. Until 1927 the motor train unit was stationed at Dudley, and only ever comprised a two-coach unit, owing to the restricted space available in the branch platform at Dudley Port High Level. Eventually the 2-4-2Ts were superseded by the Ivatt LMS 2-6-2Ts until they in turn were supplanted in 1958 by the introduction of diesel multiple units (dmus). The final service from Dudley was run on Saturday 13th June, 1964, and within a month the connection to the Stour Valley line had been severed, actually on 12th July. After removal of the track, the embankment was largely removed, for use elsewhere as infill.

Shortly afterwards, on 20th September, 1964 a fire broke out in the now redundant Sedgeley Junction box, which was attributed to an act of vandalism. The damage to the upper, timber part of the signal box was so severe that the entire box was soon demolished.

One feature at Dudley Port that will be recalled is that the large station nameboard, positioned over one of the central benches provided for passengers and retained well into BR days. This was inscribed in wooden letters with the legend: 'Junction for Dudley, Stourbridge, Kidderminster, & Stations on the Great Western Line, also Great Bridge, Wednesbury, Walsall, South Stafford & Cannock Line Branches'.

In 1957 the canal bridge over the SSR main line required renewal, which as already indicated was situated very close to the branch platform at the High Level station. The works involved removal of the old canal bridge, construction of a new bridge in concrete, and installation in the very restricted space available. The works were completed after 11 weeks, when during the night of 14th August the new bridge was moved on rollers into place.

During electrification work, the chance was taken to simplify the trackwork of the former Stour Valley line. Work began in November 1964 with the replacement of the bridge over the Great Bridge-Tividale road. Next, the old High Level station buildings were removed, and replaced by an island platform with glass-sided shelters on the platform affording only a minimum amount of protection for passengers at this rather exposed site. The running lines were slewed to run either side of the new platform. Finally, the main line signal box was removed in March 1967 as it was no longer required - its function having been taken over by the Wolverhampton power box.

Goods services using the line were rather limited, and including empty stock workings these ranged from four each way on weekdays in 1885, to four down and seven up in 1898, four down and 10 up in 1910, rising to six down and 12 up in the following year, but reducing to four down and six up by 1914. Sunday goods services over this period varied between one and three in each direction, but mention must be made of one specialized service. This was classed as 'cattle', but actually transported pigs (mostly from Ireland) to the private siding of Palethorpes' Ltd almost opposite Sedgeley Junction. These animals were of course intended to be converted into this famous firm's delicious pies and sausages. The incoming trains also conveyed vans for the finished products to shipped out later. These outgoing loads were usually contained in vans

Stanier class '5' 4-6-0 No. 45250 pauses at Dudley Port High Level with an up express in 1962. The left-hand platform face of the island platform was used for the shuttle services to Dudley. *D. Wilson*

Crewe North shed's 'Royal Scot' class 4-6-0 No. 46135 *The East Lancashire Regiment* strides away from Dudley Port High Level after a short stop with a northbound express in the summer of 1961. This photograph illustrates the northern end of the island platform, where the shuttle service for Dudley was accommodated. *D. Wilson*

dedicated to Palethorpes' use and which were prominently decorated with the company name and details of its use and Royal patronage. The first known such vehicle was allocated to this duty in March 1886, having been built in 1876 as LNWR 25 ft parcel van No. 19. This was replaced by No. 38, a 30 ft five-compartment van built in 1896, which became No. 9634 in 1910, and LMS No. 3124 in 1923. Into BR days, the vehicles used included six bogie vehicles carrying the Palethorpes' name and logo (BR Nos. M38873M to M38878M), a further two unbranded bogie vehicles (M38898M and M38899M) and at least one former Stanier CCT six-wheeled vehicle (M38735M). A further curiosity noted in August 1963 was a branded six-wheeled vehicle in WR stock, numbered W2802W. Sometimes the Palethorpes' vehicles were taken to Dudley for onward movement via the GWR lines.

In 1898 the LNWR working left Dudley Port at 12.15 pm on Sundays, and during the 1909 to 1911 period this was retimed to 12.20 pm, with an additional earlier working at 8.30 am. However, in the week before Christmas each year, there may have been daily trains leaving the factory siding usually for Camden Goods Depot in London amongst other destinations. These were very busy times indeed, as for example in the week preceding Christmas 1904 when they dispatched 10,534 boxes of sausages and pies with a gross weight of 93 tons 16 cwt 16 lb. In the following two years, the loadings for comparable periods were: 10,714 boxes (91 tons 5 cwt 39 lb.) and 12,158 boxes (103 tons 17 cwt 74 lb.). Often the full vans were marshalled in the one of the carriage sidings on the loop, so as to be ready to be attached to services passing on the Stour Valley route. All types of mixed traffic locomotives were assigned to these duties over the years, including the return empty stock workings. Indeed, by the late 1950s and early 1960s it was quite common to see express locomotives such as 'Jubilees' and 'Royal Scots' on these duties. One such working was scheduled in 1959 for the pilot engine from the 1.55 pm Birmingham-Liverpool express, usually a Crewe class '5' 4-6-0, to come off at Dudley Port and shunt the vans. It took them forward later in the afternoon to Wolverhampton High Level. It was recorded that on 11th May, 1959 this duty fell to none other than 'Royal Scot' class 4-6-0 No. 46100 *Royal Scot*. Coincidentally, the author well recalls 'Jubilee' No. 45552 *Silver Jubilee* early one Sunday morning around 1960 at Wolverhampton High Level with a string of the Palethorpes' vans.

With the removal of the track, the rather stark, open area of unused land through which it once ran has since seen the eruption of modern housing, and attempts to distinguish the trackbed are doomed to failure.

GWR Spur at Wednesbury

A spur was put in just south of Wednesbury Town station opening on 1st June, 1859, to connect the SSR to the former BWDR route (later GWR) to Wolverhampton. When constructed, this spur was laid with mixed broad gauge and standard gauge rails, but the broad gauge rails were removed on 1st April, 1869. The line curved away to the north, from just beneath where the BWDR route crossed over, to join that line a short distance west of Wednesbury Central

BR/Sulzer class '24' No. 24060 shunts empty wagons in the former LMS/GWR exchange sidings at Wednesbury on 9th October, 1975. In the background is part of the once extensive steel works of the Patent Shaft & Axletree Co. Ltd. *R. Selvey*

The goods shed constructed at Wednesbury alongside the Darlaston loop in 1863 survives to this day. In this view from March 2006 it is in use as a warehouse for a road transport business.
Author

station at a west-facing junction. Alongside the spur were created exchange sidings, actually on the curve of the spur, and on its eastern side. A connecting line ran from this group of three sidings to the works of the Patent Shaft & Axletree Co. Ltd. Two further running lines were added to the spur before 1890, and after, but before 1926 the exchange sidings were expanded further still with another group of five sidings on the western side.

The spur provided access for the LNWR to the GWR route to Wolverhampton, over which the SSR had been granted running powers via Priestfield in the BWDR Act of 1846, although it is doubtful if the LNWR, or even its successor, the LMS ever took advantage of these running powers. Into BR days, the spur was used for steel trains to the new Wolverhampton Steel Terminal which opened on the site of the former Walsall Street Goods Depot on 31st May, 1966. However, the route into it was changed to the Stour Valley line, after the closure of the former GWR route to Wolverhampton as from 6th March 1972. Nonetheless, a short piece remained in use from the former exchange sidings to the Norton Barrow scrapyard at Moxley until the early 1990s. Eventually, the West Midlands Metro route from Wolverhampton to Birmingham Snow Hill was built on the former GWR main line trackbed, and opened in May 1999. The depot for the Metro system is actually located on the site of these exchange sidings.

Darlaston to Wednesbury

As already mentioned, Parliamentary powers to construct this line were incorporated in the SSR Act of 23rd July, 1855 (Vict. 18 & 19, cap. 175) requiring completion in five years. However, time nearly ran out, and a further Bill was necessary to grant an extension of time. This was obtained in the SSR Act of 13th August, 1859 (Vict. 22 & 23, cap. 109) permitting an extension of time until 23rd July, 1862.

The required completion date was passed, seemingly without comment, and eventually the line of 2 miles and 46 chains (2½ miles) was opened on 14th September, 1863 as a single line, from James Bridge through Darlaston to Wednesbury. From this date, the former LNWR Darlaston station on the old GJR route was renamed 'James Bridge' and extended on to the Darlaston branch where a wooden platform was provided. Only one station was provided on the line, at Butcroft, conveniently near to Bull Stake in Darlaston town centre. By this time, of course, the LNWR was leasing the SSR, and so the construction was actually completed by them. This is recorded in an agreement for the working and maintenance of the SSR dated 18th March, 1861 in which the LNWR agreed to complete the construction of both the Tipton and Darlaston branches, and to be responsible for the costs. The contract for the construction of both branches was awarded to Thomas Brassey for an undisclosed sum.

Such was the volume of traffic, not only from passengers, but also goods to and from the major iron and steelworks located on the route that the line was doubled, coming into use on 22nd December, 1872.

As the line diverged from the GJR route at James Bridge station, it swung sharply westwards, then south-westwards, passing over Heath Road, and

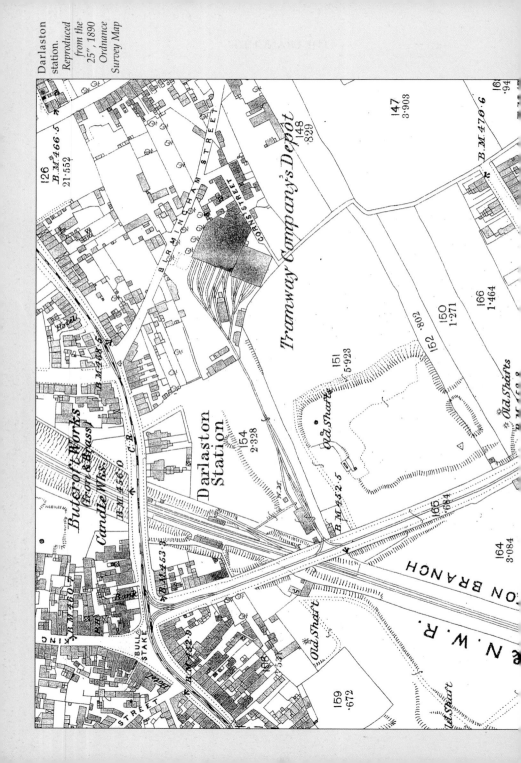

shortly afterwards beneath a narrow gauge mineral line running from collieries in the area to the Darlaston Green Furnaces of Bradley & Foster Ltd (originally the Darlaston Coal & Iron Co Ltd). These furnaces were connected to the line about ¼ mile further on, on the right, and although this connection was worked by the LNWR to the works, the company had a succession of its own locomotives for working the internal system until 1972. However, before reaching that point, on the left was the Alma Works of the nut and bolt makers Horton & Son Ltd, with siding connections on to the running line. On the opposite side of the line, the landscape was desolate with vast tracts of unused land, punctuated by the remains of old colliery workings. Passing the connection to the Darlaston Green Furnaces, the line entered a lengthy cutting of around ½ mile as it entered into the town of Darlaston, passing beneath the blue brick bridge under Walsall Road. The station was sited between this bridge and the next one, which carried Darlaston Road. No photographs have been traced of this station, but the accompanying very detailed plan from the 25 in. Ordnance survey map of 1890 enables some of the features to be ascertained. One short siding was provided on the eastern side of the down (southbound) line, behind the platform and the modest brick-built waiting room, which had a canopy over the platform. In the centre of the plan can be seen a small line running almost at right angles to the down running line. This was a narrow gauge rope-worked line, running from the siding at the rear of the down platform up to a weighbridge connected to the tramway depot, and was used for the transfer of coal from the railway to the tram depot. The main station buildings, including the booking hall, were sited on the opposite (up) platform, with the footpaths providing public entrances from both of the roads mentioned above. There was no footbridge connecting the two platforms, and seemingly no public access direct to the down platform, so presumably southbound passengers had to cross the line on a boarded crossing after having purchased their tickets, and when leaving. However, there is a suggestion that the small building on the Walsall Road bridge (shown shaded on the map), was another booking office, and that steps led from this to the platform. Beyond the second bridge, a goods loop was provided from the northbound line, amidst further desolate landscape which continued on both sides of the line as it approached Wednesbury.

But first the Old Park works of the Patent Shaft & Axletree Co. Ltd loomed up on the left, and shortly afterwards the line plunged beneath the old Holyhead turnpike road. Immediately on the right was the Albert Ironworks of James & Edward Rose, with sidings access. This firm is believed to have used its own locomotives here, but no details are known. After the Albert Ironworks closed around 1884, the sidings continued in general use until closure of the line, always referred to as Roses Sidings. Next a mineral line connecting the sprawling Monway and Brunswick works of the Patent Shaft company to its Old Park works was crossed. The Old Park works had originally belonged to the firm of Lloyds Foster & Company (established 1818), who merged with the Patent Shaft company in 1867, and so their internal railway systems, also linking to the company's own collieries in the area, were linked, although not fully until during World War I. At this time the Brunswick works were also enlarged, the ground being levelled by the contractors Perry & Co. (Bow) Ltd,

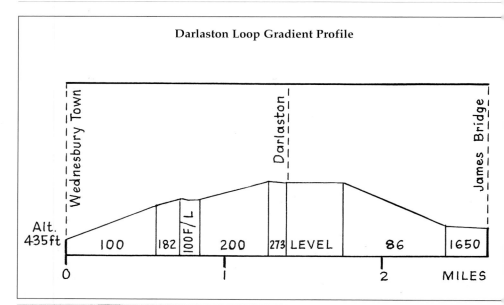

Darlaston Loop Gradient Profile

Wednesbury Town

Darlaston

James Bridge

Alt.
435ft

| 100 | 182 | 100 F/L | 200 | 273 | LEVEL | 86 | 1650 |

0   1   2   MILES

Webb 5 ft 6 in. 2-4-2T LMS No. 6704 standing in the Walsall platform at James Bridge station around 1936, propelling a push-pull train from Wolverhampton. This station was situated on the original GJR line from Stafford to Bescot, but included separate platforms for Darlaston loop trains which ceased from November 1887.   *D.J. Powell Collection/Kidderminster Railway Museum*

who used two 2 ft gauge Orenstein & Koppel 0-4-0WTs (Works Nos. 1227 of 1903, and 1229 of 1904) on this work which continued from 1917 until 1919.

In short order another line from the Old Park works came in from the left, then further sidings and connecting lines to the Monway works came in on the right. Immediately after, the line crossed Portway Lane (once a level crossing) and ran beside the gloomy Brunswick works on the right, where in 1853 the company had established a railway wheel plant. The line then ran into a cutting which continued beneath Dudley Street and then Victoria Street. Emerging from this bridge, the main goods yard and substantial goods shed in blue brick were on the left, with further sidings on the right, and the line now entered the branch platforms of Wednesbury Town station. At this point the line had completed a loop, so that the train having started from the Walsall direction at James Bridge, was now facing Walsall. Further description of this station will be found in Chapter Ten.

The passenger services on this line were intense from the start, with some 56 operating daily, although this had dropped to 48 by 1875. By 1877 the level had dropped to just 15 on weekdays, and by 1881 to just 11 (*see page 116*). Steam trams had started to operate from Darlaston to Handsworth from 16th July, 1883, and ran until 1904. More crucially for the railway, steam trams started to operate from Darlaston to Walsall on 10th December, 1884 and the depot of the South Staffordshire Tramways Company was close to the terminus at Bull Stake, Darlaston and near to the railway station. The effect on the railway was devastating, and an enquiry by the LNWR in 1883 had already learned from the station master that three or four trains a day left without passengers. Unsurprisingly, services were discontinued as from 1st November, 1887. On this date, the station on the old GJR route renamed 'James Bridge' in 1863, was renamed 'James Bridge for Darlaston'. The station at Darlaston, only one mile from James Bridge, was last used on 6th July, 1888 when it was temporarily reopened for the workers embarking on the Old Park works annual summer excursion from Wednesbury to Blackpool. Such excursions had become a regular feature for many of the larger employers throughout the country, and continued well past World War II. However, the station was finally demolished during 1889.

The first electric trams were introduced to Walsall on 24th September, 1892 and regular electric services from 31st December of the same year. In the following year the Darlaston Local Board took the LNWR to the High Court in an effort to get the line reopened for passengers. However, the case was lost, and the line remained closed to passengers.

Interestingly, the line was still operating on the 'time interval' system of signalling as late as 1884, and lacking any other information, it is possible that this continued for many further years as the line became a quiet backwater.

Goods traffic along it remained important, and whilst there were just two goods services on the line in 1867, this had risen to 11 in 1952. Even as late as 1962 there remained four weekday trip workings (as part of duties 9T44, 9T64 and 9T69 from Bescot shed) and two Saturday trips (9T44 and 9T64) to steelworks on the line. It was closed in two parts, the first being from Darlaston Junction (at James Bridge) to the Lloyds Works Siding at Fallings Heath on 24th December, 1963 thus severing the northern connection of the loop. The next

LONDON AND NORTH WESTERN RAILWAY.
TIPTON & DARLASTON BRANCHES
WAS OPENED FOR PASSENGER TRAFFIC
On the 14th September, 1863.

NEW AND QUICK ROUTE between WOLVER-
HAMPTON, (Queen Street Station,) & PRINCE'S
END, WEDNESBURY, DARLASTON, & WALSALL.

For Times and further Information, see the Company's
Time Tables.

By order,
W. CAWKWELL, General Manager.

September 3rd. 1863   987-1

Notice of the opening of the Tipton and Darlaston branches, from the *Walsall Advertiser* of 15th
September, 1863.   *Courtesy Walsall Local Archives*

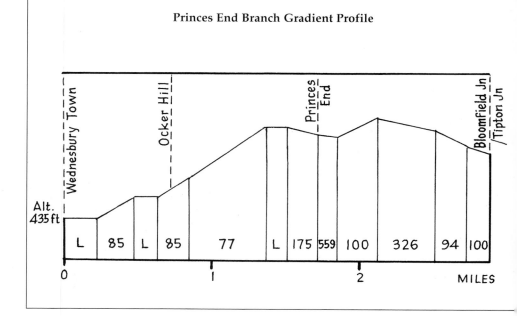

Princes End Branch Gradient Profile

closure was the section from the Patent Shaft Sidings at Wednesbury to the northern end of the line at Fallings Heath as from 1st January, 1968. This left just a short siding at the southern end of the line, most of which was used by the scrap metal firm of R.A. Giblin Ltd for access to their site, which by then also incorporated the former goods shed on the Darlaston loop at Wednesbury. They purchased their own two small diesel locomotives for shunting their yard as late as 1972, but this lasted only until 1979, when the last connection was removed. The rest of the Darlaston loop trackwork had been removed in 1970.

One railtour is known to have visited the line, organized by the Stephenson Locomotive Society, on 26th May, 1951. This was to have been powered by a Webb 2-4-2T, which members had been allowed to clean to a high standard, but this unfortunately failed on the day of the railtour. Its place was taken by Ivatt 2-6-2T No. 41226, sandwiched in the middle of a four-coach formation comprising two push-pull sets. The tour also included several other goods-only lines, such as the Princes End branch, then after reaching Wolverhampton by the Stour Valley route, a trip along the former MR line via Short Heath to Aldridge, and up the single line to Brownhills.

Part of the line through the centre of Darlaston can be traced, and indeed forms a footpath through the edge of the town, so that the site of Darlaston station can be visited. The only remains to be seen here are two former overbridges, although the goods shed at Wednesbury still survives, now in use as a road transport depot.

Wednesbury via Princes End to Tipton (the Princes End branch)

The SSR Act of 23rd July, 1855 (Vict. 18 & 19, cap. 175) authorized the original construction of this line along with the Darlaston loop, stipulating that construction should begin within two years and be complete within five years. This Act also included authorization for a chord linking the SSR at Princes End to the nearby OWWR.

The surviving records do not clearly indicate the sequence of events for this line, and are thus somewhat confusing. It seems likely that the SSR company was initially concerned only with building a branch from Wednesbury as far as Princes End, where it would make a connection with the Wednesbury Oak furnaces and collieries belonging to Philip Williams & Sons. This would make sense as Philip Williams was a major shareholder in the SSR. Indeed, a sketch plan by McClean & Stileman dated 1858 exists which shows the Tipton branch as running from Wednesbury to a canal basin at Wednesbury Oak, and gives the line as being 1 mile 40½ chains in length. Along with the earlier estimates detailed below, this suggests that at that time several plans were under consideration.

In June 1855 McClean submitted an estimate to the Board of Directors for the total costs of the 'Tipton branch', which was stated to be of 66 chains length and double track. It was to be of double track, and include two road overbridges, two road underbridges, one canal underbridge and a level crossing. This corresponds with the line from Princes End to its junction with the Stour Valley Railway at Tipton. The details were as follows:

	£	s.	d.
Earthworks	5,812	18	4
Fencing	254	2	0
Permanent Way	3,904	6	3
Bridges and level crossing	3,137	10	0
Culverts	238	5	0
Land	6,937	10	0
Contingency (10%)	2,028	5	2
Total	*22,310*	*16*	*9*

At the same time, McClean prepared an estimate for another line of double track, with a total length of 43½ chains (just over ½ mile). This was referred to as the 'Tipton SSR and OWWR line', and is therefore assumed to be the chord authorized by the 1855 Act . This was to be a line 'to junction with the OWWR at Sedgley at bridge there over of tramway from Dimock's Collieries'. In other words, it ran from a north-facing junction, just south of the OWWR Princes End station to an east-facing junction west of the SSR Princes End station.The estimate included three overbridges, one underbridge and a level crossing. The details were:

	£	s.	d.
Earthworks	3,529	3	4
Fencing	166	5	0
Permanent Way	2,573	6	0
Bridges and crossings	2,463	2	6
Culverts	225	0	0
Land	4,625	0	0
Contingency (10%)	1,358	3	8
Total	*14,940*	*0*	*6*

At a Board Meeting on 18th November, 1856 the Directors authorized a letter to be sent to the LNWR, asking what should be the course of action, in view of the imminent expiry of the 1855 authorization. However, there is no record of any reply, although subsequent events made clear the intentions of the LNWR. On 16th July, 1858 the contract bids for the Darlaston and Tipton branches were opened by the Directors, and as mentioned above, the contract was awarded to Thomas Brassey for an undisclosed sum.

However, the time granted for completion of the construction in the 1855 Act expired before a firm decision was made, and so, as for the Darlaston loop, an extension until 23rd July, 1862 was granted in the SSR Act of 13th August, 1859. Construction was certainly well under way during 1860, as the last available accounts for the SSR (up to 31st January, 1861), showed an expenditure on both the Tipton and Darlaston lines as being £7,661 11s. 9d. in the current year, with an accumulated cost of £44,066 10s. 9d. As the line was not inspected until August 1863 this suggests that there was some delay in the final completion of the line, unless it was first intended to open it for goods workings only. Unfortunately, there is no further information available on the construction of the line, nor of the chord to the OWWR, other than the report of Colonel Yolland dated 8th August, 1863 following his first inspection. He found that the works were too incomplete to permit the authorization of the opening of the line, and recommended that the opening should be deferred for one month. His comments noted that a repeating signal was required at Bagnall's crossing. He also specified that the junction with the WMR (formerly OWWR) was not protected by normal junction signals, and if these were not provided, then the junction should be taken out. This comment casts further doubt as to whether the chord was actually ever put into use, but once again there is a lack of surviving correspondence on this matter.

The chord to the OWWR is particularly intriguing as it is shown on some local maps of around 1864. The 1877 1 inch:1 mile Ordnance Survey map shows the line *in situ*. However, the First Edition 25 in. Ordnance Survey Map of 1883 reveals that only the earthworks of the line had survived by that date. The mystery over this chord is deepened by a lack of reference to it in the records of the OWWR. The conclusion is that it was built along with the Princes End branch, but closed and lifted some time prior to 1883, perhaps even before the branch was opened. Possibly it was not considered necessary as the OWWR had become part of the West Midland Railway (WMR), absorbed by the GWR in 1863, and also had a connection from a south-facing junction on the WMR (OWWR) to a north-facing junction on the Stour Valley line of the LNWR, to the west of the Tipton triangular junction. Furthermore, the GWR also had the potentially more useful connection at Wednesbury.

Board of Trade approval for the opening of the branch was eventually granted on 5th September, 1863 for the completed line of 2 miles and 51 chains (2⅝ miles). It was opened to passenger traffic on 14th September, 1863 with one intermediate station, at Princes End. A second station was eventually erected at Ocker Hill, which the Directors had authorized on 27th February, 1864 as 'a small station, to cost around £700'. This was evidently a modest affair, as it opened not long after, on 1st July, 1864.

The following report from the *Staffordshire Advertiser* of Saturday 19th September, 1863 announced the opening of the line, as well as the Darlaston Loop:

LOCAL INTELLIGENCE – WEDNESBURY
OPENING OF THE NEW BRANCH LINES – The two Branch lines from the Wednesbury Station of the London and North Western Railway to Darlaston and Tipton were opened for passenger traffic on Monday last. Wednesbury is now favoured with four lines of railway, and of necessity will become the centre into which the surrounding places will pour their passengers, and from which they may be conveyed to any part of the country. The opening of the two new lines must afford not only increased railway accommodation, but increased trade and increased prosperity to the town of Wednesbury.

On 26th August, 1865 the Board of Directors rather belatedly reviewed the Board of Trade conditions for opening of the Tipton and Darlaston branches, which included conditions that four lodges should be built at level crossings within six months of opening to passenger traffic. The Directors agreed for this work to be put in hand, but appear to have decided against the further condition that a turntable should be installed at Wednesbury. It is likely that operating conditions made this requirement unnecessary.

Fowler class '4' 2-6-4T No. 42371 passes the long abandoned remains of Princes End station with a Walsall to Wolverhampton train on 24th April, 1949. The wooden building on the down platform is probably an original waiting shelter. The poor state of the buildings in the background reflects the lack of maintenance available during the hard years of the 1930s and the subsequent austerity during World War II.   *K. Hodgkins Collection*

The SLS special of 26th May, 1951 visited the Princes End branch, and is seen here pausing in the remains of Princes End station at the heavily overgrown up platform. The down platform, on the left, had become a dumping ground for redundant track materials, although the starter at the end of the platform, was still of LNWR pattern at that time. The relatively low heights of the platforms are evident. Motive power for this special was Ivatt class '2' 2-6-2T No. 41226.

Historical Model Railway Society/ESR

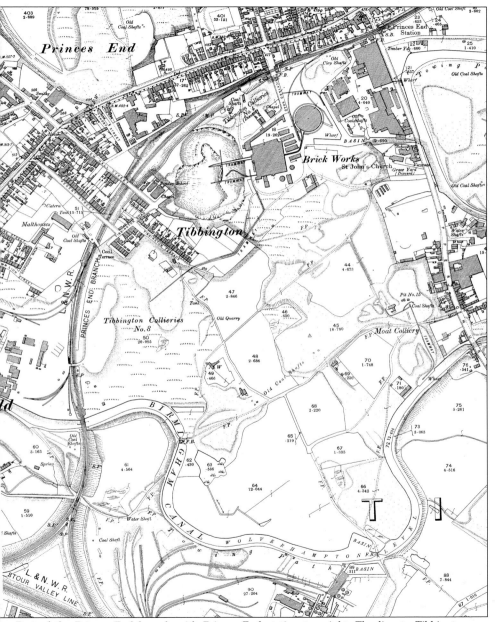

Part of the Princes End branch with Princes End station top right. The line to Tibbington Collieries & Brickworks curves south, just to the left of Princes End station. The trackbed of the mystery spur from the OWWR comes in top left and curves south to meet the SSR at Brickyard Road.   *Reproduced from the 25", 1904 Ordnance Survey Map*

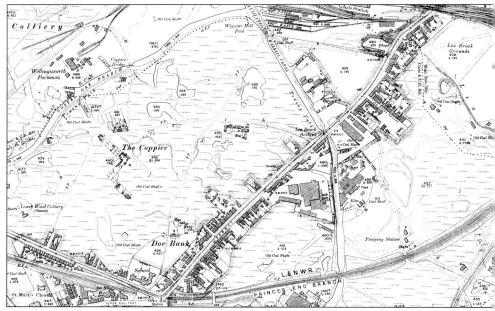

Ocker Hill station.

Reproduced from the 25", 1901 Ordnance Survey Map

A very grubby Stanier class '5' 4-6-0 No. 45065 wheels a diverted express through the remains of Ocker Hill station on 24th April, 1949. At that time the remnants of the platforms were still evident. The train has just passed beneath the short tunnel on which was situated the major junction of four roads. The large pipe over the line was a gas main from Tipton gasworks. The cutting here has since been infilled, and a residential care home occupies the station site. The large Ansells pub is long gone.

Historical Model Railway Society/ESR

At the Tipton end, a spur was installed connecting the line to the Stour Valley line at a south-facing junction (Station Junction), thereby creating a triangular junction at this point. This curve, opened on 1st January, 1883, was mostly used for freight traffic, although it was brought into use for diverted passenger trains, particularly during the early 1960s when electrification work was proceeding on the Stour Valley line further north.

A passenger service between Walsall and Wolverhampton was initiated along the line from the opening date. This is shown on page 115 in September, 1879 as totalling eight trains from Walsall on weekdays, and nine from Wolverhampton. There were no Sunday services. However, the opening of the LNWR Portobello and Pleck curves on 1st March, 1881 permitted a more direct working from Walsall to Wolverhampton. Surprisingly, the services on the Princes End branch were initially only slightly affected, as in November 1881 there were still seven trains each way (*shown on page 116*), but by November, 1887 there were just four trains each way. The down services left Wednesbury at 8.33 am, 1.30, 5.10 and 7.20 pm. Eventually the Wolverhampton trains were concentrated on the Portobello route, and this, together with the effect, already mentioned, of the introduction of tram services in the area, caused the LNWR to withdraw the passenger services as from 1st November, 1890.

The branch passenger trains up to this time were almost exclusively powered by the Webb 4 ft 6 in. 2-4-2Ts which were not fitted with push-pull apparatus, so had to run-round their trains at each end of the line. However, these were eventually superseded by the auto-fitted 5 ft 6 in. version.

A local effort to persuade the LNWR to reopen passenger services on the route was eventually successful, and on 1st July, 1895 the service recommenced. However, the Walsall to Wolverhampton services were not resumed. Instead, a shorter service was introduced from Wednesbury to Tipton and Dudley Port (High Level) on the Stour Valley line, using the 1883 curve at Tipton. This was announced in the *Midland Advertiser* of Saturday 29th June,1895 as follows:

On Monday *(1st July)* the Princes End Branch of the London & North Western Railway is to be reopened for passenger traffic. Five trains will be run each day from Wednesbury, the first at 7.53 am, and the last at 6.45 pm. The Princes End inhabitants have had their wish granted, and now why cannot the Company turn their attention to Darlaston?

The five-train service continued in 1901, and to make the best use of these short services, steam railcars were introduced some time prior to 1908. By April 1910 the service was more or less unchanged, with four from Wednesbury (at 7.38, 10.52 am, 12.55 and 3.42 pm) to Dudley Port, and five in the opposite direction (from Dudley Port at 8.50, 10.22 am, 12.20, 3.20 and 6.52 pm). The services all called at Tipton, Princes End and Ocker Hill and took between 10 and 13 minutes to complete. In addition, one service ran in each direction between Dudley and Walsall via Dudley Port (High Level), Tipton and Princes End from this time until 1914. But the service was relatively short-lived, for necessary economies during World War I enforced the withdrawal of passenger services from 1st January, 1916, and were never thereafter reinstated. The stations at Princes End and Ocker Hill were both closed from this date, but not immediately dismantled, although Ocker Hill had been demolished before 1939.

A view taken from the GWR line at Wednesbury in 1961 and looking south across the exchange sidings, in the foreground. A Stanier 'Black Five' 4-6-0 is taking the line to Princes End with a lengthy freight, and in the distance the cooling towers of Ocker Hill power station dominate the skyline.   *D. Wilson*

English Electric type '4' diesel No. D332 swings into Wednesbury along the Princes End branch with a diverted express for the north in 1962. It has just passed Ocker Hill power station.   *D. Wilson*

A seemingly unusual working, captured here in the early summer of 1962, was this WR Swindon-built single unit parcels car as it approached Wednesbury along the Princes End branch. The skyline is dominated by the cooling towers and chimneys of the Ocker Hill power station on the left, and those of the Patent Shaft steel works centre right. *D. Wilson*

Stanier 'Jubilee' 4-6-0 No. 45670 *Howard of Effingham*, of Crewe North shed, makes a fine sight as it heads a parcels train northwards along the Princes End branch near Gospel Oak in the summer of 1962. *D. Wilson*

Brush A1A-A1A No. 5544 hauls a load of full coke wagons on the Princes End branch, bound for Bilston steelworks, on 1st June, 1972. It is approaching the Gospel Oak area, near to Ocker Hill and slightly south-east of Princes End.   *D. Wilson*

A permanent way train, headed by a class '25' Bo-Bo, approaches the Gospel Oak area on the Princes End branch, heading north on 19th January, 1981.   *D. Wilson*

The double track line remained open for goods traffic, and saw considerable use, especially for coal and iron ore trains travelling to the Springvale Furnaces at Bilston, and the returning empty wagons. These furnaces had been worked by Alfred Hickman (later Sir Alfred Hickman) since 1866 until sold to Stewarts & Lloyds Ltd in 1921, and later nationalized as part of the British Steel Corporation as from the vesting day, 28th July, 1967. Iron ore traffic originated from Corby and Lamport in Northamptonshire, and in 1966/67 there was one daily train (plus the returning empties) from each of these sites to Springvale along the line. An additional daily working was from Scunthorpe to the newly-opened Wolverhampton Steel Terminal (and return empties). By 1970, there was a considerable expansion of workings along the line, with additional oil trains and other workings now proceeding to other local destinations such as the Albion oil storage depot near to Tipton on the Stour Valley route, so that both parts of the triangle at Tipton were in regular use. A summary from the working timetable for 4th April, 1970 to 4th October, 1970 shows the following traffic pattern:

	No. of workings	
Day	Up	Down
Monday	14	16
Tuesday	27	22
Wednesday	25	24
Thursday	27	23
Friday	25	24
Saturday	14	9

These include a considerable number of light engine movements, as the return workings were often not required immediately. Destinations included Corby, Toton, Milford Haven, Severn Tunnel Junction, Fawley, Cardiff, Newport, West Thurrock, Ripple Lane, South Bank (Sunderland), Scunthorpe, Sheffield, Derby, Etruria, and Mossend (Glasgow). There were no Sunday workings.

By the following year, the working timetable for 3rd May, 1971 to 3rd October, 1971 gave a quite different level of traffic:

	No. of workings	
Day	Up	Down
Monday	7	7
Tuesday	11	6
Wednesday	10	7
Thursday	11	6
Friday	10	7
Saturday	10	5

The last part of the Springvale furnaces was finally closed in 1979, thereby reducing one important source of traffic, although the adjacent Millfields Works continued until March 1983.

Locomotives used on the freight workings would have included the Ramsbottom 'DX' goods 0-6-0s and Webb 0-6-0s of the 17 in. 'Coal Engine' and

An unidentified BR Sulzer class '25' passes the signal box at Princes End with a short freight on 1st May, 1980. The driver is surrendering the tablet for the single line section from Wednesbury, and is about to enter the double track section onwards to Bloomfield Junction. The crossing gates over Lower Church Lane have already been converted to half-barrier operation with flashing lights. *D. Wilson*

The last passenger working over the Princes End line occurred on 22nd November, 1980 when an SLS railtour made up of a class '101' dmu passed along. Here we see it making its way over the level crossing at Princes End. The remains of the station platform had just about disappeared by that time. *D. Wilson*

18 in. 'Cauliflower' types during the LNWR days. The ubiquitous LNWR 0-8-0s of various configurations were well represented in the area, and a common site right up to 1963. Fowler '4F' 0-6-0s and the Stanier '8F' 2-8-0s were also a frequently seen, along with the less usual appearances of 'Black Five' 4-6-0s and BR Standard '9F' 2-10-0s. Into the diesel era, classes '24', '25', '31', '37', '45', '46', '47' and '56' were often seen along the line. The steepness of the line for down trains meant that the loaded trains, such as those containing iron ore heading for Bilston steelworks, were frequently banked from Wednesbury to Princes End. After World War II such duties inevitably fell to the LNWR 0-8-0s normally found on pilot duties at Wednesbury. These sturdy engines made a final swansong on the line on 12th December, 1964, when a visiting railtour was powered by two of them, Nos. 49361 and 49430. Earlier railtours, organized by the Stephenson Locomotive Society, passed along the line including the one in 1951 mentioned above visiting Darlaston, and also on 25th May, 1957 Stanier 2-6-4T No. 42627 provided the motive power for a further visit.

Starting from Wednesbury Town station, the line diverged from the Dudley line beyond the bridge carrying the GWR Birmingham to Wolverhampton line (originally the BWDR) and the connecting spur just beyond, and ran on to a lengthy embankment. The line crossed the small Lea Brook , which meandered through the usual dismal landscape, to join the River Tame on the left (south side) of the line. The embankment approached the Walsall Canal of the Birmingham Canal Navigation, and as it did so, a connecting line swung southwards to Ocker Hill power station, which had been opened in 1902. However, its coal was supplied entirely by the adjacent canal until May 1948 when the station was enlarged, and the rail connection put in. Even so, most of the coal continued to arrive by the canal, and the rail connection was only used infrequently until 1977 when the station was converted to oil firing. The station was kept in reserve thereafter, and used only in times of emergency, such as during the miners' strike of 1983/1984. The line had been completely buried by vegetation by this time, but this was cleared away to permit the delivery of oil to the station, which continued throughout the dispute. The power station was finally closed and subsequently demolished in 1985.

On the opposite side of the line, and also adjoining the Walsall Canal was the Leabrook Ironworks of John Bagnall & Sons Ltd. to which a connecting line was not put in until the 1930s, even though the works had been operating since before 1864. This was used until around 1980, although their two remaining Ruston diesels continued to be used purely for internal shunting until the works closed on 4th May, 1984.

After crossing the canal, the line then entered a cutting which continued into the station at Ocker Hill (¾ mile), and before reaching it, passed beneath a massive pipe. This was a 30 in. gas main running from the Mond gas works at Dudley Port to various industrial users in Darlaston, Wednesbury, Willenhall and Wednesfield. The station was located in the same cutting, at the junction of the Gospel Oak, Leabrook and Toll End Roads. The line passed beneath this major road junction in a short tunnel. The line has been infilled at the site of the station, and today a nursing home is situated on the former site, and the approaches of the line have been encroached by industrial and commercial

The Princes End branch as it headed westwards from Wednesbury in 1985, shortly before the demolition of Ocker Hill power station. The rail entrance to the power station is centre left, passing through the gate across the siding.   *K. Hodgkins*

English Electric class '37' Co-Co No. 37864 crosses the Walsall Canal of the Birmingham Canal Navigation near Ocker Hill with a steel train about 1985.   *K. Hodgkins*

developments. No goods facilities were provided at Ocker Hill, and the small station was not even connected to the telegraph system, so never became a block post. As the line continued westwards, it passed out of the cutting on to an embankment, crossing Ocker Hill Road into the Gospel Oak area. This embankment was the source of many underground fires over the years, which despite many attempts to quell, were only finally eliminated after the closure of the line, when the whole embankment was removed. On the left was Gospel Oak Colliery, and on the right a connection was made running into the Wednesbury Oak Furnaces of Philip Williams & Sons and the associated collieries. These furnaces were finally blown out around 1920, and the connection was truncated to serve other users, becoming known as Cox's siding, the access points being electrically released from Princes End signal box.This siding initially served the works of Messrs Cox, and still later Messrs Arnott, Young & Company used the site as a scrapyard for a number of years.

The line next passed over the Wolverhampton Level of the Birmingham Canal Navigation, and continued along an embankment into the township of Princes End (1¾ miles). The station was located adjacent to the town centre, and at the western end of the platforms was a level crossing over Upper Church Lane. A pedestrian footbridge was positioned nearby so as to give pedestrians a chance to cross whilst the gates were closed to road traffic, and also a means of getting from one platform to the other. The original level crossing gates were replaced on 29th September, 1974 with lifting barriers. The main station buildings were placed on the up (Wednesbury direction) platform. A 20-lever signal box with LNWR tappet frame was also positioned adjacent to the level crossing , but on the down side. The box was of typical LNWR gable-ended construction, with a brick base and wooden upper half. This box contained the Annett's Key A for control of the entry to the Ocker Hill power station siding. Key B controlled access to the siding on the up side, west of the crossing. This siding was the truncated remains of the spur, which had once led to the OWWR. Key C controlled access to the siding on the down side that originally led to the Tibbington Collieries & Brickworks Ltd, which site was latterly taken over by the Austin Motor Co. Ltd. Originally, these last three were controlled by another signal box sited on the southern side of the line adjacent to the level crossing over Brickyard Road, which it also controlled. However, when the brickworks closed in the 1920s this lane was shortened so that the level crossing no longer existed, and so the signal box was also removed. None of the station buildings and the signal box remain, but although the site of the level crossing over Upper Church Lane is easy to identify, there are no other reminders of the past.

The line now curved through 90 degrees in a cutting to face south, passing two further sidings to collieries on the right, and then recrossing the Wolverhampton Levels once more. Shortly after, and in the midst of more unused land dotted with former coal workings, the line reached Tipton Curve Junction (2¼ miles), where the lines to the north and south on the Stour Valley line bifurcated to form the triangular junction. A 20-lever signal box with LNWR tumbler frame was located in the fork of this junction, and from this point the 'up' and 'down' directions were reversed. Each side of the triangle

Johnson 0-6-0 No. 58157 propels a raft of coal wagons over the Daw End branch of the Birmingham Canal Navigation at Stubber's Green on the Leighswood branch, around 1960. The angler on the canal bank appears completely oblivious to the activity on the railway.

Bill Mayo Collection

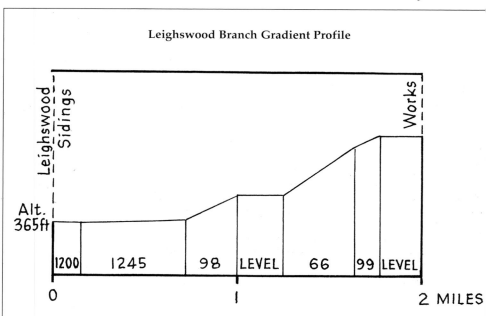

remained double track and was elevated on an embankment to the junctions with the Stour Valley line.

The line was effectively singled during 1965, when use of the down line was discontinued between Wednesbury and Princes End. Subsequently, the unused line was lifted, and the alignment of the remaining single line was slewed to the centre line of the formation for much of its length. A block post was maintained at the Princes End signal box for exchange of tokens. One final movement over the line seems to have been a Railway Correspondence & Travel Society dmu special which traversed the line on 22nd November, 1980. The line was closed completely as from 6th April, 1981, although as we have seen the portion from Wednesbury to Ocker Hill power station was left *in situ* for several more years.

The Leighswood Branch

The 1855 SSR Act also authorized construction of a line from a north-facing junction, just south of Pelsall station to the Aldridge and Coppy Hall collieries. The total length of the line was just 2 miles. Once more the powers were allowed to lapse, but this line was not built for more than 20 years, finally opening on 14th November, 1878. Construction was authorized under the LNW (New Lines) Act of 28th June, 1877 (Vict. 40 & 41, cap. 44) and apparently proceeded with little difficulty. The following report is abstracted from the *Walsall Observer & South Staffordshire Chronicle* of 23rd November, 1878:

> OPENING OF A MINERAL RAILWAY BETWEEN ALDRIDGE AND PELSALL
> On Tuesday, the 14th inst, an important event in the history of the Leighs Wood Colliery Company Limited took place – viz, the opening of a branch mineral railway from their colliery at Aldridge to Pelsall, and, as the line will afford the means of bringing other mining and manufacturing concerns in the same neighbourhood into more direct communication with the principal markets than they have hitherto enjoyed, it follows, as a matter of course, that the event is one of considerable importance to the entire district as well as to the company most closely identified with the undertaking. In the morning a sort of official visit of inspection was made by Mr. Sutton, district manager of the LNWR Company, who was met by Captain Tongue (one of the proprietors of the colliery), Mr. E. Barnett, the chief officials of the company, and other gentlemen ; and, after the remarkably fine plant had been viewed, and a visit paid to the adjacent best blue brick and tile works of Mr. E. Barnett – one of the concerns which hereafter will be connected with the railway – the first train of 20 loaded trucks was run over the line by the company's engine 'Leighs Wood', its arrival at the junction being signalled by three hearty cheers by the officials and visitors who accompanied it. The colliery, it may be added, covers 500 acres, and has seven seams (30 ft) of workable coal, and three seams of ironstone. It consists of two pits, the No.1, at Stubber's Green, known prior to its purchase by the company as the Coppy Hall Colliery, and the No.2, or Leighs Wood Colliery....By Christmas last the workings were fully opened out, and the raising of coal began.....The output hitherto has been sent away by boat, but the new railway puts the company within easy reach of Birmingham, to which the first train was dispatched on 14th inst...

The use of one or two words to spell the name 'Leighswood' appears to be optional in this area.

Johnson MR 0-6-0 No. 58157 ambles along the Leighswood branch at Shelfield with empty wagons from the Leighswood Brickworks of Barnett & Beddows Ltd.　　*Bill Mayo Collection*

Former MR Johnson '2F' class 0-6-0 No. 58157 shunting wagons at the Leighswood Brickworks around 1960. With their light axle weight, these locomotives were almost the only motive power permitted over the branch. Brickmaking kilns can be seen on the left and right of the picture, and the skyline is punctuated with colliery engines and chimneys.　　*Bill Mayo Collection*

Initially, the line was worked by the locomotive of the Leighswood Colliery Co. Ltd, but LNWR locomotives took over operation from 1st April, 1880, although the colliery locomotive (*Leighs Wood*) was permitted to work until 14th June of that year. This was an inside-cylinder Beyer, Peacock 0-6-0ST supplied new to the company in 1878.

However, the Leighswood Colliery Co. Ltd was in liquidation in 1881, and taken over by the nearby Aldridge Colliery Co. Ltd, but the locomotive was sold, as the lines to both of the collieries were then worked by the LNWR. It was used by the contractors Meakin and Dean on the construction of the second Belsize tunnel (between Kentish Town and Finsbury Park) for the Midland Railway until 1884, later finding its way to the Birtley Collieries of the Sheffield Coal Co. Ltd. The Leighswood Colliery closed in 1930, and the Aldridge Colliery in 1936, after which the company concentrated on brick manufacture. The nearby Coppy Hall Colliery had been purchased by Edward Barnett (as referred to in the newspaper report) and converted to brick manufacture, and the later company Barnett & Beddows Ltd acquired the two other colliery sites, so that thereafter the three became known as the Utopia, Empire and Atlas works.

Even in this quiet backwater, accidents occurred, and one was reported in the *Walsall Observer & South Staffordshire Chronicle* of 5th November, 1881. On the previous Monday morning, 31st October, a fireman Charles Derry James , aged 20 was killed at Leighswood Siding - so presumably actually at the exchange sidings with the SSR main line. The report stated: 'It appears that he was riding on the side of his engine, which passed so close to some trucks on another line as to crush him severely'. He died in hospital three days later.

The branch actually commenced from two sidings laid parallel to the main line about ¼ mile (actually 29 chains) south of Pelsall station, and ran as a single line towards Shelfield, where it passed through the village in a cutting, and beneath Four Crosses Road and the Lichfield Road (now A461). Moving into open countryside, the line passed by Stubbers Green and crossed the Daw End branch of the Birmingham Canal Navigation (BCN) on a plate girder bridge, with blue brick abutments, before descending to the level crossing over a lane known as Brick Yard Row. Here, all trains were required to stop, until authorized to continue by a representative of the brickworks. The inclination of the line was such that it favoured loaded trains with a descent from the colliery/brickworks to the main line. The gradients were not at first particularly taxing, even for the incoming empty wagons, as the first stretch from the main line was at 1 in 1220/1245 for ¾ mile, but then it steepened to 1 in 98 for ¼ mile, then after a further ¼ mile on level track, there were two short lengths at 1 in 66 and 1 in 99 before attaining level track for the last ¼ mile into the works. In between, where the line crossed the canal, it was approached by a very short section of 1 in 28, which fell away on the other side of the bridge at 1 in 33. This, combined with the other short steep sections, made the branch particularly difficult to work in the days of loose-coupled wagons, as even though the trains were not particularly long, some wagons would be passing over different inclinations to other wagons in the train, at the same time. Furthermore, the two very steep sections meant that the drivers had to ensure that they had adequate water in the boiler to avoid exposing the fusible plugs.

Ivatt class '2' 2-6-2T No. 41225 of Bushbury shed stands in the up platform at Pleck whilst propelling the two-coach autotrain working of the 10.50 am from Wolverhampton to Walsall on 13th August, 1958. This view illustrates the positioning of the main station building on a steel raft over the line, and the wooden construction of that building, as well as the stairs leading to the platforms, and the waiting rooms on each platform.   *R. Shenton*

The line was worked on the 'one engine in steam' system, and being of lightly laid construction, the locomotives permitted to work along it were severely limited. In LMS and BR days this meant that the normal motive power was a Johnson MR 0-6-0 of the '1142' class, from the stud kept at Ryecroft or latterly Bescot shed. These became quite a well known attraction in their later years. The main inward traffic was coal for the kilns, but there seems to have been little outward traffic, especially in later years. During its life, a maximum of two daily trains visited the line, operating Monday to Friday. Inevitably the service declined to one per day, this being 'conditional' on sufficient traffic being available.

The line closed during August 1965 when the signal box controlling the entrance to the SSR main line was also taken out of use.

The New Pleck Curve

The LNWR (New Lines) Act (Vict. 40 & 41, cap. 44) was passed on 28th June, 1877, incorporating powers to construct a new spur from the GJR at James Bridge Junction eastwards to the SSR at Pleck Junction. This new alignment thus provided the opportunity for trains from the north on the GJR route to enter Walsall without having to reverse at Bescot.

The line opened on 1st March, 1881, at the same time that the Portobello curve was opened, linking the GJR route northwards to the former MR route into Wolverhampton (High Level). Thus a more efficient service could now be offered between Walsall and Wolverhampton, which over the years was extended to Burton and Derby for selected trains. As we have seen this materially affected the Walsall to Wolverhampton service via the Princes End line, and trains travelling over the Darlaston Loop could now reach Darlaston from Walsall without travelling via Wednesbury. So the services over this route too were rescheduled. Along the curve, a new station opened at the same time, at Pleck (although Neele gives the date of opening of Pleck station as 1st November, 1881). This was situated adjacent to Pleck Road, from which the station was accessed. The main station building was situated on a deck alongside the road, and above the line. The building was constructed with wood panelling, having a tall steeply-pitched roof, with two chimney stacks protruding, each surmounted by three ornamental chimney pots. This contained the booking office, parcels office and staff rooms, so that the waiting shelters on each platform were of a rather basic nature, again executed in wood. The shelters featured short cantilevered canopies towards the platform edges. Covered wooden staircases led from the booking hall down to each platform. No goods facilities were provided. It appears to have prospered, despite the increasing tram competition at the time, but was closed as from 1st January,

Left: The outside view of Pleck station as seen from Bescot Road, Pleck on 13th August, 1958. The style of the building is most unusual, possibly reminiscent of chalets and cafeteria at the turn of the century, which were similarly executed in wood. Nonetheless, the appearance is pleasing, and the tall chimneys add distinction. Although closed in 1958, this building was not demolished until September 1972.   *R. Shenton*

1917 as part of the economies of World War I, being reopened by the LMS on 1st May, 1924. It lasted until 17th November, 1958 when it closed for the final time, and was subsequently demolished completely. At this same time, dmus were introduced into the area for the local services, as a result of which there was a service of 12 trains from Wolverhampton to Walsall using the curve, of which nine continued on to Burton. This service was axed from January 1964, but reinstated in 2000 with a service from Wellington to Walsall, which itself was completely revised as from 11th June, 2006. This then comprised an hourly service during the day, with 17 each way on weekdays and 15 on Sundays from Wolverhampton to Walsall. Only the first train of the day on weekdays ran through to Wellington, and in the reverse direction, the second and the last trains of the day started from Wellington. On Saturdays, the only train to serve Wellington was the last train of the day from that town, which was served by none on Sundays. These passenger services were entirely withdrawn as from 1st January, 2008 (see further comments in Chapter Eleven) and today the curve sees only occasional freight use.

Walsall Wood Branch

This two mile line was authorized by the provisions contained in the LNWR Act (Vict. 43 & 44, cap. 145) which attained Royal Assent on 6th August, 1880. It was constructed in 1881-1882 from a south facing junction with the SSR at Norton Junction to the Walsall Wood Colliery, passing beneath the MR line from Aldridge to Brownhills, which was also under construction, to the colliery. It continued from the colliery to connect with the MR a little further south. The line was built by John Garlick, of Saltley, Birmingham who used two locomotives on its construction. One was certainly *Minnie*, an inside-cylinder 0-4-0ST by Hunslet (Works No. 229 of 1879) but the identity of the second locomotive is not known, other than it was also a Hunslet engine, but of a larger 0-6-0ST type. Both engines were taken to Brownhills station after completion of the line, where they were auctioned on 7th December, 1882.

The locomotives of the colliery company were only used initially for shunting to the LNWR branch, but from 2nd January, 1909 the LNWR ceased to work over the line, and so the colliery engines worked through to the exchange sidings on the SSR at Norton Junction. The colliery passed to the National Coal Board on nationalization as from 1st January, 1947 and closed in October, 1964. The line was used for short period afterwards to remove stocks of coal, and other materials.

Details of locomotives used at all of the lineside industrial sites are given in *Appendix Four*.

Chapter Four

The Lease

Within six months of the completion of its main line during 1849, a group of nominally independent parties led by John Robinson McClean, the SSR Engineer, approached the Board with an offer to lease the railway. As we noted earlier, the LNWR and MR were substantial shareholders and therefore strongly represented on the Board of Directors. They did not take kindly to the idea of the line passing into independent hands, especially as this meant that traffic arrangements could be made without their prior consent, possibly with competitors, such as the GWR or the North Staffordshire Railway (NSR). The Chairman of the Birmingham Canal was also a Director, and aligned himself with the LNWR and MR representatives in rejecting these proposals put forward at two Special Meetings of the shareholders. However, the proposers were well organized and comprised many of the local shareholders, so that they were eventually able to convince the majority of the shareholders that the offer was more than they could expect from the major railway companies, who were not prepared to work the line for a guaranteed dividend. It was not unusual for railway companies to undertake to work a line in exchange for say, 50 per cent of the receipts, giving a guarantee to the shareholders of the line that a minimum dividend would be paid. Indeed the LNWR entered into such an agreement with the Shropshire Union Railways & Canal Company in the same year, which encompassed their entire business. However, the reluctance to enter into an agreement here may have been due to the relative unproven record of the SSR. Whatever the cause, their intransigence initially lost them the opportunity to work the line.

A draft 21 year lease was presented by McClean to the Traffic Committee on 25th October, 1849 which was to run from 25th March, 1850. He agreed to a deposit of £10,000 to ensure fulfilment of all payments. However, the SSR had not yet obtained Parliamentary authority to grant such a lease.

The necessary powers were included in the SSR Leasing Act of 1850 (Vict. 13 & 14, cap. 58), enabling the process to go ahead. This differed from the normal working agreements of the day as detailed above, instead establishing that any lessee would pay rent on the issued share capital of the company, and that the lessee would not be expected to pay rent on any unpaid calls, nor on any loans. The Act provided for the issued capital to be increased to £748,125 although on 31st July of that year there were unpaid calls of £39,777 11s. 10d., which increased by some £2,000 on a later call. This was subsequently amended so that the issued capital of the SSR Company was calculated as £669,375 in shares of £8 10s. 0d. each. The rent was 2 per cent of this in the first year, amounting to £13,387 10s. 0d. Thereafter it would be at the rate of 4 per cent or £26,775, increasing to 5 per cent after 14 years. The locomotive stock, rails, sleepers and chairs were to be determined later, and a valuation was calculated by Matthew Kirtley of the MR. The lessee was to be responsible for the maintenance of the rolling stock, the purchase of new rolling stock, and to provide for the restoration of the rolling stock in later years. The locomotives were said to number eight on a schedule that has not survived, with another three added before the date of the lease. Finally, the lease between McClean and the company was adopted by the Board on 21st January, 1850 and the lease signed, and became effective from 1st July, 1850. Curiously, the seal of the SSR Company was not placed on the lease until 13th January, 1851.

This was a notable landmark in railway history, as no individual had ever been authorized by Parliament to lease a railway before. It set a precedent, and the more well-known leasing of the Shrewsbury & Hereford Railway by the great Thomas Brassey followed in 1852. However, there were few that could attempt to manage a railway, let alone find the necessary finance, and so such schemes remained relatively rare.

McClean was an astute businessman, and soon realised that the company had insufficient facilities for the maintenance of the locomotives and rolling stock. He arranged for the locomotives to be sent to Crewe for the main overhauls, but Francis Trevithick, then in charge at Crewe, had no particular interest in these non-standard types and maintenance suffered. Eventually, a working agreement with the LNWR dated 10th February, 1852 came into effect on from 5th July of that year, whereby McClean subcontracted the running of the trains to the LNWR, who were then free to use whatever motive power they wished. (Neele actually gives this date of transfer as being 12th April of that year.) The SSR locomotives were transferred to the Northern Division of the LNWR, but because they remained the property of the SSR, a valuation was performed by John Viret Gooch of the Eastern Counties Railway. Thereafter, the original SSR locomotives were used alongside the LNWR Northern Division types until 1856, when it was agreed that the LNWR Southern Division would take over the running, under the command of James McConnell. On the appointed day of this transfer (unfortunately not recorded), a procession of 16 engines, all in steam, arrived from Wolverton, and the engine crews moved directly to their new steeds. Thus the green-liveried Northern Division engines were replaced by McConnell's vermilion red Southern Division types. The original SSR locomotives still remained the property of the SSR, but were renumbered into the Southern Division sequences in 1860.

Meanwhile, McClean signed an agreement with Joseph Wright, the rolling stock manufacturer of Saltley, Birmingham, who had indeed supplied many of the SSR carriages and wagons. This contract provided for Wright to maintain all of the SSR vehicles, which were listed in an inventory and valuation prepared by one Joseph Beattie as of 1st January, 1851 with a total value of £64,196. These vehicles are listed in *Appendix One*.

On 29th August, 1857 the Board of Directors agreed to extend the lease to cover the Norton and Cannock branches, both then under construction.

Throughout McClean's tenure he worked from Walsall, although the SSR head office remained at Lichfield. However, during 1858 both parties to the lease had decided that they would like to relinquish their obligations. Doubtless, McClean's many other business interests meant that he was unable to spend time on the running of the SSR, despite his very capable staff. A 'heads of arrangement' was agreed on 21st January, 1858 in which the SSR engines and

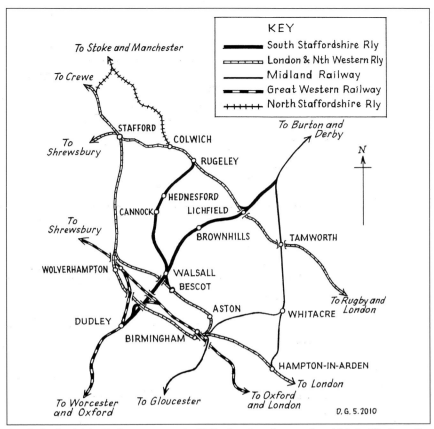

KEY

▬▬▬▬	South Staffordshire Rly
▭▭▭▭▭	London & Nth Western Rly
────────	Midland Railway
▬▬▬ ─ ▬▬	Great Western Railway
+++++++	North Staffordshire Rly

To Stoke and Manchester

To Crewe

STAFFORD

To Shrewsbury

COLWICH

To Burton and Derby

N

RUGELEY

HEDNESFORD

CANNOCK

LICHFIELD

To Shrewsbury

BROWNHILLS

TAMWORTH

WOLVERHAMPTON

WALSALL

BESCOT

ASTON

DUDLEY

WHITACRE

To Rugby and London

BIRMINGHAM

HAMPTON-IN-ARDEN

To London

To Worcester and Oxford

To Gloucester

To Oxford and London

D.G. 5.2010

South Staffordshire Railway system in 1860, showing the way in which traffic from the
north-east to the south avoided the congested lines around Birmingham.

tenders were valued at £49,486 13s. 7d. Further engines on order at the time
from Fairbairn were to be added at cost as they were delivered. Negotiations
were prolonged over the amount that McClean claimed as compensation for the
unexpired portion of the lease, and eventually an amount of £110,099 was
settled under arbitration. The lease was surrendered and a new lease granted to
the LNWR with effect from 1st February, 1860 for a period of 99 years. The
Board of Directors ratified the new arrangements on 28th February, 1861. A
formal agreement for the working and maintenance of the SSR was signed on
18th March, 1861 in which the LNWR was to purchase the wagons, carriages
and other rolling stock. Under this agreement the Board of the SSR was also to
be changed, with the LNWR being represented by ¾ of the Directors. In return,
the LNWR agreed at last to guarantee the SSR company dividends at the rate of
4½ per cent until 1st July, 1871 and 5 per cent thereafter.

This latter clause never became necessary, as the SSR became vested in the
LNWR with the passing of the LNWR (New Works and Additional Powers) Act
(Vict. 30 & 31, cap. 144) on 15th July, 1867.

Chapter Five

Unsuccessful Promotions

Compared to many other areas there were relatively few alternative schemes floated by potential promoters and/or competing railways. This was primarily because the routes north to south, and east to west between the major towns had all been taken up by 1850, either built or under construction. Reference to the 'Location Plan' (*see page 67*) will confirm that apart from the SSR, the other lines were in the hands of the OWWR (Dudley to Wolverhampton), GWR (Birmingham to Wolverhampton via Wednesbury), LNWR (Birmingham to Wolverhampton via the Stour Valley route and the GJR route, plus the Trent Valley line) and MR (Birmingham to Derby).

Great Western Intentions

The one 'thorn in the flesh' of both the MR and the LNWR was the GWR, which was still at this time trying to expand its broad gauge empire in any direction possible. Firstly, in 1854 the GWR tried to introduce a Bill for a line of mixed gauge from the BWDR line at Wednesbury to Cannock. This was noted in an SSR Directors Report dated 19th April of that year, and the proposal was roundly defeated by the SSR, doubtless with the assistance of both the LNWR and MR! On 29th June, 1865 the Wolverhampton & Walsall Railway (WWR) Act (Vict. 28 & 29, cap. 181) authorized this line to make a connection with the GWR at Wolverhampton (Low Level) as well as the LNWR at the High Level station. This was actually built, but through working from the GWR was never sanctioned. In the following year, the West Bromwich & Walsall Railway obtained its Act of Incorporation (Vict. 29 & 30, cap. 238) for a line between these two towns. However, the LNWR was able to restrict the construction powers to a line just between West Bromwich and Bescot, where without further running powers, all GWR traffic would have to be transferred to the LNWR. Evidently, this did not sit well with the GWR, and this scheme was finally dropped.

In 1866, a nominally independent scheme was promoted by the GWR as the South Staffordshire & London Railway. Whilst it was promoted as a further line to link this part of the West Midlands to London, in reality the line was an attempt by the GWR as a means of gaining access to Coventry. The main route was for a line from Wednesbury to Coventry, with a further link to Wolverhampton. This would have entailed running powers over the SSR to a junction at Walsall with the WWR (which as noted above had recently been authorized), but predated the Walsall Wolverhampton & Midland Junction Railway, and so would have been a new line from there to Coventry. The line south from Coventry would have been over the metals of the LNWR, so this part was in reality just made up to enhance the name of the promotion. The LNWR opposed it, and even before it was presented to Parliament the scheme had failed.

The GWR returned to its schemes of 1865, when the grandly titled West Bromwich, Walsall & Burton on Trent Railway was floated in 1877. This included the previous section from West Bromwich to Walsall, then running powers over the SSR through Brownhills and Lichfield City to Burton. Not surprisingly, this scheme never got as far as achieving the necessary Parliamentary powers.

In the following year, a further scheme was promoted linking the GWR to the Cannock Chase coalfields. This was the West Bromwich & Cannock Chase Railway. The railway was to run from Norton Street in the All Saints area of Hockley, Birmingham to join the SSR at Rushall, where a further line was intended to run to Cannock. The only new part of the line was from Hockley to Walsall, then running powers were then required over exisiting LNWR lines. Again the LNWR objected and the scheme was lost.

However, a similar scheme was announced in the *Evening Express* (Wolverhampton) of Tuesday 30th November, 1880, and then promoted during 1881 and 1882 as the Birmingham, Walsall and Cannock Chase Railway. A similar route was intended as in 1878, but with a further link to the BWDR at Handsworth (thus creating a triangular junction), plus access to the colliery railways in the Cannock and Hednesford areas, and a final link to the NSR at Colwich by way of Rugeley. Again this relied extensively on running powers, this time involving the MR, Cannock Chase & Wolverhampton Railway (CCWR), Littleworth Tramway, Anglesea Mineral Railway and the NSR as well as the LNWR and BWDR.

The GWR argued that coal was taking too long to reach Birmingham from the Cannock Chase coalfields (they claimed between 8 and 20 days), partly because too much coal was still being taken by canal. However, the scheme failed and this time the GWR gave up all hope of reaching Cannock.

LNWR *dithering at Lichfield*

Chapter Six deals with the attempts by the LNWR to build its line from Birmingham to Sutton Coldfield and onwards to Lichfield. Although the first part was achieved in 1862, attempts by the LNWR to complete the line to Lichfield seemed to have lost impetus after 1863, until they were revived successively in 1867, 1872, 1874, 1875, 1877 and finally in 1880. Locally, this left a feeling that the prospect was not attractive to the LNWR , and so in 1871 a local scheme was promoted as the Midland & South Staffordshire Railway, engineered by Julian Horn Tolme and A.S.Hamand with Francis Wilmott as surveyor. This was for a line of 7 miles 48 chains (7½ miles) from Lichfield to join the LNWR at Sutton Coldfield. This seems to have provided the stimulus required, as in the following year, as noted, the LNWR interest in this route was reinvigorated. The local scheme was abandoned in favour of a less risky venture by the LNWR, although this did not materialize for several years.

An enterprising scheme

In early 1872 a scheme known as the Midland, Wolverhampton, Hereford & Malvern Junction Railway was promoted as an independent concern, but seems to have been backed by the MR. The engineers were given as Butterton and Light of 17 Great George Street, Westminster and the anticipated capital was to be £1.5 million in £25 shares, with £1 payable on application. This was for a completely new railway, running from Barton & Walton (south of Burton on the MR route) to Hereford, via Longdon, across the centre of Cannock Chase to Wyrley, and then to Oxley, avoiding Wolverhampton and running to the east of Wombourne and the west of Sedgley to Wollaston, Kinver, Wolverley, crossing Bewdley from east to west, Abberley and to a junction at Martley. Here the line was to split, with the main line continuing via Bromyard to Hereford, where it would join the MR-leased line to South Wales. The other line was to run more southwards to Malvern and Malvern Link, where it would join the GWR and MR lines (the latter continuing to Tewkesbury and Ashchurch, where it would join the MR Birmingham to Bristol line). It may be appreciated that this route would have given the MR a more direct and certainly independent route to South Wales, as well as a means of avoiding Birmingham for its through traffic from the north to Bristol. This scheme failed to reach Parliament, but was revived in February 1875 and February 1876, with a further lack of success.

A rural route from Lichfield

In its edition of 1st March, 1895 the *Lichfield Mercury* carried details of an outline plan for a line from Uttoxeter to Lichfield. A public meeting on 22nd March roundly endorsed the plans and suggested future action to promote the railway. The parish council of Uttoxeter petitioned the LNWR to build the line, via Abbots Bromley, Yoxall, Newborough, Cowlishaw and Hoar Cross to Lichfield, and a deputation was sent to London to meet representatives of the LNWR at 3 pm on 15th May, 1895 in the Board Room adjacent to the Great Hall at Euston. The motion was read by Councillor S.B. Bamford of Uttoxeter in front of seven of his colleagues, plus two councillors from Abbots Bromley and six from Lichfield. It was claimed that such a line would promote the agricultural interests of the area, including important dairy farming and the transport of cattle, plus hunting, and the developing industry in Uttoxeter. Bamford & Sons, engineers were quoted as an example, and were of course, the forerunner of the immensely successful firm of JCB. Incoming traffic would primarily consist of coal from Cannock Chase.

Correspondence with the NSR was also opened, and that company responded by saying that whilst it would not oppose the building of such a railway, it would also not support it. The LNWR response was that it would also not oppose it, but equally it would not build it. The councillors engaged in lengthy correspondence during 1896 and 1897 with the firm of E.O. Preston & Company at the Bank of England in order to obtain financial support for an independent line, which was generally favourable, but not overwhelming. The

Town Clerk at Lichfield, and the Lichfield Tradesmen's Association also pledged support and made their approval public. So on 15th October, 1897 the provisional committee obtained the services of W. Seaton to prepare plans for the line. He did make some outline plans from existing Ordnance Survey maps, but detailed surveying was not carried out as it would have involved heavy expenditure. This gives us a clue that the provisional committee was not being backed by adequate financial resources at even a local level.

Nonetheless, the line was expected to join the SSR near to Trent Valley High Level station, and it was determined by this time that the line could be constructed quite cheaply under the provisions of the Light Railways Act which had been passed in 1896. It was hoped to include this in the lines submitted for approval in 1899, but by June 1898 it had become clear that local support for the line had waned. Lord Lichfield stated publicly that he could see no point in the line, and so support collapsed and the scheme was dropped.

PUBLIC MEETING.

NEW RAILWAY

FROM

UTTOXETER TO LICHFIELD.

I hereby convene a Meeting of the Citizens of Lichfield, and Landowners and Inhabitants of the neighbourhood, to be held in the GUILDHALL, LICHFIELD, on FRIDAY, the 22nd day of MARCH, 1895, at 5 o'clock in the afternoon,

To support a Memorial to the Directors of the London and North Western Railway Company to undertake the construction of a new line of Railway from Uttoxeter through Abbots Bromley, Newborough, Hoar Cross and other villages to Lichfield.

T. WALMESLEY,

Mayor.

Guildhall, Lichfield,
March 14th, 1895.

Poster for the proposed railway from Uttoxeter to Lichfield in 1895.

Courtesy Lichfield Archives

A detailed study of the LNWR platforms at Dudley on 18th October, 1952. On the right, the rather decrepit wooden stairs from the footbridge to the platform are worthy of study. A former GWR pannier tank is approaching from the north, probably with a stopping train from Birmingham Snow Hill.
F.W. Shuttleworth

Dudley GWR station platforms, facing south, in January 1956. This view shows the GWR Dudley South signal box on the platform, and just beyond the Castle Hill road bridge is a water tower squeezed against the steep embankment. A parcels van is standing in the bay platform in the left foreground.
Courtesy Dudley Archives

Chapter Six

Developments

Very few railways exist in the same format from the time they are built until the present day or the time they close. It is a process of continual adaptation to the current or anticipated traffic needs, and may involve expansion or contraction, and in some instances a mixture of both. The SSR has seen all types of development, and in this chapter we shall look at the major works associated with such developments over the years. Furthermore, it is hoped that in this way the reader will be able better to appreciate the changes taking place, rather than incorporating these into the description of the line in Chapter Ten.

Dudley

The original 1849 station at Dudley was, as we have noted earlier, of only a temporary nature, and was located on the west side of the line, north of the Tipton Road bridge and next to the original single-road goods shed. It seems to have comprised a single platform with wooden buildings, and was opened to the public from 1st May, 1850. From this the line led southwards to the burgeoning OWWR and its station by way of a single line that was to be the scene of several accidents, before common sense prevailed and the line was doubled. Before this, a new more permanent station was erected south of the Tipton Road bridge near to the OWWR station, but not connected to it, and opened probably around 1852, although no exact date has been found. This station was accessed by a path from Tipton Road, and had one platform face, but seems again to have been rather cheaply built in comparison to others on the line, and local opinion of the day regarded it as having less than ideal facilities for the traveller (which applied to the OWWR station too!). In an attempt to improve matters, the SSR constructed an additional island platform during 1855, slightly further south that was to be the site of its later more permanent station. This third station was open by July of that year. However, this structure was only of a temporary nature, and may have been an attempt to begin construction of a 'joint' station that had been talked about since 1854. The whole ensemble continued to be the source of constant local complaint.

It seems that the passing of the SSR Act on 23rd July, 1855 was pivotal, as this gave authority for the construction of a joint station at Dudley. So, at a meeting at the Queens Hotel in Birmingham on 20th March, 1856 it was formally agreed (again!) that a new joint station would be built, adjacent to, and replacing some of the OWWR station. The intention was to also resolve the problems of exchanging traffic and passengers for which both companies had rightly drawn criticism. It was agreed that the costs of the land and works would be shared equally. However, the negotiations between the SSR and the OWWR (which was notoriously short of cash) continued for several more years before anything happened. The *Wolverhampton Chronicle* of 12th January, 1859 finally reported that the project was to go ahead:

A view northwards of Dudley station in the 1950s, with the former GWR platforms on the left and the SSR/LNWR platforms on the right. The high level entrances to both platforms are evident, with the substantial connecting footbridge. A Collett '57XX' pannier tank is standing in the south-facing bay platform on the left.   *R.S. Carpenter/Kidderminster Railway Museum*

Ivatt class '2' 2-6-0 No. 46456 moves a couple of parcels vans as part of its station pilot duties at Dudley on 4th June, 1962. The tracks in the right foreground originally led to the locomotive and carriage sheds. A good view of the generous platform canopy on the former GWR platforms is given from this angle.   *B. Moone/Kidderminster Railway Museum*

NEW RAILWAY STATION FOR DUDLEY

The inconvenience of the badly constructed railway station is a fact that for some time past has become as palpable to the Oxford, Worcester, and Wolverhampton Railway Company as to passengers travelling on their line ; and it is therefore with great pleasure that we are able to announce that the prospects of having a new and commodious station are no longer problematical. This delay in not commencing the work earlier is not wholly attributable to the Oxford, Worcester and Wolverhampton Company. The South Staffordshire Railway Company, as is well known, have a joint interest in the station, and negociations [sic] have for some time been pending between the two companies for the erection of a joint station, but failing to come to any satisfactory arrangement the Oxford, Worcester, and Wolverhampton Company have determined to erect a handsome and commodious building for their own exclusive use, at a cost of upwards of £4,000. The foundations have been taken out, and it is confidently anticipated that in the course of a few weeks the building will be completed.

The new joint station was erected a little further south, and is believed to have opened shortly after this report, although no firm date has been discovered. It comprised two island platforms (one each for the GWR and the LNWR), having a footbridge connection between the two, and continuing to their own road entrances, that for the LNWR being again from Tipton Road. The southbound platform of the old (second) SSR station continued in use as a parcels platform for many years afterwards. The new station was much more in keeping with the status of the town, and the expectations of its people. The original track layout had already been modified by the installation of double track, so that pilotmen, required hitherto on the single line section from the first temporary station to the interchange, were no longer needed. McClean wrote to the Board of Trade on 30th July, 1858 to ask for an inspection of the new arrangements. After some minor changes were made, approval was given.

However, this was not really a 'joint' station, as the SSR and the OWWR had separate platforms and to a large extent entirely separate facilities for passengers and parcels. The only 'joint' feature was the footbridge linking the two island platforms. This was not destined to last, for on 6th January, 1889 there was a disastrous fire at Dudley station, reported at length in the *Evening Express & Star* the following day.

The report contained a full description of the extent of the fire and the efforts of the local fire brigade to contain the fire and extinguish the flames. The fire apparently started around 10.30 pm, in the GWR porters' room, after the last passenger trains had left the GWR and LNWR stations. The fire travelled along the footbridge connecting the two stations, and soon engulfed the GWR booking office and the entrance onto Station Road, before reaching the remainder of the GWR buildings. Efforts were directed to preventing the fire reaching the LNWR station, but their booking office, also located on the footbridge succumbed to the fire. The footbridge eventually collapsed on to the running lines, and the fire consumed some of the telegraph poles and lines in the vicinity. After the flames had been quelled, a large gang of labourers, under the direction of the GWR station master Mr Perrins, proceeded to clear the tracks so as to enable the night goods trains to pass through. The following morning a temporary booking office was installed in one of the waiting rooms. The LNWR made its own platforms available for GWR trains until other temporary arrangements could be devised

Work under way at Dudley for the creation of the new Freightliner Terminal on 30th March, 1967. The station has been completely demolished, and the running lines taken up and replaced with a new alignment seen passing through the area. The former GWR Dudley South signal box is still extant at this time, in the left foreground, but a new signal box can be seen in the top right of the picture that was to come into use later that year, and thereafter controlled all movements at this site. An English Electric class '20' diesel can be seen attached to a brake van in the centre of the picture. *Kidderminster Railway Museum*

English Electric type '1' Bo-Bo diesels Nos. 20194 and 20173 run light past the site of the original goods depots of the LNWR and MR at Dudley on 26th September, 1980. They have worked in a train to the Dudley Freightliner terminal and are running to Bescot traction depot. The site of the former goods depots can be seen to have been taken over by a dealer in army surplus road vehicles. Later it became a scrapyard. *R. Selvey*

on the GWR premises. Apart from the loss of its booking office, the LNWR buildings were badly scorched by the heat from the fire, but remained otherwise intact. Thus the LNWR buildings required only superficial repairs to the woodwork, although a new booking office was constructed adjacent to the entrance from Tipton Road. Work was soon underway rebuilding the GWR station along the same alignment as previously, but this time using mainly red brick for the principal structures. A description of the station in its final form, along with details of the workings is contained in Chapter Ten.

Prior to this event, a new goods depot was erected, opening around 1883. The original single-road goods shed continued in a minor role after the opening of the new depot, which was sited in the fork of the SSR and OWWR lines, on the other side of the Tipton Road bridge. The new structure was of blue engineering brick, and although it was served by only two internal lines contained several internal turntables at right angles to the through roads, plus three more outside. It was a commodious building, built to serve a large customer base, and for the time was very modern in its handling of goods. Four lengthy sidings were provided alongside for wagon stabling. The entire LMR and WR station and WR goods depot area was cleared during 1967, for the construction of the new Freightliner Depot, specifically designed for the handling of modern containers. This came into use in July 1967 but was not officially opened until the following 6th November. Even this piece of forward thinking had little success, and was threatened with closure as early as 1981. Efforts to find an adequate level of traffic failed, so that the last train left (for Carlisle) on 29th September, 1986. In the meantime, the 1883 LNWR goods shed, which had been designated as Dudley Town Goods from 19th July, 1950, was demolished around 1972/1973.

Wednesbury

Details of the original SSR station at Wednesbury are not known, but it is believed to have been a fairly simple affair, and possibly sited slightly further south than the later station, so as to give pedestrian and vehicular access to Potters Lane. The opening of the Darlaston loop in 1863 required additional platform space, and so the opportunity was taken to replace the original station with something that would enable easy transfer between the two lines. The resulting structure featured a central platform with faces for the westbound Darlaston loop line and the down line for Walsall arranged in a 'V' shape. The up SSR line platform was situated directly opposite the down platform, and a goods loop was arranged to pass to the rear of this platform. The provision of a goods loop would have been considered necessary as the Tipton branch via Princes End also opened in 1863, and so there would have been additional passenger, as well as goods workings, thus necessitating further line capacity. The original goods depot is believed to have been sited on the up side, where the new goods relief loop was laid. A new goods depot was constructed alongside the Darlaston loop, some 200 yards to the west of the station. A detailed description of the station is given in Chapter Ten. This new station opened with the Darlaston loop on 14th September, 1863.

LNWR 0-8-0 No. 49361 became a well-photographed locomotive during the early 1960s, and we see it here again, at Wednesbury, running light engine and about to pass beneath the former GWR Birmingham to Wolverhampton main line. Wednesbury No. 1 signal box is in the background. *S. Cartwright/Kidderminster Railway Museum*

Looking down from the former GWR line at Wednesbury, a BR class '47' at the head of a northbound freight, passes Wednesbury No. 1 signal box and over the Potters Lane level crossing, on 4th April, 1970. The down station platform is evident, although long disused by this time. *D. Wilson*

Subsequently, the growth of goods traffic, particularly raw materials for the production of steel and the outgoing steel products, necessitated a gradual increase in the length and number of sidings to the south of Wednesbury station, adjacent to the site of the former exchange sidings. This area was eventually developed as Wednesbury steel terminal opening around 1968, but was relatively short lived, closing in 1987.

It is further recorded that additional goods facilities were installed in 1917 at Mesty Croft (about a mile to the north of Wednesbury) on the site of the Crankall Waterworks Siding, that had formerly served to supply coal to the South Staffordshire Waterworks pumping station there. This is believed to relate to the provision of the up goods loop, along with the necessary signal box, and was yet another attempt to increase the line's capacity, emphasising the extent to which goods traffic had grown. It should be noted that it was fairly unusual for new projects to be entered into during these, the darkest days of World War I.

Walsall

As might be expected with a town the size of Walsall, there have been several changes to the railway structure here, and in all probability this will continue. Harking back to the days of the opening of the SSR, the first temporary station facilities were sited south of Bridgeman Street and comprised a terminus building for the line from Bescot. For the opening of the through line from Dudley to Wichnor Junction in 1849, a completely new station was built north of the temporary terminus, and on the other side of Bridgeman Street. This splendid new station, comprising one up and one down platform, was described in the *Wolverhampton Chronicle* of 11th April, 1849 detailed in Chapter Two.

The street in which the new station was situated became Station Street, not Railway Street as described therein. The style of the building was subsequently described in a variety of sources as being of Queen Anne, Italian or Italian Gothic – but whatever the name given, it was a handsome building that was destined to be overshadowed by the other less imposing buildings in what became pretty much of a back street. It was built of brick with stone facings, and had Dutch style gables and decorative finials along the roof line. The central block contained a group of seven tall, narrow windows, with a central ornamental device, and was flanked by two wings that projected outwards. Each of these had a single window and were topped by a gable end. A large grain store and goods shed was built that abutted the south end of the building, one wall of the goods shed/grain store actually forming the rear wall of the northbound (later No. 1) platform. The company offices incorporated into the station thus had direct access to this, which was connected by rail via a wagon turntable. Further tracks from the turntable led to a cattle dock, shunted by horses and capstans. There was also a stable in Station Street for the shunting horses and those used for the delivery drays, and on occasions those from the nearby canal basin would be stabled there. By 1954 the cattle dock had fallen out

The 1849 Walsall station building was in use as a parcels depot at the time of this photograph, taken on 6th October, 1952. It is intriguing that a horse-drawn delivery van was still in use at this time, painted in BR livery and numbered as vehicle M22985. This, and the lorry on the left are still advertising a trip that took place a month earlier on Saturday 6th September, to Blackpool for the illuminations for a fare of 12 shillings.

F.W. Shuttleworth

A print from a commercial postcard of Walsall station around 1890, with an LNWR 0-6-0 passing along platform 2. The original 1849 station buildings are on the left, at the rear of platform 1.

Bill Mayo Collection

of use, and was demolished in 1958, the land being used as a railway staff car park.

After the LNWR had taken over control of the SSR, the track layout through the station was changed in the 1860s to give two through roads for freight traffic, so eliminating a major bottle neck when passenger trains were standing at the platforms.

By the 1870s it was apparent that the station and the track layout was in need of a major reorganization, as a report of 5th February, 1870 stated that around 600 trains a day were passing over the level crossing at the south end of Walsall station. However, the first works at Walsall were necessitated by the introduction of MR services over the Sutton Park route from 1st July, 1879. The company had anticipated this, and had already obtained Parliamentary powers for some enlargements at Walsall station, including its own booking office and staff facilities, in the Midland Railway Act (Vict. 40 & 41) of 28th June, 1877. Also included were a new goods shed, locomotive shed and carriage sidings, but these are covered in more detail in Chapter Nine.

The LNWR proposal was to widen the lines to four through tracks from Pleck to Ryecroft and to provide additional platform capacity. Further works included the replacement of the level crossing by lowering Bridgeman Street beneath the railway, and incorporation of a footbridge between platforms. The necessary Parliamentary powers for these works were included in the LNWR (New Lines) Act (Vict. 40 & 41, cap. 44) passed on 10th August, 1877. William Baker was in charge of the project as the LNWR's Engineer-in-Chief, with Francis Stevenson as Engineer. J. Evans of Birmingham was the selected contractor for these works, which continued from 1879 until 1883. As far as is known he used at least one locomotive on this contract, an 0-4-0ST built by Henry Hughes, that was subsequently used on the Widnes to Speke widening in Lancashire for the LNWR. The new quadruple track section from Pleck to Ryecroft totalled 2 miles 6 furlongs and 7 chains (2¾ miles) and involved considerable demolition of lineside properties, and the construction of a lengthy brick-lined cutting north of Walsall station. By August 1881 two additional running lines had been brought into operation between Walsall station and Ryecroft Junction.

Local opinion concerning the inadequacy of the 1849 station was reflected in several letters to the *Walsall Observer & South Staffordshire Chronicle* of 5th November, 1881. The waiting rooms were described as 'dark and dingy', the parcels and left luggage rooms being together are 'small', and the refreshment room is 'full with six people in it, four must wait whilst two are served'. They complained of the lack of waiting room accommodation on a new platform that had been built to serve the additional running lines, and the lack of a footbridge to connect to this platform. Whilst the first mentioned complaints were certainly true, they would be addressed by the new station, under construction. The latter comments relate to a situation of work-in-progress, which again would be addressed. However, the good people of Walsall still had another two years to wait for the completion of the works.

The enlargement of the station was completed on 1st November, 1883 but was not formally opened until 1st January, 1884. The new entrance faced on to Park

The Park Street entrance to Walsall station viewed prior to the 1916 fire, showing the original glazed porte cochère.

Author's Collection

The Park Street entrance to the 1884 Walsall station shown around 1920. The ornate porte cochère is shown to advantage, and the Grand Theatre is in the right background.

Author's Collection

Street, by then one of the main thoroughfares into the centre of Walsall. A separate carriageway was provided off Park Street to the station frontage, and was provided with a porte-cochère of cast iron and glass giving cover for travellers as they alighted from their cabs. The entrance was formed by three stone archways that lined up with the three bays of the outside canopy. Inside the station booking hall were the designated booking offices of the LNWR and the MR, each with their own offices to the rear and side of the ticket windows. There was a central vaulted roof, with a decorative panel at the front, flanked by two gable roofs, one on each side. The platforms were reached by a long corridor, still at street level, which then divided to reach the footbridges across to the platforms. The corridor was of painted wood panelling to waist height, with the upper half glazed. The original down platform was retained, along with the 1849 station building. This had been converted for use as staff offices, although part was used as a dormitory for the female restaurant staff. A bay platform was provided at the northern end of this platform for trains for Rugeley, locally referred to as the 'Cannock Bay'. The adjacent goods shed had become primarily used as a parcels depot. The next two platforms were both islands, with two faces each, although the centre island also contained a north-facing bay platform, this one referred to as the 'Sutton Bay'. The bay platforms were originally used for local passenger trains, but eventually only became used for parcels trains or stabling the local push-pull units between duties. With the installation of the new island platform, the two through roads were reduced to one. This central island platform was the largest, and also contained a substantial refreshment room, which became very popular with the local businessmen. Apparently, they would regularly travel from Streetly or Aldridge to take lunch there in the years prior to World War I.

Subsequently, in 1887, a new luggage lift was installed, connecting with the corridor linking the platforms. In 1900 a 'Coffee Tavern' was opened, serving lighter meals than the restaurant.

A fire occurred at the station on 1st April, 1916 starting in the booking office and destroying part of the high level corridor. As a result the front entrance could not be used, and so the original entrance via the 1849 building had to be reinstated. Unfortunately this had occurred in wartime, and the necessary materials and men were not available to effect the required repairs, so the front entrance remained covered in tarpaulins and timber supports for well beyond the duration of the war. In fact, there seems to have been no urgency whatsoever in making the repairs - possibly caused by the inconclusive state of the railways, allied with indecision as to what improvements to incorporate into the rebuilding. Thus the good people of Walsall had once again to put up with inadequate accommodation for a number of years, even though a deputation from Walsall Town Hall had travelled to Euston in 1916 to petition for better facilities when the damaged areas were rebuilt. Eventually the reconstructed station opened on 4th November, 1923 by which time the railway had passed into the newly formed LMS, and was reported in the *Walsall Observer & South Staffordshire Chronicle* of 10th November as follows:

The Park Street entrance to Walsall station on 2nd June, 1965. The ornate porte cochère was still in good condition at this time, and it is worthy of note that BR was advertising day return tickets to Birmingham, Coventry and Derby at 4s. 6d., 12s. 3d. and 19s. 6d. respectively. *R. Shenton*

The exterior concourse at Walsall station, leading to Park Street, on 4th October, 1976. The ornate cast iron and glass work can be appreciated in this view, although sundry signs and other small structures had been added over the years to clutter the station approach. *R. Selvey*

NEW BOOKING HALL
Early Morning Opening by LMS District Superintendent
EXPEDITED FOR SHOPPING FESTIVAL

The new booking hall at Walsall Station was officially opened at 8 o'clock on Sunday morning . The function was quite informal, the huge oak entrance doors being pushed aside by Mr. J.F. Bradford, district superintendent, of Birmingham, in the presence of various railway officials, including Messrs W.A. Thomas (district goods manager, of Wolverhampton), G.A. Grimoldby (district engineer, Walsall), H. Hayward (chief clerk in the district superintendent's office), F. Butler (chief of the timetable department, Birmingham), J.W. Lazenby (tourist agent), F.W. Moll (chief of the works), W. Jones (station master), and Mr. W.B. Shaw, a member of the Walsall Chamber of Commerce Council.

At the invitation of the District Superintendent, a representative of the 'Observer' took the first platform ticket from the automatic machine, after which all the members of the party placed their pennies in the slot for souvenirs. The first railway ticket was secured by Mr. W.B. Shaw. The new building was inspected and its features generally admired.

Breakfast was served in the station restaurant, where Mr. Bradford expressed the satisfaction of the company at being able to provide Walsall with a booking hall which, he thought they would agree, was a credit to the town. It had cost £25,000. The opening had been expedited in order to assist the shopping festival, and so wished that venture every success. The LMS he added, desired to do all they possibly could to assist in promoting the welfare of the town. Finally, he appealed to all to assist in the preservation of the beautiful oak work and not to damage the stonework, for instance, by the careless striking of matches on it....

Mr. Grimoldby pointed out that as far as possible work in connection with the new booking hall had been carried out locally. The steel structure had been obtained from Darlaston, and labour was engaged in the town. The contract was given to a Coventry firm. The railway company always carried out their schemes so as to benefit in the greatest measure those out of work in the particular district....

Not mentioned in this report is that the southern outward side of the new booking hall was now broadly semi-circular, but retained most of the iron and glass porte-cochère at the Park Street entrance, still with decorative iron finials on its upper edges, whilst the roof had altered to become steeply pitched. Inside, the shape of the hall was square, it was lined with oak panelling, and of course there was now no need for separate booking offices for the MR and the LNWR. A lengthy bookstall was also provided inside the booking hall, which was 70 feet in width and the ceiling, supported by a pair of widely-spaced Corinthian pillars featured circular medallion mouldings. Surmounting the roof over the main concourse were three glass-panelled roof pitches providing light. The high level corridor leading to the platforms was retained, but was increased in width from 10 feet to 20 feet to combat criticisms that the old corridor was 'an unhealthy, irritating eyesore'.

The restaurant continued as a desirable eating place, particularly for those patronizing the Grand Theatre, which was virtually next door to the station. However, the deprivations of World War II led to a reduction in its status, such that in the 1950s it became one of the notorious BR 'buffets', serving only a selection of indifferent tea and sandwiches. The other two refreshment facilities, the 'Coffee Tavern' and an original buffet bar had already closed. Coincidental with the closure of some of the local passenger services, this too closed altogether from 16th January, 1965.

The station frontage in Park Street, Walsall in 1965. The curving shape at the rear of the booking hall is clearly evident. The platform canopies have been removed, and a start made on the installation of the overhead catenary. To the right, the Grand Theatre has made way for a replacement public house, 'The Old Grand' in the rather unlovely architecture of the 1960s.

Author's Collection

The interior of the booking hall at Walsall station on 4th October, 1976 showing the elegant wood-panelled walls furnished as part of the 1923 rebuilding. This rebuilding was necessary following a disastrous fire in 1916, and its completion was delayed by shortage of men and materials during World War I, then by uncertainty as to the future of the railways, which culminated in the Grouping of 1923.

R. Selvey

The inside of the corridor leading from the booking hall to the platforms at Walsall station, after its enlargement following the fire of 1916. This view was taken in the 1920s. *Author's Collection*

Webb 5 ft 6 in. 2-4-2T BR No. 46701 stands in Walsall station with a push-pull working from Wolverhampton on 7th May, 1952. This engine had received its push-pull equipment in 1932, but was based at Warrington (Dallam) shed, and had been temporarily transferred to Bushbury shed, to cover for unavailable Ivatt 2-6-2Ts. The train would be propelled from Wolverhampton, and pulled on its return working. *F.W. Shuttleworth*

An unidentified 'Jubilee' 4-6-0 stands in platform 4 of Walsall station having just arrived with a parcels train around 1965. The locomotive is carrying a 'light engine' headlamp code, so is presumably about to leave for Bescot shed. This fine view of the whole of Walsall station was taken from Walsall No. 1 signal box, and shows on the left, the 1849 goods shed which abutted to the rear of platform 1.   *R. Selvey*

A fine view of the permanent way depot and sidings built by the LNWR that acted as the headquarters of the district engineer and his staff. Green-liveried Ivatt class '2' 2-6-0 No. 46522 is standing in the foreground, and a good variety of departmental vehicles are stabled in and around the depot, on 10th June, 1965.   *R. Shenton*

A fairly lengthy period of further decline followed, until 1978 when the whole station was gradually demolished. The first building to be completely obliterated was the original small MR goods shed dating from around 1860, next attention turned to the 1849 station building, which was in a very poor condition by then, and was finally cleared on 2nd February, 1978. The entire demolition of the station area was completed by 1st October, 1978. The Park Street cast-iron canopy was stored by Walsall Corporation's parks department for preservation, but disappeared at an unknown date. The station was redeveloped as part of the £7 million Saddlers Centre, incorporating a retail shopping centre built above the platforms, with access available via Station Street or the shopping centre, which opened in the Summer of 1980. The platform waiting rooms and toilets were initially provided in the 'bus shelter' style of metal and glass, but these did not last long, and were replaced by more substantial structures executed in plain red brick and concrete as part of a £1.1 million facelift opening in April 1995. Apart from an imaginative curved glass screen to the footbridge leading from the Saddlers Centre to the island platform, this is altogether a most unattractive station.

Returning to the 1883 alterations, the two carriage sidings on the east side of the station were realigned and five further sidings were added, four for coal and one leading to a covered fruit and potato shed. At the rear of the carriage sidings a large water tower was constructed on a brick base, which was used as a store and mess room. Water was supplied from the tower to the three locomotive water cranes mounted at the platform ends, and to power the hydraulic lifts in the station. A boiler house alongside the water tower was added for carriage cleaning. The carriage sidings eventually proved inadequate for the longer bogie carriages introduced from around 1900, and so these had to be stabled in any available spare wagon sidings until 1925 when the MR carriage sidings became available as the result of the closure of the MR locomotive shed at Pleck. The old sidings were retained for stabling the push-pull units, and eventually for surplus wagon storage until around 1965, when all tracks in this yard were removed. The site thereafter became a car park until the opening of the Saddlers Centre in 1978, which it now occupies.

South of the station, a new larger brick-built goods shed was also erected during the 1883 expansion for the LNWR on the down side parallel to Long Street. The GWR had the southernmost and smaller portion of this lengthy building, which had one through road, and two from the south terminating inside. Details of GWR goods workings are given in Chapter Nine.

Continuing further south on the down side, the LNWR constructed a District Engineer's Department in blue brick, combining the civil engineering planning functions with workshop facilities, and supported by sidings for the associated permanent way vehicles. This was demolished in summer 2009, and new buildings erected on the same site to continue the same function, now in the hands of Network Rail and its associated contractors.

On 7th October, 1962 a new freight depot was opened on the up side, south of the station alongside Midland Road and Meadow Street, to the south of the site of the 1879 MR Goods Depot. This was intended to serve the surrounding area of 26 towns from Lichfield to Oldbury totalling around 250 square miles,

Work in progress at the old MR Walsall goods yard on 7th April, 1960 during which the stream in the foreground was converted into a culvert, and a new £500,000 goods depot erected. The original MR dedicated tracks from Walsall station serving the goods depot and continuing to the MR engine shed at Pleck run through the centre of the picture. In the background an LNWR '7F' class 0-8-0 is shunting the goods depot at Long Street. The nearest section of that depot, noticeable for its double gable, was originally owned by the GWR.   *R. Shenton*

Walsall station from the south on 26th February, 1964 showing all of the five platforms. On the left is the original SSR goods depot and station building adjoining platform 1. A dmu is standing at platform 4 with a Wolverhampton service, whilst another is stabled in the sidings alongside the coal yard on the right.   *R. Shenton*

The transitional platform buildings at Walsall station on 14th December, 1974. Although the 1889 station building at Park Street remained, the corridor, footbridge and canopied platform waiting rooms on platforms 2 and 3 have been replaced by modern structures in brick, along with modern electric lighting. However, platform 1, on the left, remained untouched at this time.

R. Selvey

BR-built class '56' Co-Co No. 56070 heads a train of loaded merry-go-round wagons out of Walsall at Albert Street, probably bound for Rugeley power station, on 26th July, 1996. The multi-storey car park bridging the line in the background is part of the Saddlers Retail Centre.

R. Shelton

Ryecroft shed being rebuilt in 1954. This very atmospheric view shows the new walls and pits being installed on the right, whilst the roofless left-hand portion of the shed continues to function for the stabling and servicing of locomotives. In view (*left to right*) are a Stanier 2-6-2T, Bowen Cooke '7F' class 0-8-0 No. 49373, Fowler '3F' class 0-6-0 No. 43410, and '7F' 0-8-0 No. 49249, whilst another '7F' class lurks behind the shed supports, and a Fowler '4F' class 0-6-0 leaves the shed yard, partially obscuring a Stanier 2-6-2T on the ashpit. On the right, two more '7F' 0-8-0s stand in the yard and a rail-mounted crane is at the head of the yard.

J. Haddock / Walsall Local History Centre

With the rebuilding of Ryecroft shed complete, this 1955 shows the shed returned to normal operations. The single pitch roof was the style favoured by BR, and was retained during the depot's life as a diesel depot. On view here are a Stanier 2-6-2T, two Stanier 2-6-4Ts, two former MR class '2F' 0-6-0s, a Fowler '4F' 0-6-0, a Bowen Cooke '7F' 0-8-0, a Fowler 'Jinty' '3F' 0-6-0T and an Ivatt class '2' 2-6-2T.

J. Haddock/Walsall Local History Centre

and cost £500,000. Subsequently, the travelling crane was transferred from the Long Street goods depot for use here. However, the move away from railborne freight meant that the depot became redundant, and the sidings were eventually taken over for the stabling of permanent way vehicles. Later, in 2000, the building was taken over by English, Welsh & Scottish Railways (EWS) as a parcels depot, but this too has succumbed and the site at present lies empty awaiting redevelopment.

The original SSR engine shed at Walsall was located on the down side of the line, a short distance to the south of the original temporary terminus, and is believed to have opened at the same time. In 1852 Francis Trevithick (LNWR Northern Division locomotive superintendent at Crewe) had ordered gas lighting to be installed in the shed, so there was evidently some direct control by the LNWR even at this early date. In 1857 tenders were invited for the construction of steelwork and a water tank. From maps of the period, the shed seems to have been gradually added to, until 1883 by which time it contained three roads and was of a rather irregular shape. A turntable was located adjacent to a coaling stage, south of the shed. It was still shown on the 1883 OS map, although by that time the new shed at Ryecroft (*see below*) was fully operational, thus giving rise to the question as to whether it was still used to some extent at that time.

In 1877 a new, much larger shed was proposed by F.W. Webb, by then the overall LNWR locomotive superintendent, to be erected at Ryecroft Junction, and was approved by the LNWR Board in October 1877. This new shed of 12 roads was of typical Webb design, with a 'northlight' pattern roof, and faced southwards at the four-way junction. It is believed to have opened by 1880. The first turntable located towards the rear of the shed on the eastern side was probably of 50 ft diameter, but was replaced by a 60 ft unit in 1933. A typical LNWR brick-built combined coal stage and water tank were also sited in the yard on the eastern side. Although this was replaced by a mechanical coaling plant incorporating a 75 ton bunker in 1937, the original structure remained, still fulfilling its role as a water tank to supply the water cranes in the shed yard. Originally, the shed was designed to hold 48 locomotives, but nearly 70 were allocated there by 1925, after the MR shed at Pleck had closed and its allocation moved to Ryecroft. In April 1952 the shed had an allocation of 54 locomotives, including the last working Webb 2-4-2T" No. 46712, which was finally withdrawn in August of that year. By this time the shed was, so typical of many at the time, in a very run-down condition, with the roof in a particularly poor state. Delays over the repair resulted in part of the roof being removed for safety reasons, but not replaced as by the mid-1950s there were suggestions that it should be converted into a diesel depot. This was eventually carried out during 1956/57, but steam continued to be serviced there until 9th June, 1958 when the locomotives and men for goods work were moved to Bescot, and for the small remaining amount of steam passenger work to Aston. Dmus had largely taken over the local passenger network by this time - hence the conversion. Locomotives allocated to Ryecroft shed immediately prior to its closure are recorded in *Appendix Three*.

The view at the north end of Walsall's platform 1, with the Cannock bay to the left. Lack of room for the signals controlling trains leaving the bay meant that the LNWR lower quadrant signals were mounted vertically instead of on a bracket, as at the end of platform 1. The rear of the booking hall is seen above the tracks heading northwards. The date is believed to have been around 1958.   *Kidderminster Railway Museum*

The old and new at Pleck Junction. The former LNWR signal box on the left was replaced (along with four others) by the power signal box (Walsall) on the right in 1965, which was still under construction at the time of this photograph on 10th September, 1964. The New Pleck Curve, opened in 1881 to connect to the GJR at James Bridge, can be seen on the extreme right.

R. Shenton

The shed was originally coded by the LNWR as No. 7, becoming LMS shed '3C' in 1935 which it retained under BR until May 1960 when it came under the Saltley district as '21F', then in September 1963 under Tyseley as '2G'. With the cessation of the local passenger services in January 1965 the location of the diesel depot became unsuitable, and so after some period of uncertainty as to whether it should be converted into an electric depot, it finally closed and by 1974 all traces had been eliminated.

During 1964-1965 a new power box was erected at Pleck, replacing five previous manual signal boxes: Pleck Junction, Walsall Nos. 1, 2, and 3, and Bescot Curve Junction and coming into use on 3rd April, 1965.

Lichfield

The situation of the original TVR and SSR stations at Trent Valley was considered as anomalous by the LNWR in the late 1860s. The TVR station lay ¼ mile to the north of the SSR line, and the SSR station some 100 yards east of the TVR line at the site of the Brookhay level crossing. Thus a scheme was prepared for an integrated station that would permit easy transfer of passengers and parcels between the two lines. A new LNWR main line station was constructed further south, so that it was partly beneath the SSR route. The original SSR station was also replaced by one over the new main line station, thus creating High Level and Low Level stations at Trent Valley. The main portion of the SSR part was sited on the eastern end of the down line (i.e. above the up main line Low Level platform), and was almost entirely of wooden construction, with lengthy half-glazed panelling along the rear edges of both platforms, to provide waiting passengers with some protection in this rather exposed position. Steps were arranged to give easy exchange between the High and Low Level platforms, with a goods lift for the transport of parcels. Water columns were provided at each end of the platforms, being served by a large water tower with red brick base located just east of the platforms, which also provided water for the columns at the Low Level station. Due to this provision of watering facilities here, none were provided at the City station.

Both levels of the new station opened on 3rd July, 1871 and the High Level continued in passenger use until 18th January, 1965, although a portion of the High Level platform canopies was destroyed by fire in the early 1960s. When it reopened on 28th November, 1988 as part of the electrified 'Cross City' route, the new High Level station accessible from both directions consisted of a single platform on the down side, even though the line is double track here, with no facilities other than a simple glass waiting shelter, and outside steps to the Low Level platforms.

The original 1849 station at Lichfield City (simply named Lichfield) was a handsome structure in the 'neo Dutch' style favoured by Edward Adams. An engraving of this building is shown on page 20. It seems to have had three storeys, and two projecting bays, each finished with the Dutch style of decorated gable. The recessed central part was given a canopy to line up with the wings, and this was the only protection available to waiting passengers, other than the

Although taken on a very murky day, this photograph is remarkable for three reasons. Firstly, it shows a goods train tackling the sharp spur from the West Coast Main Line to the SSR route northwards, at Lichfield Trent Valley - an event rarely photographed. Secondly, the locomotive in charge is former MR Johnson 4-4-0 LMS No. 395 and this type with their 7 ft driving wheels were not often associated with goods workings. Thirdly, the date - this was taken during World War II, on 28th October, 1944 when photography of railway activities was officially forbidden (and usually quite strictly enforced).   *V.R. Webster/Kidderminster Railway Museum*

This view, taken from the top of the 'parachute' type water column at the south end of the up platform, gives a fine appreciation of the wooden construction of the station platforms and buildings at Lichfield Trent Valley (High Level). Hughes/Fowler 'Crab' 2-6-0 No. 42784 is passing through with M970, an excursion from Mansfield to Dudley on 26th August, 1956.

R. Shenton

During 1960 and 1961 much work was undertaken on upgrading various structures in anticipation of the forthcoming electrification of the West Coast route. At Lichfield Trent Valley, the High Level station was partly demolished to allow the installation of a new concrete bridge section, seen here. This involved the temporary singling of the line at this point. Interestingly, the covered wooden stairs connecting to the Low Level down platform remained at this time, and are seen to advantage. The date is 24th June, 1961. *R. Shenton*

Stanier '8F' class 2-8-0 No. 48514 is eased across the temporary structure at Lichfield Trent Valley with a northbound goods train on 24th June, 1961. *R. Shenton*

The down side of Lichfield City's island platform on 23rd August, 1967 showing the semaphore signalling arrangements before conversion to colour light signalling.   *R. Shenton*

A corresponding view of the up side at Lichfield City station, also on 23rd August, 1967. Both views are taken looking north.   *R. Shenton*

internal rooms. The platform seems to have been of wooden construction, as was the opposite (up) platform, which was staggered to the south providing a boarded crossing from the end of one platform to the end of the other, in the style of the day. This platform had no buildings whatsoever. A small goods shed appears a few yards further north, which was connected to the running lines by two points and numerous wagon turntables. Further on, a wooden bridge crosses the line from Cherry Orchard to the city centre. A new road ('Station Road') had been laid to give access to the station from the city centre.

With the coming of the new line from Sutton Coldfield authorized in 1880, the station was recognized to be unable to cater for increased traffic, and so a new one was planned, about 200 yards to the south, and just north of the proposed junction for the new line. One benefit of building a completely new station was that during the construction the old one was able to continue functioning virtually uninterrupted. On 3rd November, 1884 the new station was opened and the old station closed the same day. The opening was recorded in the *Lichfield Mercury* of 7th November, 1884 as reproduced here:

OPENING OF THE NEW LICHFIELD CITY STATION

On Monday last the new Lichfield City station was opened for the convenience of passengers, although the new Lichfield and Sutton line of railway is not yet open for passenger traffic, and it is not definitely known when it will be. The opening was unaccompanied by ceremony of any kind. Although the station has been opened, none of the usual offices and waiting rooms, excepting the booking office, are ready for occupation, and until the old station has been demolished to allow for the divergence of the line the island platform itself cannot be carried any further in an easterly direction, about 200 feet now remaining to be completed. In an article on this subject published a short time ago in these columns we dilated on the vast improvement the new station would be on the old one when finished. At that time the station was in a very chaotic condition, and it was only from a sight of the plans that a definite idea could be formed of the improvement which would be effected. And this improvement is not merely ornamental as regards the station itself, but affords increased accommodation to the public in the way of offices, etc and as increased efficiency in the traffic arrangements, both goods and passengers. The booking office affords ample accommodation for the business to be transacted there. The fittings, though simple, are handsome. The ground floor is divided into three sections, the central being the entrance, from which the subway leading to the platform is approached, that to the right is reserved for the booking clerks to carry on their duties in, and that to the left forms a commodious parcels office. The floor above forms the station master's residence. Carriages waiting to take up passengers, and porters in the performance of the duty of conveying luggage to and from the trains to the cabs, etc are protected from the inclemency of the weather by a spacious portico. The platform itself presents a very elegant appearance. When completed at the eastern end it will be 1,000 feet long, and is roofed for the whole length. At the western end is a block of offices consisting of the left luggage office, porters' and lamp rooms; and another block at the eastern end contains the general waiting room, a gentlemen's waiting room, ladies first and second class waiting rooms, and the station master's office. In the centre of the platform is a broad flight of steps leading to the subway, and contiguous to it is a lift for luggage, which will be worked by an engine at the east of the station entrance. The station is well lit with handsome pendant lamps.

Thus the station comprised one lengthy island platform, with the running lines arranged to form down main, down platform, up platform and up main

BR Standard class '2' 2-6-0 No. 78038 of Bescot shed standing in the up platform at Lichfield City on 2nd April, 1955. It is about to depart with the 8.00 am to Birmingham New Street, via the Sutton Coldfield line. In the background is the malthouse of Messrs Stubbs Ltd.   *R. Shenton*

Lichfield City station from the north on Sunday 20th August, 1967. The No. 2 signal box seen at the near end of the station platform was still in use, and even the goods yard, on the right, appears to have some custom. Nearby four sets of three-car diesel-multiple-units are stabled, the nearest being by Metro-Cammell. On the left, further dmu sets have been stabled next to the former Lichfield Brewery.   *R. Shenton*

lines. The arrangement was unusual in that the down main line passed right in front of the station master's house, where normally a platform face would be expected.

The goods yard was similarly moved southwards and the opportunity taken to provide a more substantial goods shed, also of red brick construction, and sited on the down side for ease of road access. On the opposite side were Peaches Maltings and the Lichfield Brewery Company, which had rail access, and these were realigned to fit in with the new trackwork.

Actually the writer of the above press report had only a month to wait for the opening of the line from Sutton Coldfield, but his frustration at waiting for this line is easy to understand as we plough through the events of nearly 40 years leading to the completion of this new connection.

The first intentions of a railway from Lichfield to Birmingham were contained in the Birmingham, Lichfield & Manchester Railway Act of 27th July, 1846 (Vict. 9 & 10, cap. 232) which incorporated this concern and gave powers for construction of the line from the LNWR at Aston, via Sutton Coldfield to Lichfield. Any pretensions for the line to continue to Manchester must have remained in the imagination of the promoters. The line had been surveyed by John Robinson McClean, and the Directors included his colleague Richard Croft Chawner, and John Routledge Majendie (of Pipe Grange). These two had already signed agreements on 24th April, 1846 for the purchase of land in Aldridge and Swinfen with Edwin Swinfen Jervis, the Viscount St Vincent, on behalf of the company. Evidently this agreement was not carried through as the LNWR had taken over the company, and abandoned the 1846 Act. They promoted their own Birmingham & Lichfield Railway Act, passed on 9th July, 1847 (Vict. 10 &11, cap. 139) using a slightly shorter route. John Swift on behalf of the LNWR, had already signed an agreement with Jervis for the purchase of land, which was registered at Stafford County Court on 6th April, 1847. However, nothing more appears to have been done and the powers contained in this Act lapsed. The southern part of the scheme was resurrected by the LNWR with the passing of the LNWR (Sutton Coldfield Branch) Act passed on 8th August, 1859 (Vict. 22 & 23, cap. 88), which permitted the line to be built from Aston to Sutton Coldfield. This line was constructed and opened for passengers on 2nd June, 1862.

In the following year, the LNWR seems to have decided to renew its intention of reaching Lichfield by this route, and its Birmingham, & Sutton Coldfield Extension Railway Act (Vict. 26 & 27, cap. 174) was passed on 21st July, 1863. This permitted the construction of the line from Sutton Coldfield to join the SSR at Lichfield City. The promoters were Richard Henegan Lawrie, John Vessey Fitzgerald Foster, Thomas Edward Watkins and Edward Hall, with Lawrie and Foster becoming the first Directors along with Major Robert Wilberforce Bird. The company was authorized to raise £100,000 in £10 shares and have borrowing powers of a further £33,000. As a concession to Lord Jervis, a station was to be built on the approach road to Little Aston Hall. However, once more the LNWR allowed the powers to lapse.

The scheme was revived in 1872 with the passing of the Birmingham & Lichfield Junction Railway Act (Vict. 35 & 36) on 6th August of that year, and in

1874 a further Act (Vict. 37 & 38, cap. 92) gave powers for a spur from the existing line to join the MR line which crossed it at Sutton Coldfield. On 14th June, 1875 another Act (Vict. 38 & 39, cap. 52) gave an extension of time for the purchase of land and completion of the construction until 6th August, 1877. However, time came and went and so another Act was passed on 10th August, 1877 (Vict. 40 & 41, cap. 213) for another extension of time for a further two years. This time the powers were allowed to lapse completely. But the resolve of the LNWR was not quite exhausted, for the scheme was resurrected once more, with passing of the LNWR (Sutton Coldfield to Lichfield) Act (Vict. 43 & 4, cap. 10) on 29th June, 1880. This time construction finally got under way, and the line was opened to goods traffic on 1st September, 1884 and to passengers on 5th December following. The Chief Engineer for the line was Francis Stevenson, and the Resident Engineer was Mr W.T. Foxlee. The contractor for the line was Mr J. Evans of Birmingham, whose engineer was a Mr Caldwell of Manchester. At least one locomotive was used on this contract, which is confirmed by the inclusion of a wooden locomotive shed at Four Oaks in the auction on 6th July, 1885 of the contractor's unwanted equipment. However, the details of any locomotives are not known at present. This extract from the *Lichfield Mercury* of Friday 9th December, 1884 records the official opening:

LICHFIELD AND SUTTON RAILWAY

This new branch of the LNWR extending from Lichfield to Sutton Coldfield, a distance of 8 ½ miles, was opened to passenger traffic on Monday last. Considerable interest was taken on the event, not only amongst the inhabitants of Lichfield, but also of Shenstone and Sutton Coldfield, and the inhabitants of the hamlets of Blake Street and Four Oaks … We regret to say that the occasion was marred by an incident of a most melancholy nature. Whilst the bells of Shenstone church were ringing a joyous peal, and fog signals were being exploded as the first two trains passed up and down the line respectively, a man named Fields, engaged in some work at the Shenstone siding, was run over by a truck, and so shockingly mutilated that he died in the course of an hour or two.

At a considerable period before the booking office was opened at either end of the new line, a good number of passengers assembled, and the first trains were well loaded, but not to any extraordinary extent, or even to the extent that was anticipated. The engines drawing the trains were gaily decked with flags, holly, etc. … In the first place it must be mentioned that the new line has reduced the railway distance from Birmingham to Lichfield by 4½ miles, but it is noticeable that the fares have not been reduced in due proportion. The fare is now 2s. 9*d*. for a return journey of 31 miles.

However, it was not until the following 1st May that special fast trains were put on from Birmingham to Burton and Derby utilizing the shorter route now available. These are further discussed in Chapter Seven.

Chapter Seven

Working the Lines

Up to 1860

The maximum rates to be charged by the SSR for the carriage of goods and passengers had been fixed in the original SSR Act of 1846. For passengers this stipulated first class at 3*d*. per mile, second class at 2*d*. per mile and third at 1*d*. per mile. The latter effectively became the 'Parliamentary' rate, as we shall see below. The mileage rates for horses was 5*d*. each, cattle 2*d*. each, calves and pigs 1*d*. each, sheep and other small animals 3*d*./4*d*. each. Carriages were still often transported for the wealthy, using special wagons, so that they could complete their journey to their ultimate destination in their customary style, and were charged at 7*d*. per mile. Coal, coke and limestone was at 1½*d*. per ton mile, manure 2*d*., slates, clay, glass, sugar and grain at 3*d*., with cotton, wool and manufactured goods at 4*d*. per ton mile.

The first trains in 1847 were through workings between Birmingham Curzon Street and Walsall, and were worked entirely by the LNWR, as the SSR had not yet taken delivery of its own rolling stock. The earliest timetable, for 1st November, 1847 reveals four trains each way on weekdays (leaving Birmingham at 9.00, 11.00 am, 4.00 and 7.15 pm), with an equal return service (from Walsall at 9.50, 11.30 am, 4.45 and 8.00 pm). The two trains each way on Sundays left Birmingham at 8.40 am and 7.15 pm , and from Walsall at 9.40 am and 8.00 pm. The fares were 1*s*. 6*d*. (first single), 2*s*. 6*d*. (first return), 1*s*. 0*d*. (second single), 1*s*. 6*d*. (second return). Return tickets issued on Saturday were valid for return on Monday. Goods workings did not commence until 1849.

However, the SSR engines and rolling stock became available during 1849, in time for opening of the line to Lichfield, and thereafter the SSR worked the trains. An advertisement in the *Staffordshire Advertiser*, for Saturday 9th April, 1849 records the initial service:

TIMETABLE – WEEKDAYS ONLY

	am	*am*	*pm*	*pm*
Birmingham		9.00	1.15	4.00
Walsall	8.20	9.35	1.45	4.35
Lichfield	8.42	10.10	2.16	5.06
Burton		10.40	2.50	5.35

	am	*pm*	*pm*	*pm*
Burton		12.00	3.00	6.50
Lichfield	9.00	12.25	3.30	7.21
Walsall	9.22	1.02	4.10	8.00
Birmingham	9.45	2.00	5.00	8.30

FEBRUARY, 1850.

SOUTH STAFFORDSHIRE RAILWAY.

OPENED FROM BIRMINGHAM THROUGH WALSALL & LICHFIELD TO BURTON

Where it joins the Leicester and Swannington, North Staffordshire and Midland Railways; by which a great saving of mileage in Railway Communication will be gained between the South Staffordshire district and Derby, Sheffield, and the North. London Time will be observed at all Stations.

UP TRAINS.

Miles from Burton.	STATIONS.	WEEK DAYS. 1 & 2 Class.	WEEK DAYS. Parly 1 & 3 Class.	WEEK DAYS. 1 & 2 Class.	WEEK DAYS. Goods. Parly 1 2 & 3.	SUNDAYS. 1 2 & 3 Class.	SUNDAYS. 1 & 2 Class.	SUNDAYS. 1 2 & 3 Class.
	LEAVE	a. m.	a. m.	p. m.	p. m.	a. m.	p. m.	p. m.
—	DERBY	8 0	11 15	4 0	6 30	—	—	—
—	LEICESTER	7 0	10 20	2 45	5 30	—	—	—
—	UTTOXETER...	7 30	9 35	1 5	4 40	—	—	—
—	RUGELEY	8 38	12 24	4 29	—	—	—	—
—	**BURTON**	8 45	12 15	4 45	7 30	—	—	—
4	BARTON & WALTON ...	8 55	12 26	4 55	7 42	—	—	—
7¼	**ALREWAS**	9 5	12 37	5 2	7 48	—	—	—
11½	TRENT VALLEY JUNCTION	9 15	12 49	5 12	—	—	—	—
Trent	RUGELEY Arrival at ...	9 41	3 45	7 45	—	—	—	—
Valley.	STAFFORD Arrival at	10 5	2 12	8 20	—	—	—	—
12½	**LICHFIELD**	9 20	12 55	5 18	8 10	9 40	3 15	9 10
15¾	HAMMERWICH ...	—	1 5	—	8 20	9 47	—	9 18
18	BROWNHILLS	9 32	1 12	5 31	8 30	9 52	3 28	9 23
20	**PELSALL**	9 37	1 18	5 36	8 36	9 56	3 33	9 27
21¼	RUSHALL	—	1 22	—	8 40	10 0	—	9 30
23	**WALSALL** ...	9 45	1 30	5 45	8 50	10 5	3 45	9 35
26¼	NEWTON ROAD	—	1 36	5 51	8 58	10 15	3 53	9 45
29¾	PERRY BARR... ...	9 57	1 42	5 58	9 6	10 21	4 0	9 51
33¼	Arrive at **BIRMINGHAM** ...	10 15	2 0	6 15	9 20	10 30	4 15	10 0
	Leave for				a. m.	p. m.		a. m
—	LONDON...	10 30	4 0	8 8	12 15	12 30	—	12 15
—	GLOUCESTER	11 0	2 30	6 30	1 40	—	5 0	1 43

DOWN TRAINS.

Miles from Birm'm.	STATIONS.	WEEK DAYS. Parly 1 2 & 3 Class.	WEEK DAYS. 1 & 2 Class.	WEEK DAYS. 1 & 2 Class.	WEEK DAYS. Goods. Parly 1 2 & 3	SUNDAYS. 1 2 & 3 Class.	SUNDAYS. 1 & 2 Class.	SUNDAYS. 1 2 & 3 Class.
	LEAVE	a. m.	a. m. 7 15	noon.	p. m.	a. m.	a. m.	p. m.
—	LONDON	—	9 0	12 0	5 0	—	10 0	—
—	GLOUCESTER	7 0	9 38	12 35	5 5	—	—	—
			p. m	p. m.			p. m.	
—	**BIRMINGHAM** ...	10 5	1 15	4 45	8 45	8 30	2 0	8 0
3½	PERRY BARR	10 12	1 23	4 53	8 53	8 35	2 8	8 8
7	NEWTON ROAD	10 20	1 32	5 2	9 0	8 46	2 16	8 16
10¼	**WALSALL**... ...	10 30	1 45	5 10	9 20	8 55	2 25	8 25
12	RUSHALL	10 35	—	—	9 25	9 0	—	8 30
13¼	**PELSALL**	10 39	1 55	5 19	9 30	9 3	2 33	8 33
15¼	BROWNHILLS	10 45	2 0	5 25	9 35	9 9	2 39	8 39
17½	HAMMERWICH	10 50	—	*	9 40	9 14	—	8 44
20¾	**LICHFIELD**	11 0	2 15	5 40	9 50	9 23	2 53	8 53
21¾	TRENT VALLEY JUNCTION	11 4	2 20	5 45	—	—	—	—
Trent	STAFFORD Departure from	8 20	12 0	3 53	—	—	—	—
Valley.	RUGELEY Departure from	8 38	12 24	4 29	—	—	—	—
26	**ALREWAS**	11 15	2 29	5 54	10 5	—	—	—
29¼	BARTON & WALTON ...	11 22	—	6 0	10 10	—	—	—
33¼	Arrive at **BURTON**	11 35	2 45	6 15	10 30	—	—	—
—	RUGELEY	—	3 45	7 45	—	—	—	—
—	UTTOXETER...	12 25	4 40	7 15	—	—	—	—
—	LEICESTER	1 50	6 10	—	—	—	—	—
—	DERBY	12 15	3 30	8 45	1 55	—	—	—

* Calls at Hammerwich on Tuesdays.

FARES.

DAY TICKETS

BETWEEN

Birmingham and Walsall,

First Class, **2s. 6d.** Second Class, **1s. 8d.**

Birmingham and Lichfield,

First Class, **4s.** Second Class, **3s.**

Walsall and Lichfield,

First Class, **3s.** Second Class, **2s.**

CHILDREN under three years of age FREE; above three and under twelve years of age HALF-PRICE.

PASSENGERS LUGGAGE.—The Company do not hold themselves responsible for Luggage unless booked and paid for according to its value. 100lbs. weight of Luggage allowed to First and Second Class and 56lbs. to Third Class Passengers, *not being merchandise or other articles carried for hire or profit*; any excess of that weight will be charged one farthing per lb.

DAY TICKETS (not transferable) are issued from all Stations.

WOLVERHAMPTON.

OMNIBUSES leave the Red Cow Coach Office, WOLVERHAMPTON, at 9 15 and 11 45 a.m., 4 0 and 6 35 p.m. to meet the 10 30 a.m., 1 45, 5 10, and 9 20 p.m. Down Trains, and the 1 30, and 8 50 p.m. Up Trains at WALSALL, returning in connection with the 9 45 a.m., 1 30, 5 45, and 8 50 p.m. Up Trains, and the 5 10 p.m. Down Train.

McCLEAN & STILEMAN, ENGINEERS. HORATIO BARNETT, SECRETARY. J. D. PAYNE, GENERAL MANAGER.

J. R. ROBINSON, ALBION PRINTING OFFICE, DIGBETH, WALSALL.

Timetable for the northern section of the South Staffordshire Railway, as published by the SSR Company - February 1850.

Birmingham to Walsall		Walsall to Birmingham	
Weekdays	Sundays	Weekdays	Sundays
9.00 am	9.00 am	9.45 am	9.40 am
1.15 pm	7.40 pm	2.00 pm	8.20 pm
4.00 pm		5.00 pm	
7.40 pm		8.20 pm	

The second table gives departure times from Birmingham and arrivals at Birmingham from Walsall and thus duplicates to large extent the first table. The effect is that additional trains ran between Birmingham and Walsall only, at 7.40 pm (weekdays) and 9.00 am and 7.40 pm (Sundays), and in reverse on Sundays only (arrivals) at 9.40 am and 8.20 pm. The 8.20 pm weekday arrival at Birmingham is probably an error for 8.30 pm, as shown in the first table.

Seven months later, an advertisement in the *Staffordshire Advertiser* for Saturday 27th November, 1849 unfortunately ignores those trains continuing to Lichfield and/or Burton, and so gives the impression that the number of trains had shrunk from four to three each way. It is more likely that there were additional through services to Lichfield.

SOUTH STAFFORDSHIRE RAILWAY - BIRMINGHAM AND THE TOWN OF WALSALL

From Birmingham to Walsall	From Walsall to Birmingham
8.45 am 1st and 2nd class	9.30 am 1st and 2nd class
2.15 pm 1st and 2nd class	3.10 pm 1st and 2nd class
7.00 pm 1st and 2nd class	7.45 pm 1st and 2nd class

ON SUNDAYS

From Birmingham to Walsall	From Walsall to Birmingham
8.15 am 1st and 2nd class	9.15 am 1st and 2nd class
7.00 pm 1st and 2nd class	8.00 pm 1st and 2nd clas

The timetable for February 1850 (*opposite*) displays a similar level of weekday service, but the times had changed considerably, and the previous one train from Walsall to Lichfield and return had been extended to Birmingham. On Sundays the number of trains had gone from two to three in each direction, and extended to run from Birmingham to Lichfield. By October 1851 the weekday service from Birmingham to Burton had increased from three each way to five, with the one continuing from Birmingham to Lichfield. Again the times had been completely recast. The Sunday trains had gone from three to four each way, with half running from Birmingham to Lichfield and half continuing to Burton. On both weekdays and Sundays there was an identical number of trains run between Dudley and Walsall to connect with the trains to Burton and Lichfield.

One of the early government restrictions on the railways was that there should be at least one daily train each way that stopped at all stations, and where a class of fare of 1*d*. per mile was available. These became known as 'Parliamentary' or 'Parly' trains. The revenue from all trains was subject to a duty, but a remission of duty was available for such 'Parliamentary' trains. The officers of the Inland Revenue enforced the rules strictly, so that even if one station was passed, no remission of duty was permitted, even though the train contained accommodation for 1*d*. per mile travellers. The SSR reacted by

OCTOBER, 1851.

SOUTH STAFFORDSHIRE.
Birmingham and Dudley, to Lichfield, Burton, and Derby.

STATIONS.	a. m.	a. m.	p. m.	p. m.	p. m.	p. m.	SUNDAYS. a. m.	a. m.	p. m.	p. m.
BIRMINGHAM .	6 0	9 45	12 30	2 30	5 10	9 0	..	9 0	2 0	5 45
Perry Barr	6 8	9 52	12 37	2 36	..	9 7	..	--	..	..
Newton Road	6 16	10 0	..	..	..	9 15	..	..	..	..
Bescot *Junction* ..	6 24	10 6	12 53	2 52	5 28	9 23	..	9 20	2 18	6 5
DUDLEY ....*depart*	6 40	9 45	12 30	2 25	5 0	9 10	7 15	9 5	2 0	5 50
Dudley Port......	..	9 50	..	..	5 4	..	7 20	9 9	2 4	5 54
Great Bridge	6 45	9 55	12 35	2 31	5 8	9 15	7 25	9 13	2 8	5 58
WEDNESBURY	6 50	10 0	12 40	2 36	5 12	9 20	7 30	9 18	2 13	6 3
WALSALL	7 20	10 16	1 0	3 0	5 35	9 30	7 40	9 30	2 25	6 15
PELSALL	7 28	10 26	1 8	3 8	5 43	9 37	7 48	9 38	2 33	6 23
Brownhills	7 35	10 32	1 15	3 15	5 50	9 44	7 53	9 43	2 38	6 28
Hammerwich	..	10 37	..	..	5 54	9 48	..	9 48	..	6 32
LICHFIELD	7 47	10 45	1 27	3 27	6 2	✳	8 0	10 0	3 0	6 45
Trent Valley *Junct.*	7 50	10 50	1 30	3 32	6 7		8 5	..	..	
ALREWAS	8 0	11 0	1 40	3 42	6 17		8 15	..	..	6 56
Barton and Walton	8 5	11 8	1 48	3 50	6 27		8 23	..	..	7 3
BURTON	8 15	11 20	2 0	4 0	6 40		8 40	..	..	7 15
UTTOXETER	9 0	1 30	..	4 55	7 25		9 40	..	..	
LEICESTER	10 0	1 10	..	6 5	10 0		10 30	..	..	9 0
DERBY	9 0	12 0	3 20	5 0	8 50		9 30	..	..	8 5

Derby and Burton, to Lichfield, Dudley, and Birmingham.

STATIONS.	a. m.	a. m.	p. m.	p. m.	p. m.	p. m.	*On Tuesdays, Thursdays, and Saturdays only.*	SUNDAYS. a. m.	p. m.	p. m.	p. m.
DERBY	8 0	11 5	2 0	3 45	6 30			8 0	..	..	7 0
LEICESTER ...	6 45	10 0	..	2 45	5 15			7 0	..	..	5 30
UTTOXETER	..	9 50	1 5	4 40	7 3			..	..	..	6 45
BURTON	8 35	12 30	2 40	5 15	7 40			9 10	..	..	7 45
Barton and Walton	8 45	12 40	2 48	5 23	7 48			9 20	..	..	7 55
ALREWAS	8 50	12 48	2 56	5 31	7 56			9 28	..	..	8 3
Trent Valley *Junct.*	9 0	12 55	..	5 40	..			9 35	..	..	
LICHFIELD	9 5	1 0	3 10	5 45	8 10	10 10		9 40	2 0	4 45	8 15
Hammerwich	..	1 10	..	..	8 18	10 15		9 48	2 8	..	8 23
Brownhills	9 17	1 18	3 25	5 57	8 26	10 20		9 54	2 14	4 58	8 29
PELSALL	9 22	1 25	3 32	6 2	8 33	10 25		10 0	2 20	5 4	8 35
WALSALL	9 35	1 40	3 45	6 15	8 43	10 40		10 10	2 30	5 15	8 45
Bescot *Junction*....	9 45	1 50	3 53	6 23	8 55	..		10 20	2 40	5 23	8 53
WEDNESBURY	9 43	1 47	4 8	6 22	8 52	..		10 18	2 38	5 23	8 53
Great Bridge......	9 48	1 52	4 13	6 27	8 57	..		10 22	2 43	5 28	8 58
Dudley Port......	9 52	1 56	4 17	..	9 0	..		10 25	2 48	..	9 2
DUDLEY	10 0	2 5	4 25	6 35	9 5	..		10 30	2 55	5 35	9 10
Newton Road	..	1 54	..	..	9 0	..		..	..	..	..
Perry Barr	..	2 0	4 3	6 33	9 7	..		..	..	..	..
BIRMINGHAM	10 5	2 15	4 20	6 45	9 20	..		10 40	3 0	5 45	9 15

DAY TICKETS BETWEEN LICHFIELD AND

	First.	Second.	Third.		First.	Second.	Third.
WALSALL	3 0	2 3	1 6	BURTON	3 8	2 6	1 9
DUDLEY	4 8	3 6	2 4	UTTOXETER......	7 0	5 0	
BIRMINGHAM	5 0	3 9	2 6				

✳ **Runs to LICHFIELD on Tuesdays, Thursdays, and Saturdays,**
returning to **WALSALL** at 10 10 p. m.

Timetable for the northern section of the South Staffordshire Railway, as published by the SSR Company - October 1851.

making all trains stop at all stations so as to obtain the remission. Unfortunately this earned the company the title of the 'Slow-Go-Motive Railway' in the press of the day, and it was forced to restrict the 1d. per mile tickets to only certain trains, and to adopt a 3rd class intermediate fare for the remainder.

The General Manager's Report dated 18th June, 1851 mentioned that the Whitsun traffic, at this time one of the few occasions when working people were able to travel for enjoyment, had been hit by very unfavourable weather. Even so there was a healthy number of passengers, totalling some 32,279 and producing income of around £1,500. The company was evidently unprepared for this level of traffic, as it had been unable to hire additional passenger stock, and was reduced to using open goods wagons. We shall later see another occasion when this occurred.

Meanwhile the goods traffic had continued to increase steadily, and income was averaging about £500 per week. A new contract was expected for limestone from Ambergate, and the LNWR had agreed to send ironstone from Bedworth to the SSR system. A proposition had also been received from Mr Harrison for the connection of his collieries at Brownhills to the SSR, although this was eventually to be delayed for a few years. Evidence of the increased goods traffic was a requirement for further goods accommodation at Dudley.

By August 1851 arrangements had been completed for the through ticketing of passengers with the NSR and MR, thus anticipating the establishment of the Railway Clearing House by several years.

One of the early difficulties in operating the line between Walsall and Dudley was the number of old iron and coal workings that were likely to affect the stability of the railway. This had been emphasised by Captain Wynne in his inspection report, and the Resident Engineer (G. Lee) had to deal with several instances of 'crowning-in', which is where the pillars of coal left to support the surface had suddenly collapsed. In some cases, the resulting subsidence was sufficient to engulf horses and carts, and in more serious cases, whole buildings had disappeared. Where this affected the railway, it became the practice to abandon the use of transverse sleepers, and install horizontal baulk timbers until the cause of the subsidence could be more permanently fixed. As a result, several severe speed restrictions were enforced in areas known to be affected.

The Great Exhibition of 1851 recorded the extent of coal workings in the area, by the display of a single solid block of coal, weighing around 10 tons, that had been mined near Tipton. This exhibition had other effects, such as the introduction of cloak rooms at more important stations, where passengers luggage could be held as 'Left Luggage' until required - a feature not previously available, and which was subsequently introduced at Walsall and Lichfield.

In this connection, the LNWR General Manager, Mark Huish, displayed an uncharacteristic degree of generosity in making available free passes to London for all clerks and principal servants to visit the exhibition. The SSR had to make special leave arrangements in order for them to attend.

In his report dated 1st August, 1851 the General Manager continued his efforts to increase the goods traffic, planning to increase both coal and iron ore traffic for the coming Winter, to install new sidings at Dudley, and requesting approval for new cranes at Wednesbury and Walsall. It was also recorded that the former station master at Lichfield, one Thomas Brewer, had been detected appropriating excess fares for his own use, but despite overwhelming evidence against him, and after two appearances before magistrates, he was acquitted - much to the General Manager's disgust.

Reporting on the results for 1851 against those for 1850, the General Manager noted in his report of 1st January, 1852 that weekly receipts for goods were up by 35 per cent and for passengers by 30 per cent. Total average receipts for the period from 1st August to 21st December were more than £1,300 per week. Even so, the expected increase in mineral trade in the last half of the year had not happened.

On 30th January, 1852 the General Manager reported that goods were carried totalling 6,673 tons with a revenue of £1,201 in the previous month, December, and that for January the figures were 12,688 tons giving £1,906. Finished rails were now being shipped from Bagnall's ironworks at Great Bridge. A former clerk at Dudley goods depot, by the name of Milner, had been tried at Worcester County Sessions on charges of embezzlement, and having been found guilty was sentenced to transportation for seven years. These were harsh days - one wonders if he survived long enough to return.

John Payne, the General Manager, had to contend with competition from the canals as well as the other railways in the area, and it was obviously necessary to know what the opposition had planned. So, with the OWWR about to open, the General Manager made a visit to Banbury and Oxford in February 1852 to enquire about their goods carriage rates, but found that the canal companies had anticipated events, and reduced their rates in order to be more competitive.

In July 1852 McClean entered into an agreement with the LNWR known as the 'Four Towns Agreement', in which the traffic between Birmingham and Wolverhampton, and between Dudley and Walsall was dealt with as a common fund, and the proceeds shared out on an agreed basis. The purpose was to exclude the GWR from making any unwanted agreements with the SSR, and to protect the traffic as far as possible, particularly as the LNWR had previously been at a major disadvantage in that its Birmingham to Wolverhampton trains running on the old GJR route had to reverse at Bushbury Junction in order to reach Wolverhampton High Level station, until the Stour Valley route was opened to passengers in July 1852.

In 1853 James Allport became the General Manager of the MR, and immediately introduced a policy of limiting his co-operation with the SSR, which he regarded as being a part of the LNWR. From 1855, passenger and goods trains for Burton were no longer permitted to work through over the MR metals north of Wichnor Junction, so exchange sidings were laid out, and a small station and a three-road locomotive shed were provided there. The station at Wichnor Junction first appears in the timetable for April 1855 but may have been in use earlier - there was almost no local passenger or goods traffic to be gained at this rather remote location. The SSR had hoped that in exchange for surrendering the through workings, their carriages would be allowed to be worked through to Derby, but Allport would concede nothing. Thereafter all workings required the attachment or detachment of carriages to and from Burton at Wichnor, which of course, only added to journey times, and created extra expense for the SSR. The inconvenience was worsened by the constant late running of the MR trains. Frustrated at the lack of progress towards Burton and Derby, the LNWR supported the proposal for a nominally independent line, the Burton on Trent Railway, in 1859. The route lay from Wichnor Junction by way of a flyover across the MR, then running parallel with that line on its eastern side. It approached Burton across the riverside meadows, then swung north-east to enter the town, and join with the NSR at Stretton Junction. This was a revival of an earlier proposal, put forward in 1850, engineered by McClean and Stileman, and surveyed by one George Taylor. Strong opposition from the MR caused the Bill to fail in Parliament, and the proposal was dropped. But the MR had been warned that the LNWR was determined, and more serious negotiations began, eventually bearing fruit, as we shall see.

Passenger trains to and from Birmingham began using New Street station from its opening on 1st June, 1854. These trains were normally accommodated at platform 2, which was eventually converted into part of a double bay arrangement facing north, and continued to be known as the 'South Staffs Bay' until well after nationalization.

The timetable for August 1854 presents some problems, as it is difficult to sort out which are connecting services and which are through trains, and the services had increased considerably. The OWWR had opened on 20th December, 1852, and the SSR Dudley Port to Sedgeley Junction section on 2nd January, 1854 allowing LNWR trains to run through from Birmingham to Kidderminster. However, it seems unlikely that Kidderminster was a through service, as running powers from Dudley to Kidderminster were not authorized until the SSR 1855 Act was passed on 23rd July, 1855. Unfortunately, this timetable also ignores the Birmingham to Walsall services. A fair interpretation of what was available is as follows:

	Weekdays		Sundays	
	Up trains	Down trains	Up trains	Down trains
Dudley-Walsall	12	13	8	5
Dudley-Dudley Port	13	14	1	1
Dudley-Lichfield	-	-	2	2
Dudley-Burton	4	4	2	2
Birmingham-Kidderminster	8	11	2	4

The timetables published in the *Wolverhampton Chronicle* for January until August 1855 give the following level of services between Birmingham and Walsall, which also included those trains continuing on to Dudley, as they had done before the opening of the Dudley Port loop. These were as follows:

	Weekdays		Sundays	
	Up trains	Down trains	Up trains	Down trains
Birmingham-Walsall	5	6	4	6
Birmingham-Walsall-Dudley	5	4	3	3

Some of the services were retimed for the September timetable, but the overall effect was one further train each way on each of the two routes during weekdays. Sundays were not changed. Thus, the pattern in this initial period since opening had been one of a gradual increase in the frequency of services on each of the lines.

Theft of goods from railway wagons and premises has been a constant problem for all railways, but the extent that some persons will go to for a relatively small amount of money often beggars belief. Nor is this a modern phenomenon, as events reported in the *Wolverhampton Chronicle* of 12th July, 1855 proved. Three men appeared in court: William Crutchley, a breaksman [*sic*]; Thomas Smith, a pointsman; and John Craddock, a licensed victualler were charged with stealing on 12th April, 1855 150 lb. of tobacco, valued at £29 6s. 9d.

A cask of tobacco was loaded into a SSR wagon at Burton, but was missing when it arrived at Lichfield, its destination. The train had been routed to Walsall and Dudley before returning, during the night to Lichfield. A guard named Pratt was taken into custody, and confessed to his part in the theft, explaining that seeing the truck left in a siding instead of being taken into a shed, he decided to steal the tobacco. In this felony he was joined by Crutchley, a Mr Mills, the fireman of the engine, and a Mr Henderson, who has since absconded. While the train was at Walsall, Pratt and Crutchley went to Craddock's house where they got two bags, and arranged for their train to be stopped about ½ mile from Walsall station, next to the wagon so that Craddock could get into the wagon. This accomplished, they transferred the cask from the wagon in the siding to their own train which was going to Wichnor, during which journey the contents of the cask were emptied into the sacks. The empty cask was then burned in the locomotive firebox. On their return, the train was stopped at Littleton bridge, near to Cannock Chase, and the bags were removed and buried in a hole in the embankment. Unfortunately, they were spotted when they came to retrieve the sacks, and the matter reported to the police, who searched all of their homes, eventually finding the sacks at the Leopard public house at Shire Oak. All of the accused were acquitted, having given valuable evidence at the trial, except for Craddock who was found guilty and sentenced to transportation for 14 years.

In 1856 an event occurred, which whilst almost comical in some respects, was perhaps unfairly treated in the subsequent legal wranglings. A dog was in transit on the LNWR from Lancashire to Birmingham, but the guard forgot to put it out at Stafford, and so it continued to Lichfield where it was handed over to the SSR for onward movement to Birmingham. Unfortunately, the last train from Lichfield had already left, and so the dog was locked up for the night. In the morning it escaped, and was never seen again. Initially, the LNWR paid the owner's claim, but then (at the direction of their redoubtable General Manager, Mark Huish) put the claim in front of the Superintendents' Claims Arbitration Committee claiming that the SSR should bear the cost. The committee agreed with the LNWR case, even though the SSR stated that it earned no revenue from the transport of the dog.

On 1st February, 1858 the extension from Walsall to Cannock was opened, but this is outside the scope of this volume, and will be covered in Volume Two.

This had been a troublesome time for the operating management, who were really still learning how to run a railway. It had also been a turbulent time economically. The period had started with a collapse of commercial confidence in 1846, to be followed by further loss of confidence after the 1848 French Revolution. But in 1849 matters appeared a little more settled, and the business outlook appeared brighter, which was further enhanced by the Great Exhibition of 1851, which gave British businesses a real boost. However, this was not to last too long before the country was plunged into the disastrous Crimean War of 1854-1856. This had a mixed effect, providing a stimulus for some industries, but having an adverse effect on others, including railways. The cessation of the war created its own boom, but this ended the following year when a crisis in the American economy resulted in a number of bank failures in the UK. There followed a very slow recovery to the end of the 1850s, but then the American Civil War of 1861 created further instability - but that is moving too far ahead.

1860 to 1900

Having obtained the lease for the SSR in February, 1860 the LNWR turned its attention to the unsatisfactory state of affairs over the running of through trains to Burton, for which running powers had been authorized by the original SSR Act. However, not entirely believing that its rights would be upheld, the LNWR promoted a further Act in 1861 for a line from Alrewas to Burton that would be independent of the MR. This Act also proved to be a useful bargaining tool in their negotiations with the MR. So, during 1861 timings were submitted by the LNWR Traffic Department to the MR for their approval. On 1st November, the first train arrived at Wichnor Junction to be met by a large number of platelayers, and two or three MR engines in steam. One of these had been padlocked to the V crossing of the junction, thus barring the way of the LNWR train. The MR Traffic Manager, G. Needham, was also on site, having camped overnight in a saloon brought there especially for the purpose. Polite discussions were held, during which it was revealed that the MR were under the misapprehension that the LNWR had intended to arrive there with a force of 300 men, and three engines, and were intent on forcing their way into Burton. Not wishing to make matters worse, the LNWR party withdrew and were soon in touch with their head office by telegraph. Evidently the wires were buzzing between Euston and Derby, for when they returned in the afternoon, the MR force had disappeared, and way was clear to Burton. The LNWR driver entered into the spirit of things by sounding noisy and repeated 'cock crows' on his whistle as they entered the brewery town. Scheduled through trains began operating over this route as from 1st December, and goods workings from 4th December.

As a result the SSR withdrew its Act in Parliament for the independent line to Burton. This was communicated to the SSR Directors in a report dated 23rd August, 1862:

> The bill brought in by this Company for a branch to Burton on Trent was withdrawn in Parliament under an agreement with the MR Company, satisfactory to the lessee, whereby passengers are conveyed to and from your line to theirs by every train of this Company, which superseded the necessity of that measure and from which the public has materially benefitted.

The LNWR managed to consolidate its position in Burton, when it opened its own goods depot at Horninglow on 1st April, 1863 by way of a short branch from

SOUTH STAFFORDSHIRE RAILWAY.
TIME TABLE FOR JULY, 1865.

Walsall to Birmingham, (via Bescot)— 8 0, 9 5, 9 45, 10 55, 11 30, a.m., 12 10, 1 3, 2 20, 3 40, 5 45, 6 50, 8 5, 9 40, p.m. On Sundays—9 55, 10 25, a.m., 2 55, 5 30, 8 40, 9 20, p.m.

Birmingham to Walsall, (via Bescot)— 8 10, 9 5, 10 30, a.m., 12 20, 2 5, 2 40, 3 40, 5 0, 5 25, 7 0, 8 25, 9 20, 10 30, p.m. On Sundays—8 35, 9 15, a. m., 1 0, 2 55; 5 45, 8 45, 10 30, p.m.

Walsall to Birmingham, (via Dudley Port)—6 40, 7 40, 9 10, 10 5, a.m., 12 15, 1 20, 3 0, 4 15, 6 50, 9 28, p.m. On Sundays—6 30, 8 35, a.m., 12 55, 3 35, 8 5, 9 25, p.m.

Birmingham to Walsall, (via Dudley Port)—6 0, 8 45, 10 20, 11 45, a.m., 12 5, 1 10, 3 5, 5 0, 6 10, 6 30, 7 30, 8 20, 9 5, 9 50, p.m. On Sundays—9 0, a. m., 1 45, 2 0, 7 30, 8 0, 9 30 p.m.

Walsall to Wolverhampton, (via Bescot)—8 35, 9 30, 10 55, a.m., 12 45, 2 20, 3 5, 5 45, 8 50, 9 40, 10 35, p.m. On Sundays—9 0, a.m., 1 20, 6 10, 10 35, p.m.

Wolverhampton to Walsall,) via Bescot)—7 35, 8 55, 10 30, 11 0, a.m., 12 40, 1 50, 3 10, 5 20, 7 30, 9 20, p.m. On Sundays—10 0, a.m., 2 30, 8 15, p.m.

Walsall to Wolverhampton, (via Dudley Port)—6 0, 7 40, 9 10, 10 5, a.m., 12 15, 1 20, 4 15, 6 50, 7 55, 9 28, p.m. On Sundays—8 35, a.m., 12 55, 3 35, 8 5, 9 25, p.m.

Wolverhampton to Walsall, (via Dudley Port)—7 0, 8 40, 10 40, 12 0, a.m., 12 24, 1 35, 3 15, 4 25, 5 3, 6 0, 7 5, 7 15, 7 45, 9 0, 10 10, p.m. On Sundays—6 55, 9 5, a.m., 12 55, 5 0, 8 10, 9 30, p.m.

Walsall to Dudley—6 0, 6 40, 7 40, 9 10, 10 5, a.m., 12 15, 1 20, 3 0, 4 15, 6 50, 7 55, 9 28, 11 5, p.m., On Sundays—6 30, 8 35, 10 0, 12 55, a.m., 3 35, 6 35, 8 5, 9 25, p.m.

Dudley to Walsall—7 35, 9 15, 10 55, a.m, 12 30, 1 50, 3 50, 5 15, 6 35, 7 10, 8 0, 9 25, 10 45, p.m. On Sunday—7 5, 9 30, a.m., 2 25, 3 0, 6 0, 7 55, 8 40, 10 0, p.m.

Walsall to Lichfield—8 10, 9 45, 11 25, a.m , 4 20, 7 40, and on Saturdays an Extra Train at 10 10, p.m. On Sundays—7 45, 9 55, a.m., 3 30, 6 35, p.m.

Lichfield to Walsall — 8 25, 11 30, a.m., 2 30, 6 10, 8 48, and on Saturdays an Extra Train at 10 45, p.m. On Sundays—9 20, 2 25, 7 30, 8 42, p.m.

Walsall to Cannock—7 50, 9 55, a.m., 1 15, 4 25, 7 45, and on Saturdays only at 10 15, p.m. On Sundays—10 0, a.m., 6 45 p.m.

Cannock to Walsall.—9 15, a.m., 12 38, 3 12, 7 25, 8 15, and on Saturdays only at 10 45, p.m. On Sundays—12 15, 8 40, p.m.

Walsall to Rugeley.—7 50, 9 55, 1 15, 4 25. On Sundays—10 0 6 45, p.m.

Rugeley to Walsall.—8 55, 12 13, 2 50, 7 0. On Sundays—11 50, 8 15, p.m.

NOTE.—An extra Train leaves Walsall at 4 30 on Saturdays, for Rushall, Pelsall and Brownhills, returning from Brownhills at 5 0, calling at Pelsall and Rushall.

An extra rain leaves Lichfield at 11 5, on Thursdays, for Walsall.

Timetable for trains at Walsall in July 1865 from the *Walsall Free Press* of 1st July, 1865.

Courtesy Walsall Local Archives

the MR Birmingham-Derby main line, and running powers over some of the industrial lines in the town. Such was the volume of traffic generated by the Burton breweries, that although the LNWR enjoyed only a small proportion of it, this was still a considerable amount. So authorization was sought in December 1868 to build an engine shed to hold four engines, and this was duly erected, opening on 4th October, 1869. Subsequently, the MR agreed to a plan by the LNWR to build an independent branch line of 1 mile 1,510 yards (almost 2 miles), parallel to the MR main line, that would reach a new goods facility. This branch (the 'Dallow End Branch') ran alongside the Trent & Mersey Canal from a junction with the MR Shobnall branch in the south, to join the NSR line at Stretton Junction to the north of the town, and opened throughout on 1st September, 1882. It was constructed by the contractors Braddock & Matthews for the LNWR. Meanwhile, the LNWR had been pressing ahead with its intentions to reach Derby, the heart of the MR. The LNWR (Additional Powers) Act of 12th July, 1867 (Vict. 30 & 31, cap. 180) gave extended running powers over the MR to Derby. In exchange, on the same date, the MR (Additional Powers) Act (Vict. 30 & 31, cap. 144), gave the MR running powers over the whole SSR route and over the LNWR route into Wolverhampton. Goods workings by the MR to Dudley, and to Wolverhampton via Bescot commenced on 1st September, 1867. However, through LNWR passenger services from Birmingham to Derby did not commence until 1st March, 1872, having been the subject of delaying tactics by James Allport, and eventually being agreed by arbitration. Goods workings had already commenced from 1st July, 1871. Eventually, the LNWR opened its own goods facility at Derby, along with a three-road engine shed, of substantial brick construction with a standard Ramsbottom hipped roof.

Passenger services on the southern section of the SSR had reduced by September 1879 to just nine each way on weekdays and three on Sundays. The timetable on page 115 shows the services over this route at this time from which it will be seen that there were eight weekday through trains in each direction from Birmingham to Derby. Of these, five up trains and three down trains were 'fast' services with limited stops between Walsall and Birmingham. The two Sunday trains in each direction called at all stations except Lichfield Trent Valley High Level. Although Wichnor Junction is shown on this timetable, it had actually closed on 1st November, 1877 and so no trains are shown stopping there.

As the SSR had reached its target of Dudley in November 1849 and complied with the provisions of the 1846 Act, the GWR was in no hurry to complete its own line to Dudley. This 1½ mile left the GWR's main Birmingham to Wolverhampton line at Swan Village, and ran to join the SSR at Horseley Bridge Junction, with one intermediate station, at Great Bridge. Passenger services began on 1st September, 1866 running from Birmingham Snow Hill to Dudley, where they arrived at the SSR station, but after reversal, left from the OWWR station, by then operated by the GWR. This awkward pattern of operation was to continue until the cessation of services. Although running via Dudley Port (Low Level), the GWR was prohibited to stop there to pick up or set down passengers.

Relations with the NSR had always been cordial, and the LNWR (New Works & Additional Powers) Act passed on 15th July, 1866 included under Section 60

LONDON AND NORTH-WESTERN RAILWAY.

THE London and North-Western Railway Company are NOW RUNNING THEIR OWN PASSENGER TRAINS TO DERBY and BURTON, affording increased facilities for Passengers by direct Trains from those places to Lichfield, Walsall, Wolverhampton, Dudley, and Birmingham, as well as for London, Rugby, Oxford, Stafford, Shrewsbury, and all chief Stations on the London and North-Western Main Line, by connection of Trains at Lichfield (Trent Valley) Station.

Time Bills, showing the Service of Fast and Third Class Trains, can be obtained at all the Stations.

THIRD CLASS PASSENGERS are conveyed by all these Trains from Derby and Burton to Birmingham, and *vice versa*.

Parcels Receiving Offices are opened in the Towns of Derby and Burton, as well as at the Booking Offices at the Stations.

Horses and Carriages are conveyed by any of these Trains between Derby and Birmingham.

Passengers desirous of adopting this route are requested to ask for Tickets by London and North-Western Railway.

W. CAWKWELL,
General Manager.

Euston Station,
London, March, 1872.

Notice of through running of LNWR trains from Birmingham to Derby, from the *Walsall Observer* of 16th March, 1872.
Courtesy Walsall Local Archives

DERBY, via LICHFIELD, to BIRMINGHAM (Up Trains).

Stations.	Morning.							Evening.							Morn.		Even.		
LEICESTER	...	...	9 10	10 22	...	...	...	2 33	...	...	...	7 20	...	...	...	...	...	...	
Leek	...	...	7 52	10 53	...	...	...	4 12	...	6 31	...	...	...	...	...	...	...	...	
Alton	...	...	8 22	11 20	...	...	...	4 41	...	6 58	...	...	...	...	...	...	...	...	
Ashbourne	...	7 5	8 10	11 5	...	1 50	...	4 25	...	6 40	...	...	...	...	...	...	...	...	
Uttoxeter	...	7 50	8 51	11 58	...	2 33	...	5 15	...	7 35	...	...	...	...	...	...	...	...	
Derby	...	8 15	9 0	11 5	1 40	...	3 20	...	5 50	...	7 20	8 30	...	8 0	...	...	8 15	...	
Willington	...	8 26	...	1116	...	...	...	...	...	...	7 31	8 41	...	8 12	...	...	8 27	...	
Burton	...	8 40	9 18	1129	1 58	...	2 38	...	6 8	...	7 43	8 53	...	8 26	...	...	8 41	...	
Barton and Walton	...	8 48	...	1139	A	...	2 46	...	...	...	7 52	9 2	...	8 35	...	...	8 50	...	
Wichnor Junction	...	8 54	...	1144	2 14	...	2 52	...	6 21	...	7 58	9 9	...	8 42	...	...	8 57	...	
Alrewas	...	9 6	9 38	1156	1 35	2 30	...	4 2	...	6 31	...	8 17	...	...	...	...	...	...	
LICHFIELD (Trent Valley)	7 40	9 13	9 46	1159	1 40	2 35	...	4 6	...	6 34	...	8 21	9 21	...	8 54	7 20	9 9	...	
LICHFIELD (City)	7 45	...	9 57	1210	1 51	...	...	4 14	...	...	...	8 31	...	...	9 11	7 31	9 20	...	
Hammerwich	7 58	...	10 4	1216	1 57	...	...	4 20	5 40	...	...	8 37	9 34	...	9 18	7 37	9 26	...	
Brownhills	8 4	...	1010	1222	2 3	...	...	4 25	5 46	...	...	8 43	9 40	...	9 21	7 43	9 33	...	
Pelsall	8 11	...	...	...	2 6	...	...	4 29	5 50	...	...	8 46	...	...	...	...	9 36	...	
Rushall	8 14	...	...	...	2 15	2 55	...	4 37	6 0	6 55	8 55	9 50	1019	9 30	...	...	...	...	
WALSALL	8 25	9 33	1022	1235	2 24	...	...	4 44	...	7 2	8 59	...	1019	9 49	8 4	9 54	...	...	
Bescot	8 34	9 43	...	1244	2 30	...	...	4 50	...	...	9 5	...	1020	9 55	8 10	...	...	...	
Newton Road	8 40	...	...	...	2 35	...	...	4 55	...	...	9 30	...	1025	10 0	8 15	10 3	...	...	
Hamstead and Great Barr	8 45	...	...	1255	2 40	3 12	...	5 0	...	7 13	9 35	1010	1030	10 5	8 20	...	...	...	
Perry Barr	8 50	9 53	...	...	2 44	...	...	5 4	...	...	9 39	...	1034	10 9	8 24	10 8	...	...	
Witton	8 54	...	...	...	2 48	...	...	5 8	...	...	9 43	1014	1038	1013	8 28	1012	...	...	
Aston	8 58	...	...	...	2 52	...	...	...	...	...	9 47	...	...	1017	8 32	...	...	...	
Vauxhall	...	...	...	...	...	...	...	...	...	...	9 55	1025	1050	1025	...	...	...	...	
BIRMINGHAM	9 10	10 5	1045	1 0	3 0	3 25	...	5 20	...	7 25	...	...	...	...	8 40	1025	...	...	

Calls at Barton and Walton to pick up London Passengers for Lichfield Pass.
A—Calls at Barton and Walton, and on Fridays for Lichfield Passengers only, and on...

BIRMINGHAM, via LICHFIELD, to DERBY (Down Trains).

Stations.	Morning.				Evening.							Morn.	Even.		
BIRMINGHAM	6 30	9 10	1025	1125	1 50	2 30	4 25	5 30	...	7 10	9 40	9 10	2 45	5 35	
Vauxhall	6 35	...	1030	...	...	2 35	...	...	...	...	9 45	9 15	...	5 40	
Aston	6 39	9 17	1034	...	...	2 39	4 33	...	...	7 17	9 49	9 19	2 52	5 44	
Witton	6 43	...	1038	...	...	2 43	4 37	...	...	7 21	9 53	9 23	2 56	5 48	
Perry Barr	6 47	9 22	1042	...	...	2 47	4 41	...	...	7 25	9 57	9 27	3 0	5 52	
Hamstead and Great Barr	6 52	9 27	1047	...	...	2 52	4 46	...	...	7 30	10 2	9 32	3 5	5 57	
Newton Road	6 57	9 32	1052	...	...	2 57	4 51	...	...	7 36	10 7	9 37	3 10	6 2	
Bescot	7 5	9 40	11 0	...	2 10	3 5	...	5 0	5 50	7 45	1013	9 45	3 20	6 10	
WALSALL	7 10	9 45	11 5	1150	2 15	3 10	4 55	5 5	5 55	7 50	1020	9 50	3 25	6 15	
Rushall	7 25	...	1115	...	2 25	...	4 50	...	...	8 0	1030	10 5	3 35	6 30	
Pelsall	7 30	10 2	1120	...	2 30	...	4 54	5 18	...	8 5	1034	1010	3 40	6 35	
Brownhills	7 36	10 8	1126	...	2 36	...	5 0	5 24	CD	8 11	1040	1016	3 46	6 41	
Hammerwich	7 42	1013	1132	...	2 42	...	5 30	...	...	8 17	...	1022	3 52	6 47	
LICHFIELD (City)	7 51	1023	1142	1210	2 51	3 37	5 39	6 14	...	8 26	1052	1030	4 0	6 55	
LICHFIELD (Trent Valley)	7 55	1029	1145	1213	2 54	3 40	5 42	6 18	...	8 30	11 0	...	...	...	
Alrewas	8 19	1037	...	1226	...	3 50	...	5 52	...	8 42	...	1044	...	7 4	
Wichnor Junction	...	...	...	...	...	...	...	...	...	...	...	1054	...	7 13	
Barton and Walton	8 28	1045	...	...	...	3 58	6 1	EF	...	8 50	...	11 6	...	7 24	
Burton	8 36	1053	...	1241	3 16	4 5	...	6 9	6 39	8 58	...	1120	...	7 37	
Willington	8 49	11 4	...	...	...	4 14	...	6 20	...	9 9	...	1135	...	7 50	
DERBY	9 5	1120	...	1 0	3 40	4 30	...	6 35	7 0	9 25	...	...	...	...	
Uttoxeter	9 27	1146	...	2 40	...	...	5 13	...	...	7 27	...	...	...	...	
Ashbourne	10 5	1240	...	3 23	...	...	6 0	...	...	8 10	...	...	...	...	
Alton	...	1226	...	...	...	...	5 44	...	...	...	...	...	...	...	
Leek	...	1255	...	...	...	...	6 15	...	...	...	...	...	...	...	
LEICESTER	...	1222	...	4 15	...	...	7 5	...	...	...	...	...	...	...	

CD—Calls at Brownhills on Thursdays.
EF—Stops at Barton and Walton to set down Passengers from London and the South, on notice being given to the Guard at Lichfield, T.V.

WALSALL, WOLVERHAMPTON, and DUDLEY.

Stations.	Morning.							Evening.						Morn.	Even.		
WALSALL ...... dep	8 40	9 36	1030	...	1 15	...	3 15	4 45	...	7 5	...	9 10	10 5	9 53	...	7 57	10 0	...
Wednesbury	8 47	9 43	1037	...	1 22	...	3 22	4 53	...	7 12	...	9 18	1013	9 58	...	8 5	10 8	...
Ocker Hill	8 52	...	1042	...	1 27	...	...	4 59	...	7 17	...	9 22	...	O	...	O	...	...
Prince's End	8 55	9 48	1045	...	1 30	...	B	5 4	...	7 20	...	9 25	...	O	...	1 0	...	...
Deepfields	9 1	...	1051	...	1 36	...	3 31	5 10	...	7 26	...	9 31	O	111	...	9 6	...	...
Ettingshall-road	...	...	1056	...	1 41	...	...	...	...	...	...	9 36	O	116	...	9 10	...	...
Monmore Green	...	...	11 0	...	1 45	...	...	5 15	...	...	...	9 40	...	1120	...	9 15	1058	...
WOLVERHAMPTON	9 10	10 0	11 5	...	1 50	...	3 40	5 20	...	7 35	...	9 45	1058	1126	...	9 20	...	...
WALSALL	8 35	9 50	1035	...	1 5	...	3 5	4 50	...	7 10	...	9 5	10 0	...	...	7 57	10 0	...
Wednesbury	8 43	9 58	1043	...	1 13	...	3 13	4 58	...	7 18	...	9 13	1013	9 58	...	8 5	10 8	...
Great Bridge	8 47	10 3	1048	...	1 18	...	3 18	5 3	...	7 22	...	9 17	1017	10 2	...	8 10	1012	...
Dudley Port	8 52	10 8	1053	...	1 23	...	3 22	5 7	...	7 25	...	9 22	1025	10 7	...	8 16	1017	...
DUDLEY	9 0	1015	11 0	...	1 30	...	3 30	5 15	...	7 35	...	9 30	1035	1015	...	8 25	1025	...
DUDLEY	...	9 25	1020	1115	1 40	2 50	4 30	5 20	...	7 15	...	9 50	...	9 25	...	2 50	5 45	...
Dudley Port	...	9 31	1028	1123	47 2	58	4 37	5 29	...	7 23	...	9 58	...	9 30	...	2 58	5 53	...
Great Bridge	...	9 35	1031	1127	1 51	3 2	4 41	5 32	...	7 27	...	10 2	...	9 39	...	3 2	5 57	...
Wednesbury	...	9 39	1036	1131	1 53	3 6	4 45	5 36	...	7 31	...	10 6	...	9 43	...	3 6	6 1	...
WALSALL	...	9 50	1045	1140	2 5	3 15	4 55	5 45	...	7 40	...	1015	...	9 55	...	3 15	6 10	...
WOLVERHAMPTON	...	9 10	1020	1120	1 40	2 40	4 35	5 25	...	7 15	...	8 55	...	7 35	...	1 40	5 15	...
Monmore Green	...	...	1024	...	...	...	4 29	...	...	...	...	8 59	...	7 39	...	...	5 19	...
Ettingshall-road	...	...	1028	...	...	...	4 33	...	...	...	...	9 3	...	7 43	...	...	5 23	...
Deepfields	...	9 18	1032	1127	1 47	2 47	4 37	5 32	...	7 22	...	9 7	...	7 48	...	1 47	5 28	...
Prince's End	...	9 24	1038	...	1 53	...	4 43	...	...	7 28	...	9 13	...	O	...	O	O	...
Ocker Hill	...	...	1042	...	1 57	...	4 47	...	...	7 32	...	9 17	...	O	...	O	O	...
Wednesbury	...	9 30	1045	1135	2 0	2 55	4 50	5 40	...	7 35	...	9 20	...	8 40	...	3 15	6 10	...
WALSALL	...	9 40	1055	1145	2 10	3 5	6 0	5 50	...	7 45	...	9 30	...	...	...	...	...	...

B—Calls at Prince's End on Wednesdays to pick up Pass.
O—Via Dudley Port.

Timetable for trains on SSR routes from the *Lichfield Mercury* of 26th September, 1879.
Courtesy Lichfield Archives

RAILWAY TIME TABLE.

NOVEMBER, 1881.

☛ This Time Table is carefully compiled from the Companies' Tables, but of course we do not hold ourselves liable for any inaccuracy.

London and North-Western Railway.

Walsall to Birmingham, via Bescot—8 0, 8 30, 9 0, 9 35, 10 24, 10 30, 11 30, 12 28, 1 20, 2 25, 3 0, 4 5, 4 47, 5 35, 7 0, 8 10, 9 0, 9 55, 10 20. Sundays—9 45, 12 0, 3 25, 5 20, 8 0, 9 50.

Birmingham to Walsall, via Bescot—6 30, 7 45, 9 10, 10 25, 11 25, 12 25, 1 15, 1 50, 2 30, 3 35, 4 25, 5 15, 5 35, 6 30, 7 10, 8 40, 9 30, 9 40, 11 10. Sundays—9 10, 12 45, 2 45, 5 35, 8 25, 11 0.

Walsall to Bescot—8 0, 8 30, 9 0, 9 35, 10 30, 11 30, 12 28, 1 20, 2 25, 4 5, 4 47, 5 35, 7 0, 8 10, 9 0, 10 20. Sundays—9 45, 12 0, 3 25, 8 0, 9 50.

Bescot to Walsall—6 58, 8 17, 9 36, 10 53, 12 53, 1 39, 2 8, 2 58, 3 55, 4 53, 5 33, 6 3, 6 58, 7 37, 9 13, 10 13, 11 43. Sundays—9 42, 1 17, 3 16, 6 7, 8 55.

Walsall to Wednesbury—6 0, 6 50, 7 20, 8 20, 8 35, 9 40, 10 35, 11 10, 1 10, 3 5, 4 55, 5 50, 7 5, 8 53, 10 5. Sundays—7 0, 8 55, 9 50, 11 50, 3 45, 6 40, 7 57, 10 0.

Wednesbury to Walsall—8 6, 9 35, 9 39, 10 35, 11 15, 11 30, 12 35, 12 45, 2 0, 2 54, 3 0, 4 30, 4 53, 5 25, 6 40, 7 0, 7 30, 8 30, 9 25, 10 5, 11 35. Sundays—8 30, 9 43, 3 5, 4 25, 6 0, 7 35, 9 3, 11 0.

Walsall to Pleck—8 40, 10 27, 12 32, 1 15, 4 15, 4 44, 8 15, 9 5.

Pleck to Walsall—6 55, 8 14, 9 40, 10 59, 12 44, 2 2, 3 10, 4 14, 4 59, 5 38, 7 45, 8 24, 9 24, 10 20, 11 12.

Walsall to James Bridge—7 25, 7 30, 8 40, 10 27, 12 32, 1 15, 2 0, 4 15, 4 44, 5 32, 8 15, 9 5.

James Bridge to Walsall—8 11, 9 37, 10 56, 12 41, 1 59, 3 7, 4 11, 4 56, 5 35, 8 21, 9 21, 10 15.

Walsall to Wolverhampton (via James Bridge)—7 25, 8 40, 9 37, 10 27, 12 0, 12 32, 1 15, 2 0, 3 15, 4 15, 4 44, 5 32, 7 10, 8 15, 9 5, 10 15.

Wolverhampton to Walsall (via James Bridge)—6 45, 8 0, 9 25, 10 45, 11 30, 12 30, 1 50, 2 55, 4 0, 4 45, 5 25, 6 35, 7 35, 8 10, 9 10, 10 5, 11 0.

Walsall to Rushall—7 20, 11 10, 2 20, 5 12, 7 55. Sundays—10 0, 3 30, 6 25.

Rushall to Walsall—8 14, 10 13, 12 10, 2 47, 4 32, 8 40, 9 32. Sundays—9 21 am, 7 46, 9 36 pm.

Walsall to Pelsall and Brownhills—7 20, 9 55, 11 10, 2 20, 5 12, 7 55 (10 40 Saturday to Brownhills). Sundays—10 0, 3 30, 6 25.

Brownhills and Pelsall to Walsall—8 5, 10 4, 12 0, 2 39, 4 22, 8 31, 9 22. Sundays—9 11, 7 37, 9 26. Saturdays—5 40 pm.

Walsall to Hammerwich—7 20, 9 55, 11 10, 2 20, 5 12, 5 47, 7 55. Sundays—10 0, 3 30, 6 25.

Hammerwich to Walsall—7 59, 9 57, 11 54, 2 33, 4 16, 8 25, 9 16. Sundays—9 5, 7 31, 9 20.

Walsall to Lichfield—7 20, 9 55, 11 10, 11 53, 2 20, 3 20, 5 12, 5 47, 7 55. Sundays—10 0, 3 30, 6 25.

Lichfield to Walsall—7 50, 9 13, 9 46, 11 43, 2 25, 4 7, 6 34, 8 17, 9 5. Sundays—8 54, 7 20, 9 9.

Walsall to Burton and Derby—7 20, 9 55, 11 53, 2 20, 3 20, 5 47, 7 55. Sundays—10 0, 6 25.

Derby and Burton to Walsall—6 55, 8 15, 9 0, 10 50, 1 30, 3 20, 5 50, 7 20. Sundays—8 a.m., 8 15 p.m.

Walsall to Birchills, Bloxwich, Wyrley, Cannock, Hednesford & Rugeley—7 10, 8 30, 10 5, 1 10, 3 25, 5 8, 5 50, 8 0, (10 40 p m Saturdays only.) Sundays—10 5 a.m., 6 18 p.m.

Rugeley to Hednesford, Cannock, Wyrley, Bloxwich, Birchills & Walsall—7 34, 8 45, 9 35, 12 20, 3 10, 4 40, 7 15, 9 15. Sundays—8 37 am, 8 27 pm.

Walsall to Great Bridge, Dudley Port, and Dudley—6 0, 6 50, 7 20, 8 35, 9 40, 10 35, 11 10, 1 10, 3 5, 4 55, 5 50, 7 5, 8 53, 10 5. Sundays—7 0, 8 55, 9 50, 11 50, 3 45, 6 40, 7 57, 10 0.

Dudley to Walsall—7 50, 9 25, 10 20, 11 15, 12 30, 1 45, 2 45, 4 30, 5 10, 6 45, 7 15, 9 10, 9 50, 11 20. Sundays—8 15, 9 25, 2 50, 4 0, 5 45, 7 20, 8 45, 10 45.

Walsall to Darlaston—7 30, 8 40, 10 27, 12 32, 1 15, 2 0, 4 15, 4 44, 5 32, 8 15, 9 5.

Darlaston to Walsall—7 50, 9 32, 10 52, 12 5, 1 22, 3 47, 5 15, 8 10, 8 49, 10 11.

Walsall to Ocker Hill, Princes End, Deepfields, and Wolverhampton—8 20, 9 40, 11 10, 1 10, 3 5, 4 55, 7 5.

Wolverhampton, Deepfields, Princes End, and Ocker Hill to Walsall—9 10, 10 50, 12 10, 2 35, 4 5, 6 15, 8 5.

Abridged timetable for trains from Walsall in November 1881 from the *Walsall Observer* of 5th November, 1881.
Courtesy Walsall Local Archives

running powers for two daily goods trains to be run from Wolverhampton and Birmingham via Cannock and, Colwich to Stoke. A reciprocal arrangement was later made for passenger trains and from early 1882 the NSR was permitted to make through workings from Stoke to Walsall. These will be examined in Volume Two of this work.

Another line to open around this time was that from Stechford on the old L&BR route from Birmingham to Coventry to Aston on the original GJR route, This line had originally been proposed in the 1830s, but was revived to ease traffic around and through Birmingham, primarily for goods workings. It was opened for goods traffic on 7th Septermber, 1880 and for passengers on 1st March, 1882. Although it was used primarily for the Wolverhampton portions of some expresses, it was also used for through carriages from Euston to Walsall, detached at Stechford and worked forward non stop. This also provided a useful route south for the coal trains from Cannock Chase, although these were mostly dealt with differently after the opening of two new yards at Bescot in 1892. These comprised new yards for up and down directions, and to service the freight workings an eight-road engine shed was opened at the north-west corner of the yard.

At Birmingham's New Street station considerable efforts had been made to improve the traffic flow, and thus to provide additional services, with the addition of further platforms from 8th December, 1885 when the 'South Staffordshire' platform became two bays. The eastern approaches were modified in 1896, again easing conflicting traffic movements.

As detailed in Chapter Six, the new line from Sutton Coldfield to Lichfield had opened on 5th December, 1884 but was not shown in the timetables until the following January, and it was not until the following 1st May that special fast trains were run over this route from Birmingham to Derby. This caused some revision to the existing services, as many trains from Walsall then terminated at Lichfield to connect with the new services, which were also timed to connect with the NSR services from Burton to Uttoxeter.

A summary of the services in November 1885 is as follows:

	Up trains		Down trains	
Between	Weekdays	Sundays	Weekdays	Sundays
Walsall and Dudley	12	7	12	7
Walsall and Wolverhampton (via Princes End)	1	0	1	0
Walsall and Lichfield City	5	2	5+1 SO	2
Walsall and Derby	3	0	4	0
Wolverhampton and Lichfield City	0	0	1	0
Wolverhampton and Derby	0	0	1	0
Birmingham and Derby (via Sutton Coldfield)	5	0	4	0
Birmingham and Derby (via Walsall)	1	0	0	0
Birmingham and Lichfield Trent Valley (via Sutton Coldfield)	2	0	1	0
Lichfield City and Derby	1	0	1	0

SO = Saturdays only.

FLOOD AT WALSALL STATION MAY 13TH 1886

A postcard record of the flooding that occurred in Walsall station on 13th May, 1886. The carriages are standing in the Cannock bay adjacent to platform one. The rowing boat was kept at the Civil Engineering Depot at Rolling Mill Street, and brought out during these regular occurrences, so that inspections could be made. *Bill Mayo Collection*

The flood of 1931 at Walsall station was particularly severe. Here we see an inspection being made of the station, with presumably the station master taking the rear seat. This photograph was taken from the No. 3 signal box, with the corridor to the platforms overhead.

Bill Mayo Collection

The frequency between Walsall and Dudley was maintained, as the *Wednesbury Herald* for 5th November, 1887 gave 14 trains each way between Walsall and Dudley on weekdays, with six to Walsall and five to Dudley on Sundays.

Interruptions to traffic through Walsall due to flooding were regular if not frequent over the years. The problem arose from the siting of the route from the north alongside the Ford Brook (a tributary of the River Tame). As the railway approached Walsall it was actually lower than the brook, and although partly covered in, was prone to flood in times of heavy rain or snow. Such flooding was not just inconvenient, it sometimes reached 6 ft in depth at the station and curtailed all services. Serious floods occurred on 23rd July, 1872, 20th July, 1875, and 13th-14th May, 1886 and in 1931. The culvert for the brook was extended during the 1883 enlargement (*see Chapter Eleven*), and again in the 1890s, but the problem only moved and was not solved. It had become the practice to keep a rowing boat at the Permanent Way Department in Rolling Mill Street, so that when flooding occurred, a horse-drawn dray would take the boat to the station. Later, one of the Scammell 'mechanical horses' was used on this duty. A further problem arose after 1965 when the new power box was opened at Pleck to replace the several signal boxes with their mechanical operations. Previously, after the flood waters had subsided, the mechanical links and joints just needed oiling to continue as before, but the new electrical connections had to be replaced each time. More flooding occurred on 28th January, 1977, and exactly one year later. A new twin tunnel was finally driven in 1979 in an attempt to cure the problem once and for all. Unfortunately, a very heavy snowfall in the following Winter created similar flooding when the entrances to the tunnels became blocked by debris.

Returning to the passenger services, by July 1898 the pattern had changed once again, particularly in the emphasis placed on through running of trains from Dudley to Burton and Derby, as illustrated below:

Between	Up trains Weekdays	Sundays	Down trains Weekdays	Sundays
Dudley and Walsall	8	3	7	2
Dudley and Lichfield Trent Valley	2	1	2	1
Dudley and Burton	1	0	0	0
Dudley and Derby	2	0	0	0
Dudley and Stafford	0	1	0	1
Birmingham and Lichfield City (via Walsall)	0	1	1	1
Birmingham and Lichfield Trent Valley (via Sutton Coldfield)	1	0	0	0
Birmingham and Burton (via Sutton Coldfield)	2	0	5	0
Birmingham and Derby (via Sutton Coldfield)	4	0	3	0
Walsall and Lichfield Trent Valley	0	0	1	0
Lichfield City and Burton	1 + 1 FO	0	0	0
Lichfield Trent Valley and Burton	1	0	1	0
Wolverhampton and Lichfield City	1	0	0	0
Wolverhampton and Burton	1	0	0	0
Wolverhampton and Derby	0	0	1	0

FO = Fridays only

An examination of goods workings in this period reveals a complex pattern of movements and intervals between the major centres, trip workings to local sidings and collieries, but remarkably few through goods workings. As it would be tedious to list all such movements, the following table gives an overall impression of the number of goods movements including coal, mineral, general goods, empty stock, and engine and brake van movements on each average weekday or Sunday:

		Dudley-Wichnor	Dudley-Walsall	Walsall-Wichnor
July 1866	Up weekdays	24		
	Up Sundays	3		
	Down weekdays	22		
	Down Sundays	5		
November 1885	Up weekdays		40	50
	Up Sundays		4	8
	Down weekdays		41	44
	Down Sundays		4	7
July 1898	Up weekdays		36	48
	Up Sundays		5	5
	Down weekdays		32	39
	Down Sundays		4	2

This includes MR goods workings, which will be examined in more detail in Chapter Nine. One LNWR working of note was a Sundays-only milk train from Burton at 9.13 pm to London, which was routed via Lichfield Trent Valley (at 9.40 pm) where it would have used the chord to the Low Level station and attached to a through up working from the North.

1900-1947

Steam railcars were introduced on the LNWR in 1905, but their use was to be short-lived as, apart from being unpopular due to the amount of exhaust entering the passenger compartment, they proved to rather inflexible in use. From the beginning of 1906, they were put to use on the Walsall to Rugeley and Walsall to Lichfield services. Each unit contained seats for 48 passengers, and was separated into two third class compartments, one for smoking and one for non-smoking. They were soon replaced by push-pull units, where a conventional locomotive was attached to one end of the train and could be driven from either the locomotive or from a driver's compartment in the leading vehicle. A push - pull unit had been in operation on the Walsall to Rugeley and Walsall to Lichfield services since at least November 1907. This was actually in advance of its first intended use, on the Red Wharf Bay branch in Anglesey, and had been made necessary by the steam railcar, normally in use, having been taken out of service for repairs. The use of the push and pull units (also referred to by the LNWR as 'motor trains') spread rapidly, soon completely replacing the steam railcars. The shuttle services from Walsall to Dudley and Dudley to Dudley Port were so operated by 1909. An analysis of the costs of operating these units throughout the LNWR system in 1911 revealed that in this area, the receipts were the highest, and the costs the lowest of anywhere on the system. Receipts here had worked out at 1s. 8d. per mile, and costs at 6¼d. per mile. The push-pull units always ran pulling towards Dudley or Wolverhampton from Walsall, and from Rugeley and Lichfield to Walsall. The primary reason was that when standing in the Sutton bay at Walsall station, the engine would then be then nearest to the platform and furthest away from the No. 3 signal box, whose unfortunate position beneath the booking hall otherwise attracted the smoke. As there were two dedicated sets of two coaches for the Walsall-Dudley service, the second set was pressed into use during peak periods, with the engine being sandwiched in the middle of the two sets at these times.

With both the MR and LNWR sharing their routes between Wolverhampton and Walsall, from 1st January, 1909 a fairly intensive service was operated. This was part of an agreement between the two companies, signed in July 1908, to eliminate overlapping services and to pool competitive traffic. Using the Pleck curve, the old GJR route and the Portobello curve to Wolverhampton, the LNWR ran 10 trains on weekdays to Walsall (plus one Mondays only, and one Saturdays excepted), and the MR ran five. In the opposite direction, the LNWR ran nine and the MR seven. There were no Sunday trains. On the MR route via Wednesfield, the LNWR and MR each ran four trains (plus two more MR on Saturdays), and in the reverse direction, the LNWR ran four and the MR ran two (plus two more on Saturdays). The only Sunday service was by the MR over its own route, with four each way.

Although outside the scope of this book, it should be noted that Walsall also saw 13 weekday departures (14 Saturdays, and four Sundays) over the MR route via Sutton Park to New Street, and one each to Sutton Park and Penns on weekdays. Likewise, Lichfield City had eight weekday trains via Sutton Coldfield to New Street. Continuing the theme, at Dudley there were 11 weekday GWR departures for Snow Hill using the SSR line to Horseley Fields Junction, with six on Sundays.

The impact of tram competition in the Walsall area continued, as the tramway system expanded, and Rushall station closed from 1st March, 1909 as a result.

The emphasis of services from Dudley had switched by 1909 from through services to Burton and Derby to mostly local services to Walsall, where onward connections were made. By April 1910 the service between Walsall and Dudley had again increased to 15 each way on weekdays, with five on Sundays. There were 12 shuttles between Walsall and Bescot each way, operating on weekdays only, but the service to Birmingham had improved and become a little more complex. There were then 13 weekdays from New Street to Walsall, of which four travelled via Monument Lane, and nine via Aston, and this included one through carriage from Euston. In the opposite direction there were 17 on weekdays, again with four via Monument Lane and one through carriage to Euston. On Sundays there were five Walsall trains and six Birmingham trains, all via Aston. The Stechford line provided two weekday services, with one through carriage to Euston.

The services operated in May 1910 are summarized on page 123:

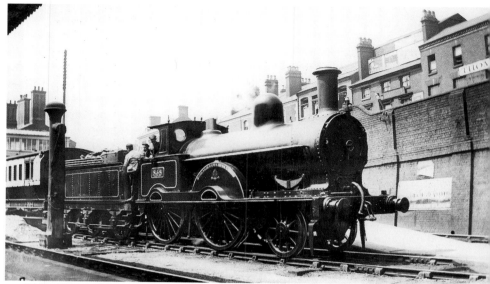

Webb 'Renewed Precedent' class 2-4-0 No. 858 *Sir Salar Jung* at the north end of platform 1 at Walsall around 1903. This engine was built in May 1897 and scrapped in July 1912. The bay platform known as the Cannock bay is to the right of the engine.   *R.S. Carpenter*

Webb 'Waterloo' or 'Whitworth' class 2-4-0 No. 632 *Ostrich* at the south end of Walsall station around 1905. Another of the 'renewals', this engine was built in June 1890 and scrapped in March 1911.   *R.S. Carpenter*

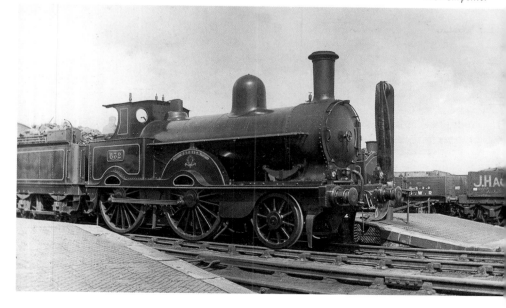

Between	Up trains Weekdays	Sundays	Down trains Weekdays	Sundays
Birmingham and Lichfield City (via Sutton Coldfield)	0	0	2	0
Birmingham and Lichfield Trent Valley (via Sutton Coldfield)	3	0	2	0
Birmingham and Burton (via Sutton Coldfield)	2	0	2	0
Birmingham and Derby (via Sutton Coldfield)	3	0	3	0
Birmingham and Derby (via Walsall)	0	0	1	0
Walsall and Lichfield City	5	1	3 + 1 ThO	1
Walsall and Lichfield Trent Valley	0	0	2	0
Walsall and Burton	1	0	1	0
Walsall and Derby	2	0	1	0
Lichfield City and Dudley	1	1	1	1
Lichfield City and Lichfield Trent Valley	3	0	3	0
Lichfield City and Burton	1 + 1 FO	0	1	0
Wolverhampton and Burton	1	0	1	0

ThO = Thursdays only, FO = Fridays only.

This pattern remained principally unchanged, except for some timings, right up until the outbreak of war in 1914.

A further study of goods workings at this time is given below, and indicates the continuing rise in traffic:

		Dudley-Walsall	Walsall-Wichnor
May 1910	Up weekdays	49	63
	Up Sundays	7	6
	Down weekdays	37	59
	Down Sundays	7	3
July 1911	Up weekdays	41	56
	Up Sundays	6	5
	Down weekdays	36	57
	Down Sundays	8	2
July 1914	Up weekdays	49	61
	Up Sundays	6	5
	Down weekdays	41	51
	Down Sundays	11	2

By May 1910 the Burton to London milk train on Sundays continued, but left Burton a little later, at 9.52 pm. On 17th August, 1911 a national strike by railwaymen began, with over 95 per cent joining in by the following day. Although severely disrupted, services were not entirely stopped, and the strike was settled on the third day, although most men did not return to work until the following day.

Further operational changes were made on 15th September, 1913 when Walsall station became a 'closed' station so that tickets were examined or collected at barriers on the station, instead of having this occur at the previous stop. This reduced the time of these station stops, and so enhanced the line capacity, particularly necessary at peak times. Platform tickets were thus required at Walsall for those desiring platform access, but not travelling.

An LNWR 'Jumbo' 2-4-0 arriving at Brownhills station with a southbound train around 1910. From the size of the crowd waiting on the platform, there was evidently an event of some importance occurring. The term 'Jumbo' for the 2-4-0s, introduced by Ramsbottom and perpetuated by Webb, was used to describe the very similar 2-4-0s of classes such as the 'Samson', 'Newton', 'Precursor', 'Precedent', 'Whitworth' and 'Waterloo'.   *Bill Mayo Collection*

An unidentified, but immaculate Webb 2-4-2T arriving at Bescot Junction station in pre-Grouping days with a passenger train typical of the Walsall to Birmingham stopping services at the time.   *R.S. Carpenter*

Only one record of any Zeppelin or bomber attacks on the line during World War I has been found. This occurred on 31st January, 1916 when around seven bombs were dropped on Wednesbury, or near the lines. Damage was inflicted on a platelayers' cabin, a goods shed, a weighing machine, a retaining wall, as well as to the permanent way and signal work, but there were no reports of any injuries. The effect on the railways in this area during World War I was nonetheless acute, with the reduction or suspension of passenger train services, especially from 1916 onwards. As we have seen this also entailed the temporary closure of several local stations, of which Princes End and Ocker Hill never reopened. The GWR services from Snow Hill to Dudley were also affected, being suspended from 29th November, 1915 until restored on 5th January, 1920. The return of the fighting forces in 1918 was greeted with considerable elation. On one occasion when the local battalion of the 5th South Staffordshire Regiment returned to Walsall, detonators were placed on the line in advance of the troop train, and the station platforms, the approach roads and the town centre filled to capacity with crowds as the troops disembarked, then paraded to the town centre Drill Hall to disband.

The government had taken control of the railway system for the duration of World War I and established the Railway Executive as the means of direction. With the cessation of hostilities, decisions had to be made as to what to do with the railway system. In 1913 the Liberal government had first mooted the idea of nationalization, and this again surfaced. But matters were not so clear cut, and so to provide time for the formulation of the future transport policy, the government control was extended until 15th August, 1921. In the end, a compromise was reached with the 'Grouping' of the railways into four main companies. This was passed into law in August 1921 with the passing of the Railways Act and the process began. The MR and LNWR, former rivals, became part of the new LMS as from 1st January, 1923.

With the 'Grouping' only months away, in July 1922 the pattern of services on the northern section had understandably changed considerably. Derby was now served on weekdays by only one train from Birmingham via Sutton Coldfield and Lichfield, and two in reverse. But there were then six from Walsall, and seven returning. No trains ran to Burton only, and none to Derby on Sundays. There were two on weekdays from Walsall to Lichfield City (plus two more on Saturdays) and three to Lichfield Trent Valley, with the reverse direction being one less, and two each way on Sundays from Walsall to Lichfield City. There were six weekday workings between Lichfield City and Trent Valley stations, with five on Saturdays, but none on Sundays. The service from New Street to Lichfield City via Sutton Coldfield had increased compared to the pre-war level, with 10 down and nine up trains on weekdays, plus two each way terminating at Sutton Coldfield, but still none on Sundays.

LNWR services on the Walsall to Wolverhampton routes had increased overall, as despite only one during weekdays on the MR route from Walsall, there were 19 on Mondays, 18 Tuesday to Fridays and 20 on Saturdays on the LNWR route. In the opposite direction there were 19 on each weekday on the LNWR route and two on the MR route. Just one ran each way on Sundays, this using the MR route.

A charming study from around 1912 at Brownhills station, as a Lichfield-bound train arrives. The elegant platform lamp on the left can be seen to include an internal station name for the benefit of passengers travelling at night.   *R.S. Carpenter/Lens of Sutton*

Fowler LMS '4F' class 0-6-0 No. 4106 rounds the bend in front of Ryecroft shed, Walsall with a Burton to Walsall local train composed of three non-corridor coaches, in June 1936.
E. Talbot Collection

The MR had expanded its services on the same Walsall to Wolverhampton routes even more so, as despite there being only two on weekdays from Walsall and one return, there were now three each way on Sundays, all using the LNWR route. But the MR now ran through trains from New Street via Sutton Park on its own route, continuing from Walsall to Wolverhampton on the LNWR route, thus avoiding the necessity for reversal in Walsall. These totalled three up and four down trains on weekdays. There were also services from New Street terminating at Walsall using the Sutton Park route, giving four down and six up trains, and a further one each way between Walsall and Sutton Park. None of these latter services ran on Sundays.

Meanwhile, the Walsall to New Street services via the LNWR route continued with frequencies similar to those of the pre-war period. There were 13 down trains on weekdays (plus one from Stechford), with 14 on Saturdays, and four on Sundays. The up trains comprised 17 on weekdays (plus one to Stechford), 16 on Saturdays and five on Sundays. Of these five each way ran via Monument Lane, but none on Sundays. The shuttle services between Walsall and Bescot continued with 10 each way on weekdays only, and from Walsall to Dudley with 12 on weekdays and four on Sundays. These latter services were particularly popular for theatregoers from Walsall and Wednesbury travelling to Dudley Opera House, which was replaced after a fire in 1936 by the Dudley Hippodrome. These venues were conveniently sited right next to the station. In the reverse direction, the Grand Theatre, right next to Walsall station, also attracted passengers to the SSR line trains.

The GWR route from Snow Hill to Dudley continued at a slightly higher frequency of 12 to Dudley and 13 return, but the Sunday services no longer ran.

In the inter-war years, many working class families from the Walsall area managed to take a summer holiday that cost nothing. This involved working as hop pickers in the fields of south Worcestershire and Herefordshire, and to get there the LMS put on additional carriages to their regular service trains. Special fares were available, but the normal practice was for the hopyard owners to provide travel vouchers for the pickers to exchange for tickets at the stations where they embarked. These passengers had to travel in the designated carriages, as these would be transferred at Dudley to be attached to GWR trains. Furthermore, on their return many were found to have uninvited visitors, as having spent a couple of weeks sleeping in very rough accommodation, they had often become infested with various fleas and bugs. This was not something that the LMS wished to pass on to its other passengers, and so these carriages were regularly fumigated.

Walsall station became a centre for incoming milk supplies, much of them from farms adjacent to stations on the northern section of the line around Lichfield, and until about 1930 there could often be seen a large collection of the standard 17 gallon milk churns, awaiting collection by the local dairies. Soon after this date the dairies found that using their own road transport to collect the milk directly from the local farms was more convenient. However, the Walsall Co-operative Society opened a new dairy in Midland Road on 10th July, 1937 and the LMS began deliveries using milk tankers on low loading wagons. The tankers were unloaded at an old cattle ramp siding at the Tasker Street end, and a railway lorry then took the tankers to the dairy, returning with the empties.

Three LNWR Daimler buses lined up outside the depot at Brownhills around 1913. The ones to the left and right are Commer 34-seater 32 hp registration numbers BM 2597 and BM 2598, and the centre one is Milnes Daimler 34-seater registration number LC 6707. Each bears a different destination board.   *Author's Collection*

LNWR omnibus BM 2597 at Boney Hay in 1913 .   *J. Tinsley*

During World War II, bombing raids were directed on Walsall on several occasions. In 1940 several houses and commercial property in the area north of Ryecroft received damage. Two houses at the end of Highbridge Row were destroyed in an attack on the Norton Junction marshalling yards. Passenger services were once again severely disrupted in this period, some by enemy action, and many by the temporary reduction or suspension of timetabled trains. The goods traffic over the route somehow managed to continue, although it must have been incredibly difficult to operate, especially at night during the frequent 'blackouts'. Shunting, train formation, and locomotive servicing must have been particularly hazardous. Even walking about the stations was fraught with danger when there were no lights, which is where the practice of painting the platform edges white originated.

At the end of the war, the whole railway infrastructure was absolutely worn out, both the track and buildings, as well as virtually the entire rolling stock. Nevertheless, some semblance of normal services was soon resumed, and with the prospect of nationalization the future seemed assured. The LMS became part of British Railways with effect from 1st January, 1948.

Omnibuses

The LNWR first started to use petrol-driven omnibuses on its country routes in North Wales, replacing horse-drawn vehicles on the route between Holywell town and the railway station, and then introducing them on a new route, from Connah's Quay to Mold. In 1912 the company built a garage for its omnibuses at Brownhills, near to the Wyrley & Essington Canal wharf, and began services on 1st October of that year. Initially the route was from Brownhills to Norton Canes and onwards to Hednesford. Two Milnes-Daimler double-deck omnibuses were purchased from the Associate Omnibus Company of London, and painted in the LNWR passenger carriage livery of plum and custard. As was the custom of the time, the upper deck was open, which must have been especially uncomfortable in Winter as passengers would only have been used to a slower speed with horse-drawn vehicles, even if they were limited to 12 mph. These first two vehicles retained their London registrations (LC 9930 and LC 6707) and were numbered 11 and 12 in the LNWR fleet.

On 16th June, 1913 a further route was added, this time from Brownhills via Chasetown to Hednesford, and two further vehicles obtained. These were of 32 hp Commer manufacture, but featured the same seating capacity (34), and the usual open top deck. They carried the registrations BM 2597 and BM 2598, and the LNWR fleet Nos. 45 and 46, which indicated the extent to which the LNWR had expanded its road interests. However, World War I intervened, and inevitably the services were withdrawn as from 17th April, 1915 with the vehicles being commandeered for use in France. The LNWR never resumed its omnibus services after the war, and in July 1919 the routes were taken up by Walsall Corporation who introduced a regular Walsall to Hednesford service via Brownhills.

The time is August 1948 and shortly after nationalization, Webb 2-4-2T No. 46654, carrying the name of its new owners, stands in Dudley station at the former LMS platform having just arrived with the two-coach push-pull working from Dudley Port.   *L.W.Perkins/F.A. Wycherley*

The Webb 2-4-2Ts were familiar sights on the push-pull workings in the Walsall area for many years, and as BR No. 46757, this was one of the last in service. Here it is propelling a train from Dudley to Walsall at Great Bridge station (renamed Great Bridge North one year later) on a murky 13th July, 1949. In common with most former LNWR locomotives, no smokebox numberplate was ever fitted by the LMS or BR.   *Historical Model Railway Society/ESR*

1948-1965

Most of the passenger services had reverted to the pre-war level by 1953. A review of departures from Walsall in the Working Timetable for 21st September of that year reveals the following pattern:

Destination	Monday-Friday	Saturday	Sunday
Dudley	7 (RM)	7 (RM)	-
Burton	2	2	-
Lichfield City	2	2	-
Lichfield Trent Valley	1 (RM)	1 (RM)	-
Birmingham New St (via Aston)	14	14	5
		(+ 2 unadvertised)	
Birmingham New St (via Monument Lane)	3	2	-
Birmingham New St (via Sutton Park)	4	5	-
Vauxhall (via Aston)	2	1	-
Coventry (via Monument Lane)	1	1	-
Wolverhampton (via Portobello)	6 (incl. 2 RM)	3	-
Stafford (via Rugeley)	2	2	-
Rugeley Trent Valley	12	13	7
Rugeley Town	1 (RM)	1 (RM)	-
Brownhills	1	-	-

RM = Rail motor (push-pull working)

In addition, there was one down empty stock movement passing through every day, which on Saturdays ran as the 1.35 am Birmingham Central goods to Longsight (Manchester). There was also one parcels train in each direction on Mondays to Saturdays from Birmingham New Street, and one down from Sutton Park (Mondays excepted).

The departures from Lichfield City were as follows:

Destination	Monday-Friday	Saturday	Sunday
Lichfield Trent Valley	-	2	-
Derby	1	1	-
Burton	6	7	-
Walsall	4	4	1
Dudley	-	1	-
Wolverhampton (via Walsall)	1	1	-
Birmingham New St (via Walsall)	-	1	1
Vauxhall (via Walsall)	1	1	-
Birmingham New St (via Sutton Coldfield)	12	12	3

At Dudley the situation was:

Destination	Monday-Friday	Saturday	Sunday
Dudley Port High Level	7 (all RM)	6 (all RM)	-
Walsall	6 (4 RM)	8 (5 RM)	-
Birmingham Snow Hill (WR trains)	13 (9 RM)	14 (9 RM)	-

Webb LNWR 2-4-2T No. 46654 runs out of Dudley Port High Level station (seen in the right background) with a shuttle service to Dudley in July 1949. It is just crossing the Birmingham Canal Navigation on the girder arch bridge. *M. Whitehouse Collection*

Stanier 'Jubilee' class 4-6-0 No. 45638 *Raleigh* of Longsight shed powers a Birmingham to Manchester express out of Dudley Port High Level in July 1949. The locomotive has received its new BR number following nationalization the previous year, but has not yet received the new owner's name on its tender. In the bay platform, LNWR 2-4-2T No. 46654 waits with the 'Dodger' to Dudley. *M. Whitehouse Collection*

The Western Region (WR) peak hours services from Snow Hill to Dudley usually comprised suburban non-corridor stock hauled by either a Collett 2-6-2T of the '5101' class or a '57XX' class 0-6-0PT from Tyseley or Stourbridge Junction shed. Off-peak services were handled by the former GWR diesel railcars, usually operating singly. The other 'rail motor' services continued to be steam-hauled.

Off-peak services included attractive evening return fares from most stations, which were particularly popular for persons wishing to do some evening shopping in Wolverhampton or Birmingham, where the stores remained open until 8.00 pm during weekdays, and some as late as 9.00 pm on Saturdays.

One incident that related to the SSR route, but did not actually occur on it, was the infamous crash at Sutton Coldfield on 23rd January, 1955 of a York to Bristol express, which had been diverted southwards at Wichnor Junction to Lichfield because of engineering works on the MR line. The express, headed by 'Black Five' 4-6-0 No. 45274 took the sharp curve at Sutton at twice the permitted 30 mph limit and derailed, with much loss of life.

The first generation 2-car BR dmus were introduced on the Birmingham to Lichfield services via Sutton Coldfield in March 1956. The new service proved immensely popular, and the 2-car units (mostly Park Royal and Derby Lightweight designs) were transferred to the Birmingham-Walsall services in June 1958 and replaced by 3-car units. A new service from Wolverhampton through to Burton was also introduced at this time, featuring the dmus. The level of such services was completely recast with a much more intensive service, particularly between Lichfield City and Birmingham New Street. The introduction of the dmus involved the closure of Ryecroft shed, as from 31st May, 1958, when the remaining freight and pilot steam locomotives were transferred to Bescot, and the passenger engines and men to Aston shed on the following weekend. The shed at Ryecroft was subsequently completely rebuilt to become a diesel depot, specifically handling the dmus. By October of that year, a single car parcels unit (No. M55998) had been allocated to Ryecroft for regular workings to New Street and Coventry.

The effect of these changes can be seen in the timetable for the period 17th November, 1958 to 14th June, 1959, enabling a useful comparison at Walsall:

Destination	Monday-Friday	Saturday	Sunday
Dudley	13	13	-
Burton	9	9	-
Lichfield City	3	2	-
Lichfield Trent Valley	1	1	-
Birmingham New St (via Aston)	19	20	9
Birmingham New St (via Monument Lane)	2	1	-
Birmingham New St (via Streetly)	1	2	-
Vauxhall (via Aston)	1	1	-
Euston (via Monument Lane)	-	1	-
Wolverhampton (via Portobello)	19	25	-
Rugeley Trent Valley	20	20	9
Stafford (via Rugeley)	1	1	-
Brownhills	1	-	-

LNWR '7F' class 0-8-0 No. 49099 proceeding towards Walsall station on the down slow line through platform 1, with a haul of empty coal wagons, undoubtedly destined for the Cannock Chase collieries. Walsall No. 1 signal box is just visible on the left. The date is 7th May, 1952.

Kidderminster Railway Museum

Ivatt class '2' 2-6-2T No. 41244 passes Pleck on the up fast line with a three coach push-pull working from Walsall to Wolverhampton around 1955. On the left is the District Civil Engineering Depot built by the LNWR. *R.S.Carpenter/Kidderminster Railway Museum*

Ivatt class '2' 2-6-2T No. 41223 at Dudley station on 1st September, 1956 in charge of the shuttle service to Dudley Port High Level. The engine was always marshalled at the south end of the set on these duties. *F. Hornby*

Collett GWR '57XX' class 0-6-0PT No. 8742 shunting a rake of wagons at Dudley station on 30th July, 1957. The driver has just pulled the wagons out of the former LMS goods yard at Dudley, and the imposing Dudley Town goods shed is visible in the left side of the photograph. On the right-hand side, vans can be seen parked in the original 1850 platform, by then used as a parcels platform. *Author's Collection*

This shot of 'Princess Coronation' class Pacific No. 46251 *City of Nottingham* on the up 'Shamrock', emphasises the speed at which the major expresses negotiated Lichfield Trent Valley station. The well-protected platforms of the High Level station are well shown here.

E.M. Johnson Collection

Bowen Cooke 0-8-0 No. 49246 runs into Wednesbury with a class 'K' pick-up freight from the Dudley direction on 28th May, 1960. Fellow class member No. 49275 pauses on the right in the middle of shunting duties in the yard adjacent to the spur connecting to the GWR route to Wolverhampton, as the fireman takes time to peruse his newspaper. The two lines disappearing middle right are the lines to the Princes End branch. The Baguley diesel shunter belonging to The Hill Top Foundry Co. Ltd can be glimpsed above the middle three conflat containers of the pick-up goods.

Transport Treasury/R.C. Riley

At this time there were a further five up and six down weekday empty stock workings, with four up and six down on Saturdays, and one up and two down on Sundays. Parcels traffic had increased to four each way on weekdays, two up and three down on Saturdays, but none on Sundays.

At Lichfield City the departures were:

Destination	Monday-Friday	Saturday	Sunday
Lichfield Trent Valley	5	4	-
Burton	10	10	-
Walsall	2	1	-
Wolverhampton (via Walsall)	10	10	-
Birmingham New St (via Sutton Coldfield)	26	26	7

There was one further empty stock working in each direction on weekdays, with two up and one down on Saturdays, and one up on Sundays.

At Dudley the departures were still mostly steam-hauled, except where the ageing GWR railcars were still used on off-peak services to Snow Hill:

Destination	Monday-Friday	Saturday	Sunday
Walsall	13	14	-
WR trains: Birmingham Snow Hill	17	17	6

The use of dmus had spread to most of the passenger services by 1962, with just a few of the peak hours' services remaining as steam-hauled. The off-peak dmus from New Street now operated at roughly hourly intervals, with some continuing onwards to Rugeley or Stafford. The picture at Walsall for the period 10th September, 1962 to 16th June, 1963 was as follows:

Destination	Monday-Friday	Saturday	Sunday
Dudley	13	14	-
Burton	9	9	-
Lichfield City	2	2	-
Lichfield Trent Valley	2	2	-
Birmingham New St (via Aston)	21	22	7
Birmingham New St (via Monument Lane)	1	1	-
Birmingham New St (via Sutton Park)	5	5	-
Vauxhall (via Aston)	1	1	-
Euston (via Monument Lane)	1	1	-
Wolverhampton (via Portobello)	19	25	-
Stafford (via Rugeley)	1	1	-
Rugeley Trent Valley	20	21	9
Brownhills	1	1	-

The through train for Euston departed at 7.54 am. Empty stock workings had been reduced a little to two up and one down (plus one on Mondays only) on weekdays, Saturdays were two up and three down, and Sundays were one up, three down. One of the Saturday down workings (at 6.20 am) actually conveyed railway staff to Walsall. The parcels workings had further increased to six up and seven down workings on weekdays, with four up and five down on Saturdays, but still just the one up on Sundays.

Stanier class '8F' 2-8-0 No. 48712 struggles up the 1 in 60 grade south of Sedgeley Junction towards Dudley with a long freight in the Summer of 1961. The signal box can be seen in the background towards the rear of the train.   *D. Wilson*

A stalwart of the heavy freight services in the area, one of the Bowen-Cooke 0-8-0s usually referred to as 'Super Ds' tackles the climb from Horseley Fields Junction to Dudley Port in 1961. It is just about to pass beneath the bridge carrying East Park Lane.   *D. Wilson*

Stanier class '3' 2-6-2T No. 40173 seen on the climb away from Sedgeley Junction with a short parcels train from Walsall to Dudley in the early Summer of 1961. *D. Wilson*

The exhaust from Saltley's '8F' class 2-8-0 No. 48256 almost obliterates the goods shed at Great Bridge North as it blasts its way southwards on a rather wet day in 1962 with a class 'D' partly-fitted freight. *D. Wilson*

'Royal Scot' class 4-6-0 No. 46108 *Seaforth Highlander* is seen in 1962 with a southbound express, diverted because of electrification works on the Stour Valley line. It has just passed Bescot and is approaching Wednesbury in the Mesty Croft area.   *D. Wilson*

An unidentified Ivatt class '2' mogul passes Mill Lane, Walsall with a stopping train for the Lichfield direction around 1962. In the distance, the direct line linking the former MR Sutton Park line to the Walsall to Wolverhampton line crosses the Lichfield line on a plate girder bridge.
                                                                R. Selvey

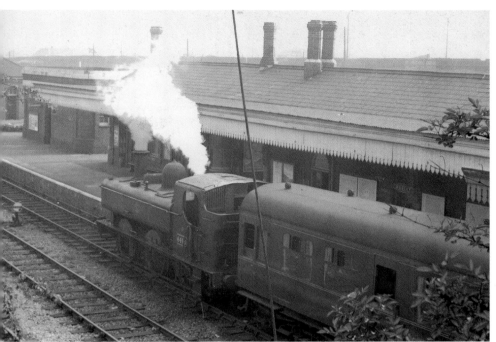

Looking down from the footbridge at Dudley station as Hawksworth '64XX' class 0-6-0PT No. 6418 stands at the former LNWR platform, having just arrived with a push-pull working from Birmingham Snow Hill. This travelled via Swan Village, Great Bridge South and Horseley Fields Junction, and thence over the SSR route to Dudley.   *B. Moone/Kidderminster Railway Museum*

An unidentified Stanier '8F' class 2-8-0 sets off with a southbound freight into the sunset on 1st May, 1963, passing the Sedgeley Junction signal box on the right. The splitting signals are for the branch to Dudley Port High Level station and the Stour Valley line, which diverged behind the photographer.   *D. Wilson*

Ivatt class '2' 2-6-0 No. 46445 assists LNWR '7F' class 0-8-0 No. 49361 with a lengthy southbound freight, consisting mostly of steel, on the up slow line near to Walsall No. 1 signal box, seen in the background. The date is 16th September, 1964. *R. Shenton*

Double-headed Bowen Cooke '7F' class 0-8-0s Nos. 48895 and 49430 haul a southbound goods near to Pleck Junction, Walsall on 13th October, 1964. Both locomotives carry the yellow diagonal stripe on their cab sides, indicating that they are not to work beneath overhead electric catenary. *R. Shenton*

At Lichfield City the departures included a still further increase in those to New Street :

Destination	Monday-Friday	Saturday	Sunday
Lichfield Trent Valley	5	3	-
Burton	10	10	-
Walsall	1	1	-
Wolverhampton (via Walsall)	10	10	-
Birmingham New St			
(via Sutton Coldfield)	33	32	12

There were a further three up and three down weekday empty stock workings, plus one up and three down on Saturdays, but none on Sundays. Most of these empty stock workings are attributed to having to move the empty dmus for their first and last workings of the day from the depot (normally Ryecroft).

The WR trains from Dudley were now worked by 3-car dmus, mostly those built by the Gloucester Railway & Carriage Works, whilst the Walsall services were then mostly dmus with Derby Lightweight 2-car units prevailing, although peak services just survived as being steam-hauled. The sole Dudley Port service (7.50 am from Dudley, and 8.08 am return) was normally worked by a dmu in between turns from Dudley to Walsall:

Destination	Monday-Friday	Saturday	Sunday
Walsall	13	14	-
Dudley Port High Level	1	1	-
WR trains: Birmingham Snow Hill	17	17	6

Freight continued its dominance of the line, mostly comprising seemingly endless coal trains from the Cannock Chase pits via Norton Junction, or Anglesea Sidings (plus of course, the Cannock and Hednesford areas) to the yards at Bescot, and the returning empties. An examination of the 1962 Working Timetable reveals something like 25 weekday coal trains in the up direction from the pits to a variety of destinations. Several coal trains reversed direction to take the left-hand line at Ryecroft Junction on to the old Wolverhampton MR route as far as Birchills power station. Towards Dudley, coal trains were banked up from Great Bridge, either by the familiar former LNWR 0-8-0s, or latterly by Stanier '8Fs', as they headed for Pensnett sidings and Stourport power station. Iron ore continued to Round Oak steel works, along with other steel products, which also found their way to Dudley, Brierley Hill and Wednesbury. Other through workings have been described in the section on the Princes End line. An increasing number of freight workings from the North to Washwood Heath were being routed through Walsall and on to the Sutton Park MR route to join the MR line from Derby at Water Orton. This was particularly useful for those through workings that were ultimately travelling south to Bristol and the West Country or to South Wales. Parcels services from Walsall to Dudley had to run into that station, before reversing into the former LNWR goods shed alongside the OWWR route to Wolverhampton. At the northern end of the line, there were several daily workings taking the spur from Lichfield Trent Valley High Level

A view from the High Level station at Dudley Port looking down into the Low Level station on 19th June, 1965 as Stanier '8F' class 2-8-0 No. 48662 passes with a lengthy haul of coal, probably bound for Stourport power station. The exhaust from the engine assisting in the rear can be seen just above the second road bridge. The Low Level station had been closed for two years by this time, as evident by the weeds encroaching on the platform.   *D. Wilson*

BR Standard class '4' 2-6-0 No. 76086 takes the up slow line at Pleck Junction with a load of steel, probably destined for Round Oak steel works, on 13th January, 1966. Despite the advancing overhead wires, the semaphore signals remain in use.   *R. Sheldon*

to reach the West Coast Main Line at Low Level. These included some from Burton to Swansea, Pontypool Road, Hereford, Shrewsbury, and Stafford, as well as Crewe and Wellington to Wichnor. One through working of note was the 9.15 pm York to Birmingham Curzon Street fish train, which ran every day including Sundays. There were also some workings from the North then taking the Sutton Coldfield line at Lichfield. For example, in 1957 there was a daily pick-up freight from Aston goods to Lichfield and return, plus two northbound coal empties from Aston, one southbound coal train, and two goods workings from Wichnor Junction also to Aston Goods, one of which also ran on Sundays.

Then there were the considerable number of local trip workings, notably from Bescot yards, to the various engineering works along the SSR route. On a daily basis in 1962 these totalled 13 from Bescot, four from Dudley, eight from Lichfield, two from Walsall and five from Norton Junction. The workings from the Palethorpes' Siding at Dudley Port continued with one outward train each day in 1962/1963.

Pigeon specials had long been a familiar sight at Walsall, often loaded to as many as 10 vehicles, with such far away destinations as Bath, Templecombe or Weymouth. But most of the pigeons were carried in just one parcels or full brake vehicle attached to ordinary passenger trains, which would then be transferred to a main line train at New Street station, and probably required further marshalling as it wound its way to the required release point. However, the introduction of dmus from 1956 onwards made this impractical, as such vehicles could not be attached, and so steam-hauled specials had to be run, which was a costly exercise. Inevitably, BR chose not to continue with this traffic, and in any case road transport was becoming much more preferable with the improvement in the nation's road network, and so this ceased entirely in 1964.

This photograph is reproduced from a postcard, showing an obviously posed and extremely clean LMS 'Jubilee' 4-6-0 with a rake of Palethorpes' vans of both bogie and six-wheel configuration in front of the factory.   *D. Wilson*

The 'Pines Express'

The line into Walsall from the GJR route at James Bridge Junction had seen the passing of only one prestigious express train on a regular basis over the years. This was the 'Pines Express', which continued its journey from Manchester to Bournemouth (and vice versa) over the Sutton Park MR line to Water Orton, where, as we shall see, it ran either southwards via New Street station, or via the Camp Hill line.

This train began life in 1927 as the 10.00 am from Manchester London Road to Bournemouth, with the northbound service leaving Bournemouth at 10.20 am. Southbound it called at Walsall from 11.45 to 11.50 am to change engines, on Mondays, Fridays and Saturdays. Northbound it called at around 3.15 pm, also to change engines, but only on Saturdays. The object of performing the engine changing at Walsall was to eliminate some of the congestion that otherwise occurred in New Street station, and enabled the train to avoid the station completely by travelling over the Camp Hill line. The train received its name as from 28th September, 1927 and although carriage roofboards proclaiming this distinction were usually carried, it rarely carried a headboard on the locomotive smokebox - the normal appellation for named trains.

A portion from Liverpool was attached at Crewe, and detached in the opposite direction, but from 1930 this ran as a separate train, also calling at Walsall to change engines, on Saturdays only. However, in 1933 the train was routed to travel over the Stour Valley line from Wolverhampton to Birmingham on every day, and so avoided Walsall. In 1934 the train received some new rolling stock, including kitchen/thirds, which remained with the train until the end of steam haulage in 1962. The 'Pines' resumed its original routeing and timing in 1937, although the northbound service left Bournemouth some 15 minutes later. Another service, taking the original 10.20 am departure time from Bournemouth, was for Liverpool, and this now also called at Walsall. Unfortunately, World War II intervened, and the 'Pines Express' was suspended from 11th September, 1939 until the cessation of hostilities, being reintroduced on 6th May, 1946. The following harsh winter, amongst other things, caused a further suspension of the train from January 1947 until Easter of that year.

Thereafter the train left Manchester at 10.25 am, calling at Walsall only on Saturdays in both directions. In 1957 there were further changes when the Manchester departure time became 10.15 am, and another service, the 9.25 am from Bournemouth to Manchester and Liverpool also called on its way north.

The engines working the southbound service were based at Crewe North shed but worked through from Manchester, coming off and going on to Ryecroft shed for servicing, and were replaced by engines from Saltley shed for the next phase of the journey as far as Bath. Once serviced, they returned to take over the northbound train. But after the closure of Ryecroft shed to steam in 1958 the engines had to travel to Saltley for servicing. In its original days, the train was usually hauled between Manchester and Crewe by an LNWR 4-6-0, usually a 'Prince of Wales' or an 'Experiment' class, but often a '19 in. Goods' (which was more of a mixed traffic engine), and even a 'Claughton'. It was not

'The Pines Express' at Walsall station in 1961. The 'Patriot' 4-6-0 No. 45524 *Blackpool* has arrived from the north, and is about to be relieved by 'Jubilee' 4-6-0 No. 45647 *Sturdee*, which is waiting in the Cannock bay with a fully-coaled tender. The 'Jubilee' will take the train southwards to Bath where it will be relieved for the last stage of the journey over the Somerset & Dorset line to Bournemouth. *J. Haddock/Walsall Local History Centre*

unknown for a pair of LNWR 4-4-0s to turn up on this working, or even an LMS Compound more than likely piloted by another 4-4-0. Certainly these were used on the southern leg, along with the LMS developments of the MR 4-4-0s as pilots or in tandem. Double-heading of this train was commonplace on both the northern and southern legs, as it was frequently strengthened by additional carriages, especially in the summer months, and often reliefs were run. Whilst the engine changing was taking place, the kitchen car would have its gas refilled from the trackside pipes. From the mid-1930s the southern portion came to be dominated by Saltley's allocation of the Stanier class '5' 4-6-0s, and increasingly the northern portion was given over to either one of these, or a 'Patriot' or 'Jubilee' 4-6-0, or any combination. With the advent of dieselization and electrification, Crewe North amassed a sizeable allocation of BR Standard 'Britannia' class 4-6-2s, which appeared in the closing years of the northern section of the train. However, the last working of this famous train through Walsall occurred on 8th September, 1962 when Stanier 4-6-0 No. 44659 left with the northbound train.

The Sutton Coldfield 'Motorail' service

A further working of note was the introduction of the Sutton Coldfield to Stirling car sleeper service, which ran via Lichfield City and Wichnor to Leeds then over the Settle and Carlisle line to Scotland. This was introduced for the summer 1958 timetable, with departures on Sunday and Wednesday evenings, returning on Monday and Thursday mornings. The fares were £14 10s. 0d. for driver and car, with additional passengers at £5 adult and £3 child, and featured a full sleeper service. The passenger vehicles were marshalled in the former terminus platform of the original 1862 Sutton Coldfield station, with the car vehicles loading on an adjacent siding. This, therefore, involved some complex movements, as the passenger vehicles were first backed out by the train engine on to the running line, then run forward into the main down platform. A second engine then had to withdraw the car vehicles and attach these to the passenger carriages in the platform.

By 1961 the service had changed to run outward on Sunday, Tuesday and Thursday mornings, returning on Monday, Wednesday and Friday mornings, but the driver and car fare had risen to £19 10s. 0d. There was no service during the winter months. For example, the times from Sutton Coldfield in the winter 1962/63 working timetable were:

		Winter	Summer
Tuesday	9.40 pm	11th Sep., 1962 only	7th May-16th Jun., 1963
Thursday	9.40 pm	10th Sep.-4th Oct., 1962	18th Apr.-16th Jun., 1963
Sunday	9.43 pm	10th-30th Sep., 1962 only	21st Apr.-16th Jun., 1963

Return workings were at 8.35 pm from Stirling over the same periods, departing on the previous evening in each case. Before each departure, and after each arrival there was a further empty stock working to the carriage sidings at Vauxhall & Duddeston.

Over the following years, the service was expanded across the country, and two new destinations, Newton Abbot and St Austell, were added and certain of the Stirling services were continued to serve Inverness.

The service lasted until the end of the summer timetable in 1972, for which time (22nd May to 16th September) it consisted of:

Departures			Arrivals		
Sunday	23.15	Stirling		18.25	St Austell
Monday	23.15	Stirling and Inverness		19.45	Stirling
Wednesday	13.10	Stirling		05.50	Inverness and Stirling
Thursday	23.15	Stirling		05.50	Stirling
Friday	23.15	Newton Abbot		19.35	Stirling
Saturday	23.15	St Austell		19.30	Newton Abbot

Of course, the southbound workings to Newton Abbot and St Austell do not interest us here, as they worked south from Sutton Coldfield, and so not over our line.

Motive power for these trains was provided by Aston shed, and was given as a minimum of class '5', which meant that it was often powered by a Stanier or Standard class '5' 4-6-0, but equally more often by something larger such as a 'Jubilee', 'Patriot' or 'Royal Scot' if available. Eventually, loadings became so good that more power was needed, and in 1959 two BR 'Britannia' 4-6-2s, Nos. 70046 *Anzac* and 70048 *The Territorial Army 1908-1958* were allocated to Aston specifically for this duty. Later, on one occasion one of Holbeck's Gresley 'A3' Pacifics, No. 60077 *The White Knight*, turned up on a southbound working, and it wasn't until it reached Aston shed that it was realised that it was not authorized to have worked the route. It was hastily, and quietly , returned on the next working.

Excursions

The SSR had taken a keen interest in developing excursion traffic right from the start, with the running of attractively priced trains at Whitsun time to the festival in Lichfield known as 'The Lichfield Bower'. This was actually a medieval pageant , 'The Court of Array', that had been revived in 1816 being more of a recreation than having any religious significance. It had become very popular, and the crowds flocked to it. But on the first occasion, in 1849, being short of covered rolling stock, the company decided to use open wagons with planked seats. This was not popular, and so when the next occasion arose, they used cattle wagons. However, when the train was stationary, onlookers started to 'moo' at them !

Not deterred, the company used proper carriages thereafter, and arranged for trips to the Shrewsbury Show Fair on 23rd June and to the Coventry Show Fair on 24th June, 1851 and a cheap trip to Alton Towers *(the original)* around these dates.

The company developed Lichfield as a popular destination for sightseers to visit the cathedral, putting on special trains for school children and adults. The next target was Dudley Castle, which John Payne identified as a good tourist destination for the people of the Black Country. In 1850 he arranged for entertainments in the castle grounds, and illumination of the caverns beneath that had been created by many years of limestone working. His next intention was to obtain a lease of the grounds so that they could be even more developed for leisure activities. This seemed to be going to plan with the full agreement of Lord Ward's agent, but the municipal authorities objected on the basis that the accustomed freedom of access to the castle would be ended.

The development of the castle and eventual opening in 1937 of a zoo in the grounds was left to others to proceed with, but the successors to the SSR reaped some satisfaction from its ultimate popularity. Special trains were often put on at Bank Holidays from the West Midlands locality, and eventually it became a favourite destination for a day out from the East Midlands and as far away as Lincoln, Wakefield and other towns in South Yorkshire. There were many special trains to Dudley for this purpose, and even up to the closure of the line, these could be seen throughout the Summer Saturdays. Usually, the motive power was provided by the excellent mixed traffic 'Black Fives', but Stanier and Hughes/Fowler 2-6-0s, as well as Stanier 'Jubilees' and the humble Fowler '4F' 0-6-0s often appeared on such workings. From Eastern Region points, LNER 'B1' 4-6-0s and 'K3' 2-6-0s were a frequent sight. Most such trains were brought in by Burton men, often with men from Ryecroft or Bescot sheds as pilotmen.

The Whit Monday specials from the Birmingham area to Lichfield for the Bower Day continued right through to the early 1960s, by then being formed of dmu sets.

Individual organizations arranged excursions for their friends and workmates, as a small advertisement in the *Lichfield Mercury* of Friday 27th June, 1879 showed:

On Monday 7th July 1879 the Committee of Lichfield Working Men's Association and St. Mary's Men's Society are running a day trip from Lichfield City at 6.00 am to Blackpool and return at 7 pm. Fares for adults are 4s. 6d., children under 12 years and Sunday School scholars are 2s. 6d.

Many employers arranged special holiday excursions for their employees during the 19th century, and this certainly occurred throughout this area. For example, in the *Walsall Observer & South Staffordshire Chronicle* of 1st August, 1881 it was reported that Job Wheway of the Birchills Hame and Chain Works took his employees on their annual outing, by train to Blackpool on 25th July, 1881. The train left Walsall at 5.00 am and arrived back at 2.00 am the next morning, having also picked up passengers at Bloxwich. This was certainly a long day - but then most working people were not able to take a week's holiday at that time.

Another report, this time from the *Midland Advertiser* of Saturday 6th July, 1895 emphasised the length of the day:

MESSRS JAMES RUSSELL AND SONS, WEDNESBURY
ANNUAL EXCURSION

To rise at three o' clock in the morning, wash and dress in order to enjoy a day out at the seaside is not altogether a pleasant performance, yet this was what was necessary for those who intended accompanying the Crown Tube Works popular excursion on Monday, which this year was destined to go to that well known pleasure metropolis of the north - Blackpool. As in former years there was a large number of excursionists, several other firms joining in the trip, including the staff of the *Midland Advertiser*, who in view of preparing for the forthcoming general election wished to enjoy a day by the side of the sea waves. Special arrangements had been made with the London and North Western Railway company to convey the trippers to Blackpool, and about four a.m. the first of two heavily laden trains left Wednesbury via Ocker Hill, Princes End and Wolverhampton for the north. Ten minutes later the second consignment followed, and once the pit mounds and slag heaps of the district were lost sight of the party settled down, some for another hour or two's sleep, some whiling away the time by a game of cards, while others discussed the political situation or viewed the scenery that abounded at every hand. Through Stafford, Crewe, Warrington, Preston and other places the train steamed, until shortly after eight o'clock the company landed at their destination. Upon arriving, the first consideration with the majority was breakfast, and soon the many eating houses and restaurants were made aware of their arrival. This over, the company separated in groups to visit the many and varied places of interest, for these are so numerous that it is impossible to pass a dull moment whilst on pleasure bent. If there is a more popular watering place in the northern half of the kingdom than Blackpool we certainly do not know it. There are bigger seaside towns without doubt, and there are towns which are more affected by the classes, but for downright and through going popularity among the great masses of the people Blackpool undoubtedly outdistances all competitors, which is not to be wondered at when it is borne in mind that over one million sterling is sunk in the resorts of amusement in it, and for a town whose population is not more than 28,000 this is remarkable …

Just before the departure, the happy but weary trippers made their way to the Central Station, and once comfortably ensconced in their carriages a start was made for home. Workmen who had not met since morning, compared their views of the place, and one and all seemed unanimous that the destination had been well chosen, and was one more to be added to the very successful trips in connection with this local firm of tube makers.

From many of the carriages sounds of music (?) emanated, thus disturbing the very good intentions of going to sleep which many had formed early in the day. Arriving at Warrington full advantage was taken of the five minutes' stoppage for a 'refresher', and at Stafford, where the tickets were collected, this performance was repeated. The trains were timed to reach Wednesbury at 12.50 and 1 am respectively, but it was 1.40 and 2.5 before the trippers were landed at home, all having spent a delightful day's out. The committee and secretary (Mr. Walter Ellis) left no stone unturned to ensure the comfort of the excursionists, and a word of praise is due to them for the complete manner in which the whole of the arrangements were carried out. The Crown Tube Works band, under the leadership of Mr. A.E. Barnsley, accompanied the trip, and at intervals during the day played selections of music which considerably added to the enjoyment of an outing which will be long remembered as one of the best ever held in connection with Messrs. James Russell and Sons' Crown Tube Works.

The LNWR ran many excursions to a whole variety of destinations and for a large number of differing events, as indeed did their successors, the LMS and BR. The following are a selection of advertisements placed in the *Lichfield Mercury*:

Friday 13th April, 1900
League Football Match - Aston Villa vs Nottingham Forest
On Saturday, April 14th 1900.
AN EXPRESS HALF DAY EXCURSION will run as under to NOTTINGHAM, via Burton and the G.N.R.
The train leaves Birmingham (New Street) 12.20, Vauxhall 12.24, Aston 12.28, Sutton Coldfield 12.35 and Lichfield City 12.50 pm.
Fares for the double journey - Third Class Only 2/9.
The return train will leave Nottingham (London Road) at 10.50 pm the same evening.

Friday 13th April, 1900
WARWICK CASTLE, JEPHSON GARDENS (LEAMINGTON), KENILWORTH CASTLE.
On Easter Monday, April 16th, 1900.
A Cheap Day Excursion will run to Coventry, Kenilworth, Warwick (Milverton) and Leamington.
The train leaves Lichfield (City Station) at 10.20 am, Brownhills 10.30, Pelsall 10.35 and Walsall 10.45.
Fares for the double journey - Lichfield 2/9, Brownhills, Pelsall and Walsall 2/3.
The return train will leave Leamington (Avenue) at 7.0 pm, Warwick (Milverton) at 7.3 pm, Kenilworth at 7.10 pm; and Coventry at 6.50 pm the same evening.

Friday 2nd February, 1928.
Saturday 11 February 1928.
From Lichfield City to Witton (for Aston Villa vs Sheffield United football match) at 1.4 pm. Fare 1/10d.

Friday 9th February, 1928
Monday and Tuesday, 12 and 13 February 1928 to Bromford Bridge (Birmingham Steeplechase). Leaves Lichfield City at 11.20 am (2/1d).

Friday 16th March, 1928
Monday and Tuesday, 19 and 20 March 1928 to Wolverhampton (Steeplechase).
Leaves Lichfield City at 11.20 am (2/1d), Hammerwich 11.27 (1/9), Brownhills High Street 11.32 (1/6), Pelsall 11.37 (1/6), Walsall 11.37 (1/3).

Fowler '4F' class 0-6-0 No. 44078 is the motive power for this half-day excursion from Wolverhampton to Alton Towers on 2nd August, 1953 as it nears Lichfield Trent Valley (High Level) from the south-west. Such affordable excursions were popular at that time, and for many people were the only holidays away from home that they were likely to have. *R. Shenton*

On 13th November, 1954 the Stephenson Locomotive Society ran a special railtour of West Midlands lines to celebrate the centenary of the opening of the BWDR/OWWR line from Birmingham Snow Hill to Wolverhampton Low Level. Included in its route was a visit to Walsall, where we see Collett '14XX' class 0-4-2T No. 1438 in charge. To the left is the original 1849 SSR station building on platform 1. *B. Moone/Kidderminster Railway Museum*

Friday 16th March, 1928
On Saturday 24 March 1928 to Nottingham (for Nottingham County vs Wolverhampton Wanderers football match).
Leaves Pelsall at 11.55 (3/6), Brownhills 12.4 pm (3/6), Lichfield City 12.15 pm (3/-).

Friday 10th August, 1928
Sunday 19 August 1928.
At 11.40 am from Lichfield City to Ashbourne (3/-), Thorp Cloud (3/-), Alsop-en-le-Dale (3/6) and Buxton (4/-).

Friday 17th August, 1928
To Scarborough on Saturday, 25 August, leaves Lichfield City at 5.10 am (13/6).
But bookings can be made to Scarborough for 4, 6 or 8 days from 24/6d.
Sunday 26 August 1928 to Alton (for Alton Towers) from Lichfield City at 11.40 am (3/-).

Friday 24th August, 1928
On Sunday 2 September 1928 from Lichfield City at 11.00 am to Rhyl (5/-), Colwyn Bay (5/6), and Llandudno (6/-).

Interestingly, the July 1914 working timetable showed a scheduled excursion 'for the season' leaving Dudley at 1.10 am each Saturday for Blackpool, and returning at 12.45 am on Sunday. After this trip, it can be imagined that Sunday would definitely be 'a day of rest'. This scheduled trip indicates the popularity of the resort, and emphasizes that this was as much holiday away from home as most working folk were likely to enjoy at that time.

The annual illuminations in the Arboretum at Walsall became more of a feature from the 1950s to the present day, eventually rivalling the more well known attractions at Blackpool for their inventiveness. These illuminations had started off very modestly in 1875 with a display of candles in coloured glass vessels suspended from the arboretum trees, and running for just two weeks at the end of September. More recently, the illuminations run until the end of October, with further attractions in the form of a 42 ft Ferris wheel and modern laser lights. BR saw this as an opportunity to advertise 'evening excursion' fares from Birmingham and the surrounding area, so that while there were no special trains put on for this event, there were certainly many extra passengers on the evening services. The illuminations were last held in 2008, and are unlikely to be repeated until 2012 at the earliest, with this date relying on finding suitable Lottery funding.

Other local excursions originating in the West Midlands made their way over SSR tracks towards Dudley, heading for the popular local beauty spots of Stourport and Bewdley. Many such half-day excursions came from Birmingham Snow Hill and other GWR stations to the south, via Swan Village and Great Bridge. Right up until the late 1950s, such was the frequency of Summer Saturday holiday travel, that as a way of avoiding traffic bottlenecks in the Midlands, many long distance holiday trains used this route on their way to South Wales and the West Country.

One enthusiasts' railtour on 13th November, 1954 was made in connection with the anniversary of the opening of the BWDR/OWWR from Birmingham to Wolverhampton. It comprised Collett '14XX' class 0-4-2T No. 1438 from Stourbridge Junction shed with two 70 ft auto-trailers, and started from Birmingham Snow

Stanier 'Jubilee' class 4-6-0 No. 45656 *Cochrane* is seen here at speed about to enter Lichfield Trent Valley (High Level) on 20th February, 1954 with a special working M911 from Newcastle to Smethwick. This was run for the benefit of Newcastle United football supporters attending a match with West Bromwich Albion.The massive brick base for the water tank supplying the water columns at this station is dominant on the left. *R. Shenton*

Racing towards Hammerwich on 10th April, 1955 is Hughes/Fowler 'Crab' 2-6-0 No. 42756 working excursion M961 from Mansfield to Dudley for the zoo. *R. Shenton*

Stanier 'Jubilee' class 4-6-0 No. 45656 *Cochrane* takes the Walsall line south of Lichfield City station on a snowy day, 10th January, 1959 with a football special from Rotherham to Witton.

R. Shenton

Fowler '4F' class 0-6-0 No. 44202 is passing Mill Lane, Walsall with the return working of an excursion from the East Midlands to Dudley Zoo around 1960. It has just passed the interesting double banner repeater signals.

R. Selvey

During 1959 and 1960, the restored LMS compound 4-4-0 No. 1000 was used on a number of special trains, mostly for railway enthusiasts. Here it is seen leaving Lichfield Trent Valley after a water stop, with an SLS special from Birmingham to Derby works and Toton running shed. The author was on board this train, so one of the many protruding heads may be his ! The chord linking to the West Coast main line can be seen curving away on the extreme right.

R. Shenton

Hill. Amongst the many lines visited that day were the SSR lines from Walsall to Wednesbury, along the Princes End branch, thence to Dudley Port High Level (reverse), Sedgeley Junction (reverse) and back to Snow Hill via Swan Village.

A Stephenson Locomotive Society (SLS) railtour on 25th May, 1957 also traversed the Princes End branch, then continued through Wednesbury to Walsall and Norton Junction, over the Norton branch to East Cannock and Rugeley, eventually returning to Birmingham via Burton, Lichfield and the Sutton Coldfield line.

Further railtours were inevitably made as the lines in the area became due for closure. Two are recalled, both using LNWR 0-8-0s of which there were still a few working examples even in 1963 at Bushbury and Bescot sheds. One was run on 2nd June, 1962 and hauled by 'Super D' 0-8-0 No. 48930 on a route that started from New Street station and continued to Sutton Coldfield (reverse), Aston, Stechford (reverse), New Street, Soho South, Perry Barr, Bescot, Pleck curve, Wednesbury Town, Ocker Hill, Princes End, Soho, New Street.

A year later, on 22nd June, 1963 another 'Super D', this time No. 49361, was used on a SLS railtour from New Street to Selly Oak, Camp Hill, Saltley, Walsall, Bescot, Dudley Port, Wolverhampton Low Level, Walsall, Darlaston, Wednesbury, Walsall, Norton branch, Rugeley Trent Valley, Lichfield Trent Valley and Soho Road back to New Street.

Slightly earlier, on 23rd March, 1963, a 3-car dmu special organized by the Locomotive Club of Great Britain had also visited many minor lines in the West Midlands, including the Pleck Curve, the Dudley Port Loop, the Bescot Curve, and the SSR main line between Bescot and Dudley Port. This special started from and terminated at Birmingham Snow Hill.

On 3rd September, 1963 a Metropolitan Cammell 3-car dmu working from Aberystwyth to Derby travelled via Shrewsbury, Stafford and down the Trent Valley line to Lichfield, where it used the chord between the High Level and Low Level lines to continue its journey north. This is the only known instance of a passenger train traversing this chord, although it seems likely that there were others over the years.

The empty stock of the SLS special run on 2nd June, 1962 in connection with the centenary of the Sutton Coldfield line is seen here, headed by former LNWR Bowen-Cooke 0-8-0 No. 48930, and tailed by a Stanier 'Black Five'. It has just entered the old MR goods yard near to Walsall station, prior to stabling. *R. Shenton*

An unidentified Stanier mogul drifts into Dudley Port Low Level on a bright summer day in the early 1960s with an excursion. Judging from the number of persons waiting on the platform, this had originated locally and was about to pick up many more day trippers, probably headed via Dudley and Worcester to a resort on the North Devon coast, or even South Wales. Such day trips were extremely popular, especially for those persons unable to be able to afford a full week's holiday away from home. The original wooden down side waiting shelter is about to be demolished, and its replacement is under construction just beyond. In the meantime, a temporary structure is visible in the foreground.

P.B. Whitehouse

Burton shed's 'Jubilee' class 4-6-0 No. 45712 *Victory* heads an excursion for Dudley Zoo through Great Bridge North station in 1962. Even in its last year of service, the station staff attempted to brighten the very urban setting with bedding plants and painted edgings. *D. Wilson*

Bescot's double chimney 'Black Five' No. 44766 piloting 'Jubilee' 4-6-0 No. 45618 *New Hebrides* out of Walsall and past the permanent way depot at Pleck, with an excursion from Nottingham to Dudley Zoo on 6th August, 1963. *R. Shenton*

Locomotives

The SSR Land & Works Committee had requested McClean on 7th June, 1848 to seek quotes for two goods and four passenger engines and tenders from Hawthorns of Newcastle, E.B. Wilson of Leeds, Sharp Brothers of Manchester, and Bury, Curtis & Kennedy of Liverpool. There are no surviving records of the quotes obtained, but over the next few years locomotives were purchased from a variety of manufacturers suggesting that either there was no great distinction between the various quotes, or that the preferences were made on some other criteria, such as delivery times, as all locomotive manufacturers were particularly busy during these years. Later, on 3rd November, 1855, the Board of Directors received quotations from Beyer, Peacock for two six-wheeled locomotives complete with tenders at £2,750 and authorized their purchase. These were delivered as Nos. 22 and 23. A quotation from Fairbairn for six engines at £2,950 each was approved by the Board on 5th June, 1857 and related to engines Nos. 24 to 29. This completed the early locomotives built for SSR, which eventually comprised 29 engines. Details of all of these locomotives are given in *Appendix Two*.

As part of the 1852 running agreement with the LNWR mentioned in Chapter Four, they took over the working and maintenance of all SSR engines and merged them into their Northern Division stock, although the SSR engines remained the property of the SSR. Thus, the LNWR Northern Division supplied engines of their own and SSR origin from July 1852. In fact, an arrangement had already been in place since McClean had taken over in 1850, as he had experienced some difficulty with having adequate motive power, and had hired in locomotives from the LNWR (both Wolverton and Crewe) at the rate of £5 per day, plus one shilling per mile over 100 miles. For example, Wolverton had made available four engines in April 1852.

The original locomotives of the SSR numbered 16 by this time, and were supplemented by further types up to a final total of 29 in 1858.However, many of the earlier engines were notoriously unreliable, and so the number undergoing repair at any one time led to serious shortages of motive power almost continuously. This became so bad in December 1855 that three trains were withdrawn, and the following month six more engines were loaned from Crewe, but made little difference. It should be remembered that whilst the LNWR was running the trains, it was the responsibility of the SSR to provide the engines. By March 1856 there were nearly 600 wagons stranded around the SSR system, with no means of moving them. Eventually, the LNWR Southern Division was able to loan two engines.

Then as from 21st April, 1856 the LNWR Southern Division took over responsibility for running the trains, and 16 of their engines were brought up from Wolverton in steam. The crews moved directly from their SSR engines to these and continued their day's work. These are believed to have included 11 'Mineral Engines', 0-6-0s newly-built by Stothert, Slaughter & Co. of Bristol, which had not been well received on the Southern Division. It was considered that they would be more suitable to the SSR, 'where the loads were big and the distances short'. These were newly renumbered 54 to 64 (originally 321 to 331), which were allocated to Walsall and Wichnor sheds. The SSR engines numbered 21 by this date.

At the time of this latter changeover, Neele mentioned three locomotives, *Sylph, Saracen* and *Stork* from the Northern Division. The first was actually one of the SSR locomotives, No. 14, but *Saracen* was a Ramsbottom 'SFB' (short firebox) class 2-2-2 built in April 1852 for passenger work, carried the distinctive running number 1 and was replaced relatively early, in 1861. *Stork* was a Ramsbottom 2-4-0 of class 'SFB Goods', carrying the running number 136, that was rebuilt into a 2-4-0T in September 1867. In June 1882 it went on to the duplicate list as No. 1972 and was scrapped in April 1884.

As part of the agreement of 21st January, 1858 transferring the lease to the LNWR, the locomotives (23 by then) were purchased by the LNWR for £49,486 13s. 7d., and an order for six Fairbairn 0-6-0s was also taken over. Valuations were performed annually, and often half-yearly, as part of the normal accountancy procedures. So we can usefully learn that on 31st July, 1861 McConnell valued the SSR carriages at £12,398 and the locomotives at £51,282. It would be expected that the unreliability of the original SSR engines would have resulted in them being disposed of quite promptly, but evidently the standard of subsequent repairs carried out at Wolverton must have been adequate, as they mostly soldiered on for another 10 or 15 years.

It is probably fair to say that most of the Ramsbottom types, comprising classes of 2-2-2, 2-4-0, 0-4-2 and 0-6-0 would have seen use on the lines before 1859. The Southern Division types comprised mostly locomotives of similar wheel arrangements (including the useful mixed traffic class 'M' 0-4-2s, such as No. 741 that worked regularly between Wichnor and Birmingham in 1862), plus a number of 4-2-0s and 4-2-2s for express work. Certainly by 1872 the Birmingham to Derby trains were often worked by former Northern Division 2-2-2s alongside former Southern Division 2-2-2 'Small Bloomers'. One of the original distinctive differences had been that the majority of Northern Division goods and passenger engines were named, whereas those of the Southern Division rarely carried names. That other primary distinction of the liveries (Northern in green livery, Southern in either green, or some briefly in a dark red) was lost with the repainting of all types into black (the famous LNWR 'blackberry' black) under Webb from about 1873, and brass number plates were introduced. Passenger and mixed traffic engines were lined out in red, white and blue with varying styles, but goods engines were unlined. Meanwhile, the distinction between the two divisions had been abolished in 1862, but even so the old order was inevitably continued for a few more years. The last McConnell design of 0-6-0 was turned out from Wolverton in 1863 (10 of his 'Express Goods' Nos. 1056 to 1060 and 1071 to 1075), and thereafter Crewe products became the mainstay of motive power. The production of Ramsbottom engines, especially his very successful 17 in. 'DX' class of 0-6-0 goods engines gradually took over. Various types of tank locomotives were used for shunting and trip work, many having been converted from goods tender engines, such as the early 'Crewe Goods' 2-4-0s and Ramsbottom 'DX' 0-6-0s. Webb's most successful 0-6-0 designs of 17 in. 'Coal Engines' and 18 in. 'Cauliflowers' became the most numerous on the LNWR system, and thus well

Standing again at Walsall's platform 3 around 1903 is Ramsbottom 2-2-2 'Lady of the Lake' class No. 754 *Ethelred*. Built in November 1862 this engine was rebuilt by Webb in January 1899 and survived until July 1907.   *R.S. Carpenter*

Webb 'Dreadnought' class divided drive 2-2-2-0 compound No. 648 *Swiftsure* at Walsall around 1903. These controversial engines earned disparate reputations for both their speed and their reliability. This engine was built in June 1888 and scrapped in October 1904. The glazing of the corridor running between platforms 2 and 3 can be seen above the platform awning.

R.S. Carpenter

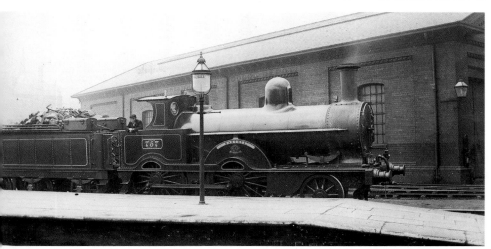

Webb's replacements of Ramsbottom's 'Samson' class 2-4-0s were known as 'Waterloo' or 'Whitworth' class engines. Here we see No. 757 *Banshee* in its later form at the south end of Walsall station around 1905. It was built as a 'replacement' in January 1892 and scrapped in 1908.   *R.S. Carpenter*

Webb 'Renewed Precedent' class 2-4-0 No. 1748 *Britannia* at Walsall's No. 3 platform around 1905. Dating from July 1889 this engine was another 'renewal' of a Ramsbottom 'Newton', originally built in October 1866. It survived to appear in LMS livery as No. 5016, and was not scrapped until June 1928. The corridor from the Park Street entrance can again be clearly seen above the canopy, and lurking beneath the booking hall, on the right, is the almost subterranean No. 3 signal box.   *R.S. Carpenter*

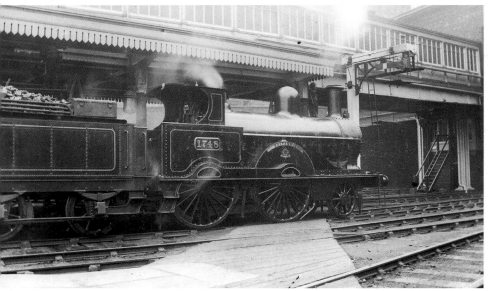

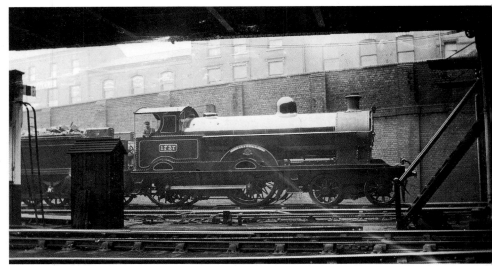

Whale 'Precursor' 4-4-0 No. 1737 *Viscount* at the north end of Walsall station. This engine was built in March 1905 and converted in October 1922 into a 'George the Fifth' class, in which form it lasted to become LMS No. 5316 and was withdrawn in July 1936. However, in this view from around 1905 it is in original condition. The stairs to the right lead to Walsall No. 3 signal box.

R.S. Carpenter

Webb 5 ft 6 in. 2-4-2T LMS No. 6757 at Ryecroft shed in May 1948 shortly after nationalization. These engines were the mainstay of local passenger work in the area for many years.

Kidderminster Railway Museum

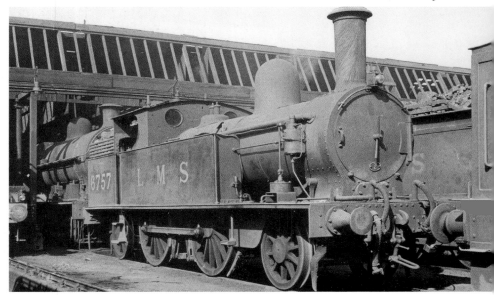

Webb 17 in. 'Coal Engine' 0-6-0 No. 8088 passing Ryecroft Junction with a southbound coal train in August 1935. This engine had a long and interesting career, being built in May 1873 as LNWR No. 2085, and moving to the Railway Operating Department of the Army in 1917 to see war service. It returned in 1923, and was given its LMS No. 8088 in January 1928 and renumbered 28088 by January 1937. It was allotted BR No. 58320, but was withdrawn in July 1948 before this could be applied. *LNWR Society*

Webb 17 in. 'Coal engine' 0-6-0 LMS No. 8308 passing Ryecroft Junction as a light engine in August 1935. This engine was built in October 1892 as LNWR No. 2092, but was placed on the duplicate list in January 1916 as No. 3183. However, it continued in use, but did not receive its LMS number until March 1928 and was renumbered as 28308 in 1940. It was finally withdrawn in June 1948, not receiving its allotted BR number 58358. *E. Talbot Collection*

Bowen Cooke '7F' class 0-8-0 running light engine on the up line from Walsall to Bescot. This was the first part of the SSR to be completed, opening on 1st November, 1847. The two lines on the left are part of the route to Wednesbury and Dudley which ran parallel for over half a mile until connecting at Pleck Junction. *RCTS/PMB Collection*

A Bowen-Cooke 'Super D' 0-8-0 ambles southwards in the Summer of 1961 along the SSR main line at Goldshill near Wednesbury with a very light load of one container wagon, a covered van and a brake van. *D. Wilson*

represented on the SSR system for goods work. Express and semi-fast passenger work became the province of his various types of 2-4-0 ('Samson', 'Precedent', 'Precursor', 'Jumbo', 'Newton', and 'Whitworth' classes), eventually yielding to the 4-4-0s of such classes as the 'Precursors' and Bowen-Cooke's 'George V'. Local passenger workings were dominated by the Webb 4 ft 6 in. and 5 ft 6 in. 2-4-2Ts for a very lengthy time, right past nationalization, when they were still seen on the Walsall - Dudley 'Dodger' or 'Dasher'. LNWR No. 1468 (BR No. 46757) was long associated with the area, and the last member of the 5 ft 6 in. class (BR No. 46712) was withdrawn from Ryecroft shed in August 1954. However, after the Grouping the MR 0-4-4Ts from the MR Pleck shed were frequently used on the Walsall – Dudley 'Dasher', although eventually this service reverted to the exclusive use of the Webb 2-4-2Ts.

Webb's 0-6-2 side tank version of the 'Coal Engines', known as the 'Coal Tanks', were also frequently used on both goods and passenger workings. George Whale's 'Precursor' 4-4-0 and 4-4-2T 'Precursor Tank' were not numerous, but were also seen regularly on workings from Birmingham New Street. They were largely superseded by the Bowen-Cooke inside cylinder 4-6-2Ts introduced from 1910 onwards. The express 4-6-0s 'Experiment' and 'Prince of Wales' classes may only have seen duty on this line in their closing years, but Whale's '19 in. Goods' 4-6-0s would have been more familiar on the long distance goods and other mixed traffic duties. Much of the local coal traffic eventually passed into the hands of the several different classes (and rebuildings) of the 0-8-0s by Whale and Bowen-Cooke, this time lasting right up until 1964.

Into LMS days, the ubiquitous Fowler '3F' and '4F' 0-6-0s were allocated to Ryecroft shed, as were several Johnson MR '2F' 0-6-0s for use on some of the lightly-laid colliery branches. These latter engines survived on this light work until 1962, when the last four (Nos. 58123, 58124, 58185 and 58218) were withdrawn on 7th July and noted stored at Bescot shed, their duties having been taken over by the Ivatt and BR class '2' 2-6-0s. Local passenger work was handled by a stud of the unpopular Fowler 2-6-2Ts, as well as some of his more successful 2-6-4Ts, and former MR 4-4-0s. After the arrival of Stanier on the LMS, his more successful 2-6-2Ts proved their worth locally, as well as his larger 2-6-4Ts, along with Ivatt moguls of classes '2' and '4', and the occasional Fowler or Johnson MR 4-4-0 that was lingering in the area, until the introduction of dmus from 1956. The push-pull units, worked hitherto by the Webb 2-4-2Ts, were taken over by Ivatt 2-6-2Ts and latterly by one or two of the BR Standard variety of this design in the '84000' series. One short-lived experiment occurred with the transfer to Ryecroft shed in March 1954 of one of the small class of nominally Stanier-designed 0-4-4Ts, No. 41902 on the push-pull duties. It seemed to have performed with a reasonable amount of success on these workings from Walsall, and stayed until April 1956. Indeed, it shared a special shuttle service from Dudley via Walsall to Sutton Park for day trippers on Easter Monday 1955 with Ivatt tank No. 41279. The heavy coal workings continued to employ the 0-8-0s, but eventually Stanier '8Fs' could be seen in use. However, the BR '9Fs' were rarely evident. In fact, the BR Standard designs were not frequent visitors to the line. The semi-fast and express workings that

The locomotive seen here ambling into Lichfield Trent Valley (High Level) had an interesting history having been built originally in 1886 as a Johnson '1562' class 4-4-0, but was 'renewed' by Fowler in 1924 with new frames and cylinders as a '483' class engine, eventually receiving its BR number 40364 in December 1951. This three-coach local passenger service is the 9.17 am Wolverhampton High Level to Burton, and comprises a mixture of corridor and non-corridor stock. *R. Shenton*

Fowler 2-6-4T No. 42421 is seen here having its tanks replenished from the 'parachute' type water column at the end of the up platform at Lichfield Trent Valley (High Level), whilst working a local passenger service from Derby to Birmingham New Street, via Walsall. The wooden construction of the platform is clear in this view. *R. Shenton*

Fowler '4F' class 0-6-0 No. 44518 with a northbound stopping passenger train, has just passed the site of Ryecroft engine shed on the right, part of which was being cleared by this time, probably during 1963. *R. Selvey*

This Hughes/Fowler 'Crab' 2-6-0 No. 42799 is heading an excursion for Dudley Zoo in 1962, and has just passed the Palethorpes' siding and loading platform at Sedgeley Junction. *D. Wilson*

Ivatt class '4' 2-6-0 No. 43119 approaching Lichfield Trent Valley (High Level) with an excursion from Lincoln to Dudley for the zoo and castle on 13th April, 1952. In the background can be seen Lichfield Trent Valley Junction signal box that controlled access to the chord linking to the West Coast main line, as well as the level crossing over Burton Old Road.   *R. Shenton*

Burton shed's Ivatt class '2' 2-6-0 No. 46454 runs past Wichnor Junction signal box with a three-coach local passenger train for Burton, consisting of LMS non-corridor coaches, around 1956.
R.S. Carpenter

The Stanier class '3' 2-6-2Ts were not an altogether successful design, but were a distinct improvement over the earlier Fowler variety. Nonetheless they had an important role to play in the LMS and BR eras, and this one, No. 40080 is seen on 16th March, 1959 at Dudley station, having been fairly recently outshopped from Derby works.   *R. Shenton*

Stanier class '4MT' 2-6-4T No. 42659 approaches Ryecroft Junction with a two-coach stopping train from the Lichfield direction around 1960. Unusually, the two coaches are former LNER Gresley corridor stock. The south to east spur linking to the former MR Sutton Park line is in the background.   *R. Selvey*

Bescot shed's Stanier class '5MT' 2-6-0 No. 42957 passes Ryecroft Junction with a haul of coal in metal-bodied 16 ton wagons in Spring 1964. The line to Cannock, and the south to west spur linking to the former MR line to Wolverhampton are on the left.   *R. Selvey*

Stanier class '5' 4-6-0 No. 45253 passes through the cutting at the approach to Lichfield City station with a football excursion from Nottingham Midland to Smethwick Rolfe Street on 8th February, 1958. Although the cutting is faced with bricks at this point, beyond the bridge in the background the rough hewn sandstone remains.   *R. Shenton*

Stanier 'Jubilee' class 4-6-0 No. 45603 *Solomon Islands* passes through Lichfield Trent Valley Low Level on the up through line with a southbound express in the mid-1950s. The SSR line High Level station can be seen behind the train. *G. Coltas*

Stanier '8F' class 2-8-0 No. 48450 heads northbound through Great Bridge North in the summer of 1962 with a load of empty coal wagons. Interestingly, the first three wagons contain 'coal boxes' usually only used on canal barges to prevent breakage of the coals during the persistent manual loading and unloading necessary in that form of transhipment. These 'coal boxes' almost certainly identify the originating collieries as being on Cannock Chase. A fellow '8F' stands in the up goods loop on the left, waiting to assist southbound trains up the grade to Dudley. *D. Wilson*

Brush class '31' A1A-A1A passes through the remains of Wednesbury Town station on 1st June, 1972, with a southbound haul of iron ore, almost certainly bound for Bilston steelworks. The up platform has almost completely disappeared, as have most of the buildings from the down platform.
D. Wilson

BR Sulzer Bo-Bo No. 25032 passes the site of Dudley Port Low Level station on 7th January, 1981, with a string of empty mineral wagons, probably from Round Oak steelworks. It has just passed beneath the Stour Valley line, and under the concrete replacement footbridge that connected the two platforms at the low level site.
D. Wilson

existed were more often than not the preserve of Stanier's 'Black Five' 4-6-0s, although other types did turn up, such as the Hughes/Fowler 'Crab' and Stanier moguls, 'Jubilees', 'Patriots' and 'Royal Scots'. The LMS Pacifics were not permitted on the route.

Into the diesel era, most of the types introduced by BR have been seen on the route, as many were allocated to Bescot and often visitors were borrowed for some of the shorter turns. By this time, the local passenger workings were all in the hands of the succession of dmus, and so diesel locomotives tended to appear only on goods workings, with classes '20', '25', '31', '37', '40', '44', '45', '46', and '47' predominating. Local shunting and some trip work was in the hands of the seemingly everlasting '08' class of 0-6-0 diesel-electric.

Rolling stock

The SSR Land & Works Committee requested McClean on 16th November, 1847 to determine the cost of four engines, 300 waggons and 16 first and third class carriages. He responded to the Finance Committee on the following 17th January that the total cost would be £50,250 with delivery by the following 1st January, 1849 which would have been in time for the opening from Walsall to Lichfield. On 23rd April, 1848 the Land & Works Committee authorized the purchase from Wrights of Saltley of the following vehicles:

2	First Class carriages at £365 each
6	Second Class carriages at £250 each
6	Composite carriages at £305 each
6	Third Class carriages at £205 each
4	Luggage vans at £165 each
2	Horse boxes at £158 each
2	Carriage trucks at £110 each

These were to be subject to a 7½ per cent discount, as negotiated by the LNWR. The SSR first class carriages carried the company's coat of arms, which depicted the shields of the towns of Dudley, Walsall and Lichfield in a combination to reflect the railway's connection with those towns.

Subsequently, on 29th September, 1857 the Board of Directors accepted a tender from the Patent Shaft & Axletree company for 300 wagons at a total cost of £31,360. There are no further records of rolling stock purchases at this time, but from the various comments made concerning traffic problems, it seems that the SSR was desperately short of passenger rolling stock in particular. As already mentioned, it became necessary to use open wagons fitted with wooden planks for the benefit (?) of passengers, who it was hoped would not be unduly concerned. But tastes in travel were changing fast, and the company soon realised that they could not expect paying passengers to put up with such crude discomfort. It seems that they had to resort to hiring stock from other railways, notably the LNWR, but even they were not going to make available their best stock. Only when the LNWR took over the running of the trains were these matters finally and successfully put in order.

'Peak' class 1Co-Co1 No. D67 approaches Alrewas with a diverted parcels service in September 1964. The flat countryside in this area is the result of the flood plain of the River Trent.

C. Shepherd

An unidentified BR class '47' is seen here at the site of Great Bridge station on 18th November, 1973, apparently working wrong line, but more likely engaged on engineering work. The station had completely disappeared by this time, but the presence of the class '25' in the goods yard, plus the considerable number of wagons, indicated that rail traffic, notably of steel, was still healthy at this time.

D. Wilson

Even so, the LNWR rolling stock was not in the forefront of design in the country. Their own four-wheeled stock was initially used on the line, probably until around the 1880s when six-wheeled vehicles became available. Despite the obvious and pressing safety issues, the LNWR continued with the use of Clark & Webb chain brakes on the majority of their vehicles, but had finally reduced the number still in operation to 225 by the end of 1891, and just 15 by 30th June, 1892. Simple vacuum brakes had initially been fitted from the early 1880s, and the LNWR were somewhat tardy in adopting the automatic vacuum brake, as although they had agreed to do so in 1886, they had none so fitted by 30th June, 1887 when these were being fitted by other railways. Matters were taken out of their hands, when an Act of Parliament was passed giving the Board of Trade the necessary powers to compel all railways to fit some form of automatic continuous brake to those trains carrying passengers. So it was that efforts were made to improve the situation, and by the end of 1891 there were 718 engines so fitted, 5,948 vehicles with these brakes, and a further 989 fitted with through pipes. Six months later there 975 engines fitted to work the automatic vacuum brakes, 6,587 vehicles with them and 732 fitted with through pipes.

By the early 1900s bogie stock was common on long distance LNWR trains, and some would have been in use on the SSR, although the six-wheeled vehicles would have continued on the local services. Passengers had to make do without heating until the early 1900s when this was gradually introduced. The LNWR finally withdrew second class accommodation as from 1st January, 1912 although most other railways had long since abandoned this class, with the MR leading the way in 1875.

Non-corridor stock continued on local passenger services, right up to the end of steam services, although sets were also made up from former express stock that had been downgraded as a result of the introduction of more modern vehicles over the years.

Withdrawal of passenger services

This chapter closes with the recording that passenger services were withdrawn from the following lines with effect from 18th January, 1965:

Lichfield City to Wichnor Junction
Walsall to Lichfield City
Walsall to Water Orton, via Sutton Park
Walsall to Wolverhampton, via Pleck
Walsall to Rugeley

Earlier, the Walsall to Dudley line had closed to passengers from 6th July, 1964 at which time the Dudley to Dudley Port services were also withdrawn and Dudley LMR station closed. The WR services from Birmingham Snow Hill to Dudley had been withdrawn three weeks earlier, as from 15th June, 1964, at which time Dudley WR station closed. (In fact the WR Birmingham division was transferred to the LMR in January 1963, but for the purposes of this book it is convenient to continue the distinction.) All of the intermediate stations on

The final services from Birmingham Snow Hill to Dudley were operated by dmus, and here we see a Metropolitan-Cammell two-car set that has just joined the South Staffs line at Horseley Fields Junction, in 1961. The junction can be seen in the background, with the former GWR line climbing steeply away to the right, and opposite, almost at the top of the embankment is the signal box controlling the junction.   *D. Wilson*

Collett '5101' class 2-6-2T No. 4158 runs into Dudley Port Low Level station with a through four-coach passenger train from Birmingham Snow Hill to Dudley on 15th May, 1964. Unusually, the first two vehicles are a former LNER Gresley set. The modern brick-built waiting room on the up platform replaced an earlier structure built mainly of wood.   *D. Wilson*

each of the routes closed on the same dates as the related routes. Thus the only passenger services to remain on any portion of the SSR were Birmingham New Street to Walsall from Bescot Junction, and the short length of line from the junction at Lichfield City to the station for the services from New Street via Sutton Coldfield.

There was little in the way of public outcry at the time of these closures, and most did not even receive any local press coverage. Just one has been located, that of the *Lichfield Mercury*, of Friday 22nd January, 1965, in which it was recorded that the last train from Lichfield City to Wolverhampton was the 7.20 pm from Lichfield City on Monday 18th January, 1965, composed of a two-car dmu. There were only a handful of passengers. During the past year there had only been seven trains per day between Burton, Lichfield, Walsall and Wolverhampton, compared to double that in the previous two years. Mr W.A. Ramm, station master at Lichfield City, said that there were never more than 100 passengers per day, and these were mostly in the peak hours of morning and evening. Most other trains during the day ran empty. Trent Valley High Level closed as a result, but there were no redundancies at Lichfield City. The driver was recorded as Ernest Pritchett (62) and the guard was Benjamin Daniels (68). The Walsall Locomotive Society placed a wreath in the driver's cab, and took photographs.

A Burton to Wolverhampton dmu formed by a two-car Derby Lightweight unit approaching Alrewas in September 1964.   *C. Shepherd*

Chapter Eight

Accidents and their Effects

Accidents are almost inevitable on railways, as in life generally, but in researching for this book, it became evident that there were a disproportionate number affecting this line - especially in its early days. This opinion is not based on any statistical analysis, just on experience in researching railway histories. Normally, such incidents are insufficient to warrant more than occasional attention, but in these circumstances, it has been felt more appropriate to allocate a chapter to those that have been discovered - and to see what lessons were or could have been learnt. This is not an exhaustive list - these have only come to light by chance, and there are almost certainly many more.

The start of the SSR goods service through Great Bridge on 1st March, 1850 included an interchange with the canal traffic at the basin of the Birmingham Canal. However, the sidings into the basin were laid on a falling gradient, and although wooden stopblocks were provided at the end of the sidings, and numerous cautionary notices had been erected to prevent heavy shunting, this still occurred. The inevitable results were that wagons finished up in the canal. A heavy stone stopblock was tried instead of the wooden one, but this too suffered the same fate. The Resident Engineer, a Mr Walker, tired of the constant clearing up operations, and dispensed with the stopblocks altogether, reasoning that if the men knew there were none they would take more care. This brilliant piece of psychology worked, and there were no more wagons deposited in the canal. However, removing safety to instil responsibility would not be a popular move today.

The following incident occurred on Saturday 14th June, 1851 and was included in the General Manager's Report Book:

> On Saturday morning last a train arrived at the top of the Dudley Incline, with fortunately only three passengers, but instead of passing over the points at the dummy siding, the driver stopped the train on these points and disconnected his engine, leaving the carriages on the incline. The guard being in his van behind the train, found his break [sic] would not work, and consequently the three carriages and van proceeded down the Incline, on the wrong side at the rate of about 15 miles per hour – the train did not come to rest until it had passed Wednesbury station; two of the three passengers jumped out, whilst the train was in motion, but without receiving any particular damage. No claim or complaint has been made. I am of the opinion that both the driver and the pointsman are guilty in this case and should be punished. It is miraculous that the descending train should not have met a coming train in its progress and to have caused a double collision. I have written to Messrs. Wright & Company with reference to the construction of their breaks and their share of the liability. It suggests to me the necessity of having breaks on most of our carriages, as well as a telegraph bell between Dudley and Great Bridge, which is far more necessary there than at Bescot.

Carriages were equipped with chain brakes throughout by the 1860s, but these were not automatic, and it was not until the 1893, after a period of equipping many engines and carriages with the simple vacuum brake, that the LNWR could state that almost all of their engines and passenger stock were equipped with the automatic vacuum brake. The electric telegraph was first installed on the SSR on its Walsall to Bescot section in 1849, so whilst it could have been installed throughout by this time, it was evidently not felt necessary. Eventually, of course the telegraph was installed along the entire SSR route mileage, although at what date this was completed is not known, but is thought to be by 1860.

Another incident occurred shortly after, and the following is again abstracted from the General Manager's Report Book, dated 1st August, 1851, but unfortunately does not give details of the cause of the accident:

> An accident happened to our goods train from Bescot to the north on 23rd July, in consequence, as is alleged by the LNWR of some defect in one of our iron wagons (No. 112). Much damage has been done – say –
> Six Ince Hall waggons totally destroyed
> Two SSR waggons irreparable
> Four SSR waggons very much damaged
> Seven LNWR waggons smashed to pieces
> Two LNWR waggons considerably damaged
> As well as a quantity of goods injured.

On Wednesday 10th December, 1851 a passenger fell under the wheels of a moving train whilst attempting to board it at Wednesbury, and subsequently died. The inquest recorded 'accidental death', and this was probably correct in this instance.

Another item from the General Manager's Report Book, dated 30th January, 1852, gives the following account:

> A slight collision took place at Bescot on Saturday last, 24th instant between the 8.45 passenger train and two LNWR goods wagons which were placed on the middle road at Bescot, but blown forward by the wind until they obstructed the main line at the points, the result was the empty wagons were thrown off the line and the question of liability arises in consequence of this station being managed by the LNWR.

This illustrates the lack of brakes on most of the goods wagons, which were normally prevented from running away on gradients by the use of scotch blocks. However, these had their limitations, as being made of wood, in use they became grooved and it did not need a great deal of effort to move a wagon over the scotch block once it had become so worn.

This seems to have been a particularly unfortunate period for the railway, as the Report Book also contains the following entry:

> An accident occurred at ½ past 2 o'clock on Christmas morning to our goods train at Wichnor Junction; the driver had passed through with the greater portion of our train through the points on to the down line of the Midland Railway when a Midland goods train approached on the same line and ran through our train, severing it in two. The matter has been fully inquired by the authorities of the Midland Railway, and the whole blame was found to rest with their driver, who was discharged. The Midland Railway will consequently pay all expenses.

In his report dated 23rd April, 1852 the General Manager made the following rather curt entry :

We had the misfortune to kill a young man 18 years of age (Joseph Harper, a cleaner in the employ of the Loco Department) on Sunday the 18th instant at Walsall, getting between the buffers of two wagons of coke when the engine was in motion - a verdict of accidental death was returned by the Coroner's Inquest.

Many people came into railway employment at this time without any appreciation of the speed of railway movements and potential dangers. It was a fact of life at this time that employees were expected to look after themselves, as we shall see from the numerous tragic events and the inevitable verdicts of 'accidental death' at the subsequent inquests. Even rudimentary training at this time seems to have overlooked the obvious human failings, although there were many instances of carelessness, often arising from persons becoming 'over familiar' with their occupations. One possible contributory cause of accidents was being intoxicated, which was strictly forbidden, and strictly enforced by the SSR company.

Two further entries on the same date are of interest in this vein, as although not recording an accident, it does show that the company was making some effort to avoid incidents:

It is desirable to furnish three crossings and three junctions with time pieces for the better protection of the line - We now have several watches on hand in consequence of the alteration in the engine drivers.

As the time interval system was still in use at this time, this seems to be an eminently sensible move – or even, perhaps essential.

One of the goods engine drivers (John Anderson) from the Northern division of the LNWR has on two occasions passed at a furious rate and in a most reckless manner the danger signal at Lichfield and Pelsall, as well as having refused to attend to instructions and used language of defiance. The things cannot be permitted and I consider it is my duty to have the man taken before the Magistrates to answer for the offence; but the great delicacy necessary under present circumstances in dealing with the drivers belonging to the LNWR renders this a proper question for the serious consideration of the lessees.

One can understand the need for delicacy in this regard, as the lessee had subcontracted the running of trains to the LNWR by this date. It would seem that a joint approach by both the SSR and LNWR managements would have been appropriate at this time – but whatever was adopted the principle of ensuring the safety of trains was evidently of prime importance, and rightly so.

On 18th June, 1852 another solemn, but surprisingly brief report recorded:

I am sorry to have to report that Harry Stringer (one of our platelayers) was killed on the Dudley Incline on May 24th. A verdict of accidental death was returned and no blame attached to the company.

The entry for 13th August, 1852 included a ray of hope in its conclusion:

I am sorry to have to report two accidents to passenger trains, by collisions, since my last communication; one at Bescot on July 5th by which two passengers (Mr Scrivin and Mr Perry) were injured, and a sum amounting, with Doctors' Bills, to £30 will probably cover the expense.

A second occurrence, took place at Hammerwich on July 27th by which several persons are more or less injured but do not anticipate more than a few trifling claims. The insurance company as well as the Board of Trade has been duly informed.

Recommend continuing the telegraph to Alrewas Junction and fitting breaks to 3rd class carriages. Am preparing a Rule Book for the line.

We shall see below further comments on the introduction of an SSR rule book.

A passenger train was waiting at Dudley Port (Low Level) on 29th July, 1853 waiting for a connection from the Stour Valley line at the High Level station, when it was run into at the rear by a freight train. The driver of the freight train insisted that the signal was not at danger. There was no contradictory evidence, and it appears that a porter was standing in for the normal signalman, which may have accounted for the lapse, although the porter denied that he had not set the signal correctly. An alternative cause was that the distant signal levers were at the far ends of the platforms and passengers may have interfered with them, as they used the boarded crossing from one platform to the other.

The standard regulation as to signals was that the danger (red) stop signal must be exhibited at stations as a protection for five minutes after the passing of any train or engines, and the caution (green) signal for five minutes more, after which the alright (white) signal would be displayed.

The company were let off somewhat lightly by the inspector in this case; they promised to put up a footbridge, and to bring the whole of the levers together, which would have prevented any unauthorized interference.

In under two months, on 19th September, 1853, another accident took place, this time at Wednesbury, where a passenger train ran into the tail of a goods train. The distant signal was properly exhibited, but was only 370 yards away from the home signal. The company maintained that because the driver had failed to stop at the red home signal, he had thus broken the rules. However, the Board of Trade Inspector, Lieutenant Tyler took a different view, saying that the distant signal should have been 500 yards away instead of 370. As the goods train was 1¼ hours late, the telegraph should have been adopted to give some information as to the state of the line. Furthermore, as there were 36 passenger and 20 goods trains between Wednesbury and Great Bridge in 24 hours, the timetable wanted rearranging. Also, he reported that the SSR had no rule book of its own; the staff were using MR rule books, while the drivers had LNWR books! Finally, the driver had made no attempt to stop at the red home signal, and he noted that there was a general laxity in observing this regulation.

The General Manager contented himself with a reply to the effect that, as his men had to work over the MR and LNWR lines, the rule book of each company was required, and while the Board of Trade objected to the use of two rule books, the suggestion actually called for three to be supplied ! He decided to issue an order that no signals are to be exhibited at distant signal posts unless it is intended that drivers shall stop, and if the red signal is shown, drivers must stop at it, and if line is clear draw ahead. As we have already seen, the General Manager stated just over a year earlier that he was in the process of compiling a rule book for the SSR. This was eventually introduced in 1855 when John Payne took over as General Manager, and was quite succinct as to what employees were not allowed to do. There was to be no tipping, guards were not allowed to go roof hopping, and intoxication was not only punishable by instant dismissal, but also by criminal proceedings. More prosaically guards were empowered to stop passengers exposing themselves - which it is believed was more to do with the lack of lavatorial facilities than any perceived sexual threat! Of greater significance was the eventual creation and introduction of a nationally agreed rule book by the Railway Clearing House in 1876.

The company was evidently only too aware of the failings of its staff, and made some efforts to redress the situation. For example, it was noted that on 9th August, 1854 McClean authorized the not inconsiderable payment of £10 10s. 0d. to Mr Keenan, the station master at Dudley Port, for his prompt action in preventing an accident.

The *Wolverhampton Chronicle* of Wednesday 4th October, 1854 reported an incident which led to the court appearance of one of the railwaymen :

COLLISION ON THE SOUTH STAFFORDSHIRE RAILWAY
EXAMINATION AND COMMITTAL OF A GUARD, YESTERDAY (TUESDAY)

On Friday, soon after the train which leaves Walsall for Dudley, at 9.35 a.m., entered the Wednesbury cutting, it came in violent collision with a luggage train, proceeding in the same direction, by which the seats in several of the carriages were torn from their supports, and about thirty of the passengers were bruised, contused, and violently shaken, but none, fortunately, severely injured. The guard of the passenger train was not so fortunate ; for, looking out at the moment to learn the nature of the obstruction signalled to him by the driver's whistle, he had his collar bone broken, and was otherwise injured about the head and face.

It appears that the luggage train, which was a heavily laden one, should have been shunted at Brownhills until the passenger train which subsequently came into collision with it had passed. Instead of that, it kept on its way at about 14 or 15 miles an hour, passing the Walsall station at 9.35 a.m., just previous to the arrival of the train from Burton, which was a few minutes behind time that morning. It proceeded at this rate until passing the signal post at the Wednesbury junction with the Grand Junction Line. Thereafter its speed slackened, and, on entering the Wednesbury cutting, it came to a standstill, or nearly so. The guard, John Dance, went back, but not, it would seem at the most, more than a hundred yards, placed a fog signal on the rails, and held out a red flag. These were noticed by the driver of the passenger train, who shut off the steam, applied his break, signalled to the guard to apply his break, and then jumped off the engine. The break of the guard's van was applied by Mr. Coates, the stationmaster at Great Bridge, who happened to be riding in the van at the time. These precautions broke the force of a concussion which, from the brevity of the notice, they could not altogether prevent. The fact that the cutting is entered by a curve from the extremity of which nothing in the cutting can be seen, added alike to the difficulty and danger, and but for the promptness with which the steam was shut off, and the breaks applied, a great sacrifice of human life must inevitably have taken place.

The guard of the goods train was immediately given in custody of the police, and was brought up at the West Bromwich Petty Sessions, on Saturday, charged with neglect of the company's rules. He was remanded to the Wednesbury Petty Sessions, at which he was examined yesterday (Tuesday), before the Rev. W. Kerr, and T. Walker, Esq. Mr. Sill, from the office of Messrs. Doignan and Hemnant, prosecuted on behalf of the South Staffordshire Railway ; and the accused was defended by Mr. Moore. Mr. Sill stated that, by the rules of the company, the accused should have gone back 800 yards with hand and fog signals, and had he done so the collision would have been avoided. The rules of the company were found on the accused when he was taken into custody, and it was proved by the evidence of a number of witnesses that he had not gone back a hundred yards. The majority of the witnesses were of the opinion that the goods train was in motion at the time of the collision, but going at a very slow pace. The other portions of the evidence were a recapitulation of the circumstances described above.

The case being closed for the prosecution, and Mr. Moore having intimated that he would reserve his defence, the prisoner was committed for trial at the ensuing Quarter Sessions ; but admitted to bail, himself in £50, and two sureties in £25 each.

Given that the time interval system was still in use here, this incident was caused by the incompetence of the goods guard. Really, the time interval system should have been replaced by then, and it was not until 1884 that the whole of the passenger lines were working on the absolute block system, with two minor exceptions. These were the Horseley Junction to Dudley Port section which was worked on the permissive block arrangement, and the Darlaston Loop which continued on the time interval system. The latter lost its passenger service in 1887 and was therefore exempt from the requirements of the 1889 Regulation of Railways Act, which made the block system compulsory for all lines having passenger traffic. Indeed, the expense of providing for this requirement may well having been an influencing factor in the LNWR resistance to subsequent efforts to reopen the line to passenger traffic.

Working the single line section between the SSR station at Dudley and the OWWR station gave rise to a number of collisions on this section. One such occurred in October 1854 with a repetition occurring in May 1855. The latter collision gave rise to injuries to 40 persons, and a strong report from the Board of Trade Inspector, as a result of which a pilotman was thereafter employed on all trains passing over this single line.

Another incident was reported in the *Wolverhampton Chronicle* of Wednesday 27th December, 1854:

FATAL ACCIDENT ON THE SOUTH STAFFORDSHIRE LINE
On Wednesday an inquest was held at Brownhills, before W.W. Ward, Esq., coroner, on the body of John Johnson, a labourer, 54 years old. The deceased lived near Brownhills, and it appeared that on Saturday night he left home to pay a small debt. An engine driver named John Holt, who left Burton with the 8.14 train on that night, observed something on the line near Brownhills, and informed the stationmaster of it on arriving at Pelsall. A man was sent from the Brownhills station, who found the deceased lying on the line ; his left arm was cut off at the elbow, and the right side of this head was fractured. He was then quite dead. Verdict, 'Accidental death'.

Trespass on the railway has forever been a problem, and despite continual warnings the tragic results continue to shock, but never sufficiently for the problem to be eliminated. Trespass may have had some bearing on a fatal accident which occurred at the level crossing in Bridgeman Street, Walsall on 6th March, 1855 when a man was knocked down by an engine and killed. This was the subject of an enquiry by the Government Inspector, Colonel Yolland and in his report dated 17th March, 1855 he was uncertain as to whether the man had been using the level crossing, or whether he had been making his way from the end of the station platform to the level crossing. He recommended that a footbridge should be installed at the site of the level crossing, which latter should be closed to pedestrians. This was done, but either out of sheer idleness or possibly believing it to be quicker route, pedestrians still continued to use the crossing rather than climb over the footbridge. Eventually the level crossing was replaced by an underpass for both pedestrians and vehicular traffic, during the widening of 1883.

Another incident occurred in December 1854 in the cutting to the north of Walsall station One goods train waiting to enter the station was run into by a following goods train; the resulting wreckage blocked the opposite line. A third goods train, passing at that time, hit the debris and was derailed, killing the driver. The Inspecting Officer, Lieutenant Tyler, blamed the SSR for lack of proper staff, as the signals at one place had been given by a platelayer's wife, and at another by a girl of 13 years of age. In any event, they were either not observed or not obeyed by the drivers and the collision ensued. Apparently one of the drivers had never been over the line before, and the other footplatemen implicated in the affair had been on duty for 19, 21 and 26 hours at a stretch. It is difficult to see from this distance in time, how such poor management could have been tolerated, and indeed matters were inevitably taken in hand to at least try to reduce such a combination of circumstances. The new rule book, reduction in working hours, and more responsible supervision were all eventually, and perhaps somewhat slowly, introduced.

The *Walsall Observer* of Saturday 20th March, 1875 reported an incident at Walsall station, which showed the initiative of several railway employees in dealing with the situation:

At about 5.00 am on Wednesday morning, John Smith, a wagon examiner in the employ of the London & North Western Railway was going to work at the railway station when he found one side of the ticket office and the adjacent lobby, that was for first and second class passengers, in flames. The hose was fetched but there was difficulty in putting it to work. A couple of locomotive engines were brought along the line from the shed and stationed alongside the office. The water was then taken in bucketfuls from their tanks and poured upon the fire, which was soon subdued.

For some accidents the company could not be held responsible. In the next example, the unfortunate person had even ignored his workmates' heedings of the danger he was creating for himself, as recorded in the *Wolverhampton Chronicle* of 17th May, 1876:

THE FATAL ACCIDENT AT WEDNESBURY
On Thursday an inquest was held by Mr. Hooper, at the London and North Western Inn, Wednesbury, touching the death of Edward Bear (46), who lived at Lea Brook Square, and who was killed on Tuesday morning *(9th May, 1876)* at the Wednesbury Railway Station, on the London and North Western Railway. It appeared that the deceased was employed by the Gloucester Waggon company to repair some waggons at Wednesbury.On the morning mentioned, about half past twelve o'clock, he was engaged with a young man named Smith in repairing the last of a number of empty trucks which stood in a loop of the railway company's line leading to the Great Western Station, there were nearly fifty trucks behind him, and the one he was engaged upon was in front of him. An engine came along the siding, and notwithstanding that, Smith, immediately he heard the whistle blow ran from between the trucks and called to the deceased to get out of the way, the latter persisted in doing something to the draw bar of the waggon. The delay was fatal ; the

engine struck the trucks which were behind, and the unfortunate man was crushed by buffers of the two trucks between which he was stood. His chest was smashed, and his ribs penetrating his heart, death was almost instantaneous. Smith, when questioned by the Coroner, said that the deceased was warned by several shunters to get out of the way, and that he ought to have repaired the waggon in a siding, and not on the branch of the line on which there was constant traffic. - The jury returned a verdict of 'Accidental death' - the deceased leaves a wife and eight children.

At this point it is perhaps worth reflecting that although the number of accidents on the SSR were certainly above average, the general level throughout the country was still very high. For example, in 1875 there were 1,290 persons killed on the railways of which 134 were passengers, 765 were railway officers or servants and 391 were classified as trespassers or suicides. Of this total, 19 were considered to have been killed by circumstances beyond their own control, which leaves a massive 98.5 per cent as having contributed to their own demise!

In the same period, there were some 5,755 persons injured of which 1,806 were passengers, 3,618 were railway officers or servants and 331 were trespassers or (presumably attempted) suicides. Here again, 1,212 were considered to have contributed to their own injuries, representing a slightly more credible 79 per cent. However, it should be borne in mind that in compiling these statistics, it was generally considered that persons had a more general responsibility to look after their own safety, whereas today it almost entirely believed that someone's safety is somebody else's duty.

Returning to further incidents, on Saturday 31st May, 1879 an accident occurred at Bloomfield Junction, where a Walsall to Wolverhampton train overran the junction there to collide into a passing Liverpool to Birmingham express. That there were no deaths is quite remarkable, as the *Wolverhampton Chronicle* of 4th June, 1879 reported. The actual report was very extensive, including interviews with some of the victims and a detailed list of those injured, together with their injuries. The following extracts are those which contain the most relevant details:

SHOCKING RAILWAY ACCIDENT AT TIPTON
27 PERSONS INJURED, AN EXPRESS TRAIN CUT IN TWO

On Saturday night last an accident of the most alarming character, and unfortunately resulting in injuries more or less serious to a large number of persons, occurred at the Bloomfield Junction, on the London and North-Western Railway, about five miles from this town. The junction referred to is situated between the two stations of Deepfields and Tipton, and is formed for the running of trains to and from Walsall on the Princes End loop branch to the Stour Valley Line. The accident was caused by a local passenger train from Walsall running into a through express train from Liverpool to Birmingham. The express train is timed to arrive at Wolverhampton at 7.23 p.m., and to go out for Birmingham and the south for 7.26, but from what we can learn the train on this occasion was some nine minutes late, and this was the case also with the 'local' from Walsall. The latter, however, had proceeded on its journey all right until within a short distance of the junction, when the driver noticed the signals against him to allow the express to pass. And he at once applied the brake to lock the wheels of his engine - one of the small tank kind much used for running local passenger trains - but owing to the rails being wet and slippery, and there being a slight decline to the junction the wheels failed to bite the rails, and the train was carried along to the Stour Valley line ... That the driver made desperate efforts to stop the engine when he saw the danger is evident from the fact that the rails for some distance were thickly covered with sand, which had been deposited from the engine with the view of obviating the slipperiness. The signals at the junction are worked by means of Saxby's interlocking apparatus, the principle being that when the signals of the main line are raised the signals for the branch are lowered simultaneously by the same action of the lever … Just at this moment the express came tearing ahead at terrific speed, the main line here also being on a slight decline, which rises again on going into Tipton Station. The engine and three of the coaches passed the point of danger in safety, but the Walsall engine struck the next almost at a right angle. The engine, which was running tank end first, was brought to a standstill by the force of the impact, and the sides of the express passenger carriages, as they came along, catching the tank, had huge pieces cut clean away. Four of the carriages were thrown off the metals and fell in different positions across the two lines of rails, completely blocking the road at this point. One carriage - a third - was thrown upon its side on the down line, a composite carriage fell across the up and down lines, another carriage was considerably damaged by rolling over, and the passengers were all more or less injured, several having very narrow escapes from death. Just after the accident occurred, the 6.55 slow passenger train from Birmingham came up in the opposite direction, but the brakes being promptly applied the train was brought to a standstill within twenty yards of the overturned coaches. The front portion of the express had also been pulled up by the engine-driver after going a short distance. The guard's van and two coaches at the end of the train remained on the metals, probably owing to their wheels having been locked with the patent brake. Every effort was at once made by a number of passengers who had escaped injury with the officials to rescue those unfortunate persons who were imprisoned in and beneath the partly demolished coaches … As soon as it was possible to do so after the whole of the persons had been rescued from the overturned coaches, a special train was made up, and several of the injured and those passengers who wished to go forward were conveyed to Birmingham … Breakdown gangs *(from Wolverhampton, Birmingham and Walsall)* were quickly on their way to the scene of the accident, and at once commenced to remove the debris, the work occupying them until a quarter past eight o'clock on Sunday morning….It should be added that at the point where the Princes End branch intersects the main line the two sets of line are carried on an embankment, and one of the coaches fell partly off the line and hanging over the embankment, and it is said that two children and a man were precipitated from one of the compartments down to the bottom of the embankment. Another coach fell on top of a platelayer's hut, situated on a piece of land at the junction of the two sets of line, and the sleepers of which it is built sustaining it in the position in which it fell. Those coaches which felt the full force of the collision were wrecked in a most curious manner, and it is really astonishing that some of the passengers in them escaped with their lives … An examination of the Walsall engine shows that, in addition to the injury to the buffer, the boiler leaks slightly through the straining of the plates. The driver of the Walsall train has been suspended pending an enquiry which will be held in the course of a few days by Mr. Sutton *(district superintendent).* An enquiry will also be held by one of the inspectors of the Board of Trade, but the date upon which it will take place is not yet known….During Saturday night and yesterday many thousand persons visited the scene of the collision, and the Tipton police had considerable difficulty in maintaining order, particularly on Saturday night.

Subsequently, Colonel Yolland was appointed to investigate this accident. His conclusions vary somewhat from the above press report, but he criticised the signalman for accepting both trains into his section, although only the express had been given clear signals to proceed through. The local train had not received a 'caution' at the distant signal, and so was proceeding on the assumption that the next signal (for the junction) would be clear. Because of inadequate sighting of these signals, when the driver applied his brake he could not stop, but fortunately reduced the speed of his train to about 5 mph at the moment of impact. The express train was, in fact, only travelling at about 15-20 mph.

Furthermore, Colonel Yolland was also strongly critical of the layout of the junction and the siting of the signal box. It transpired that he had inspected the Princes End branch (including the junction) in 1863 prior to its opening - so he was concerned that he could be criticised for approving the poor layout. On further investigation, he was able to prove that the junction had been moved 171 yards north since his inspection in 1863. The signal box was now some 340 yards from the junction, and in no position to adequately supervise intersecting movements. Initially, the LNWR denied making any changes, but eventually conceded that the junction was revised soon after his 1863 inspection.

The junction layout was altered soon after, and the signal box resited.

On 5th November, 1881 the *Walsall Observer & South Staffordshire Chronicle* included letters complaining at the lack of waiting room accommodation on the new platform that had been built on the far side of the station, especially after the fatal accident to a Mr Woolley who had been run over whilst trying to reach this platform via the boarded crossing instead of the new footbridge. The boarded crossing was never intended for the use of passengers, and even though warning signs may well have been displayed, the use of such crossings was commonplace at many of the smaller stations, and may have persuaded Mr Woolley to use it, especially if he was making a last minute connection.

Although of widely differing nature. the next three instances have all the classic elements of pure accident mixed with a degree of 'over - familiarity'.

The 27th October, 1883 issue of the same newspaper included the following report:

FATAL ACCIDENT ON THE RAILWAY

On Wednesday Mr. A.A. Fletcher (the borough coroner) held an inquest at the Cottage Hospital, on the bodies of James Walters (55), Alexandra Street and Samuel Davis (52), Portland Street, who were killed on the London and North Western Railway at the Pleck, the previous day. Mr. Stoker (from the office of Mr. Sutton) and Mr. Stevenson (stationmaster) represented the LNWR Company, and Inspector Rousby the North Staffordshire Railway Company.

Herbert Yates, Oxford Street, Pleck deposed that he was a platelayer, and was employed by the LNWR. On Tuesday morning he was working between Davis and Walters, who were also platelayers, on the line at Pleck Junction. It was about twenty minutes to ten, and the Birmingham and Wolverhampton trains came towards them together. They were both going in the same direction, and were nearly abreast of one another. The smoke and steam from the Wolverhampton train was blowing across the line, so that the witness and the others could not see the Birmingham train. As the Wolverhampton train passed him witness just turned his head, to see if anything was coming. Seeing the train upon him he jumped, but it caught him on the shoulder, knocking him aside. When the trains had passed, he saw Davis lying in the six foot and Walters in the four foot. Witness went up to the men, and found that Walters was dead, but Davis was still living ... Witness thought he heard a whistle before the train was upon them, but he was not sure. It was a very windy morning, so the whistle might have sounded without him hearing it ... Both the deceased men had been platelayers for a considerable time. The lines run parallel for Birmingham and Wolverhampton for some distance, the latter turning out just past the place where the accident happened ... No warning of the approach of a train was given to platelayers except the sounding of a whistle. That was always sounded, and the men had to look out for themselves ... William Jackson, Stoke-upon-Trent, engine driver in the employment of the North Staffordshire Railway Company, deposed that he was driving the train from Walsall to Birmingham on Tuesday morning. He saw nothing of the men on the line until Yates suddenly rose, about a foot in front of the engine, and just got clear of the buffer beam. Immediately afterwards he heard a spade or something rattle against the engine. He thought they had run over something, and therefore brought the engine to a standstill. On walking back along the line about 150 yards, he found Walters, who was dead.

Mr. Stoker said ... that platelayers had to move about, sometimes two or three of them extending over a couple of miles. When there were serious repairs or gangs of men signals were put up ; but when odd men were at work, as these had been, that could not be done.

Charles Wright, Darlaston Road, Pleck, ... was at work about 300 yards from the accident. He saw the Wolverhampton train coming, and saw the signal off for the Birmingham train also. The platelayers could have seen that signal if they had looked up. The Wolverhampton train was about 50 yards in front of the Birmingham train, and he could not see the latter in consequence of the smoke and steam ... Witness said that platelayers did not work at that work in foggy weather. Deceased could have seen the signal of they had looked, and it was their own fault that they did not. The platelayers were always supposed to look after themselves ... A verdict of 'accidental death' was returned.

Walsall station continued to attract accidents, as this report from the *Walsall Observer & South Staffordshire Chronicle* of 18th October, 1884 recalled:

FATAL ACCIDENT AT WALSALL STATION
On Thursday night, a shocking and fatal accident occurred at the LNWR Station, Walsall, to Mr. George Dunn, of the Cannock Chase Colliery. Deceased, who had the return half of a ticket from Brownhills, and had been making some purchases at the railway bookstall, was going to the 5.57 express for Lichfield, when it started. He ran to the train and attempted to get but failed, and fell under the carriages. The alarm was immediately given, and the train was stopped, but not before the unfortunate man had been frightfully mangled - his skull being smashed and his body and limbs dreadfully cut. Dr. Monkton, of Rugeley, who was on the platform, attended to the deceased, but death had been instantaneous. The body was removed to the Queen's Hotel to await an inquest. On the body being searched a number of letters and papers were found upon him, and established his identity. We deeply regret to learn that the deceased, who was a man widely known and highly respected, leaves a widow and six children to mourn his sudden and terrible death.

The following incident was reported in the *Lichfield Mercury* of Friday 21st November, 1884:

THE FATAL ACCIDENT ON THE RAILWAY AT LICHFIELD
On Friday afternoon an inquest was held by the Borough coroner (Mr T.H. Stanley) at the Cottage Hospital, Walsall on the body of William Mason Wiseman (20) of Lichfield, who died at that institution on Thursday week. Mr Stoker (Birmingham) and Mr Stevenson (Walsall) were present for the railway company.

Thomas Wiseman of Cannock, signalman, identified the body as that of his son, who was a porter, in the employment of the LNWR at Lichfield. Deceased had previously been in the same employment at Cannock, having been in the service for three years altogether.

John Johnson, station master at Lichfield City station, deposed that he was on duty on Thursday morning when the train arrived at 8 o'clock from Walsall for Derby. There were two cattle trucks to go on by the train, and it was part of the duty of the deceased to attach these trucks to the train. The train was a little late, and witness directed the driver in running on to the siding to fetch the trucks. Deceased was engaged with the trucks, the shackles of which he would have held ready to attach it to the train when it came up. Witness was directing the driver of the engine, and did not see the deceased; but he suddenly heard some shouting, and ran to the trucks where the deceased was. The train had been going just gently along. When witness got to the deceased, he had been got off the line, the train then being at a standstill. Witness sent for a doctor, who said that it was a very bad case. Everything was done for him which was possible, and then he was sent on to the Walsall Cottage Hospital by express engine at once. Deceased had repeatedly coupled trucks before, and indeed was rather quick and clever at it ... In reply to a juror, witness said that the permanent way was quite clear, except that there was a scotch block to stop the trucks when necessary beside the line. Deceased caught his heel against the block, and that was what threw him to the line. Witness had cautioned both deceased and the other porter about getting in and out to attend to the couplings while trains were in motion ... John Heber Cook, Lichfield, porter at LNWR Lichfield and had been for over ten years. Witness was on duty ... and saw the train being shunted to fetch the trucks. The train was due out, and was sent into the sidings for the two trucks. Deceased was between the train and the cattle wagons, calling the train back to them. The scotch block mentioned was not ten yards from where the cattle wagons were. The train went up towards the deceased very slowly – about 2 ½ miles per hour. Deceased walked backwards as he called the train to come towards the trucks, and then stepped into the four foot way. Deceased took hold of the coupling chain of the trucks, and as he stepped along with them, he tripped over the scotch block, and fell across the right hand rail. Two wheels of the last carriage in the train passed over the deceased, who was seized by the witness and dragged out. Deceased appeared sensible, but was only greaned [sic]. It was against the rules of the company to get between carriages for the purpose of coupling them while they were in motion, but it was done by the men at times.

The jury returned a verdict of 'accidental death', suggesting that the company should as much as possible dispense with scotch blocks.

On 1st July, 1887 George Hall (1 year 7 months) was crossing the boarded walk at Pelsall with his six-year-old sister, when his foot became stuck between the rail and one of the boards laid for the crossing. A passenger train from Walsall came into sight, the driver whistled and applied his steam brake (the train was not fitted with continuous vacuum brake), but could not stop in time and ran over the infant, who was killed. The inquest on 4th July, 1887 returned a verdict of accidental death, but recommended the installation of a footbridge. The footbridge was duly installed. In all cases where the driver has been unable avoid a collision with someone on the track, one feels sympathy for the driver, and especially in this particularly distressing incident.

The following two incidents both underline the problem of being near to the track, even to experienced railwaymen:

On 29th December, 1893 Jarvis Garner (signalman at Brownhills station) was killed on his way home. He walked along the line, as his duties included extinguishing the signal light at Norton Junction. Several goods trains were shunting at this time, and his attention was diverted so that he did not see a passing passenger train, which knocked him down and killed him.

On 19th January, 1894 William Charles Lockley (platelayer) was killed at Norton Junction, when his attention was drawn to a passing passenger train, so that he did not see an approaching coal train, which knocked him down and killed him.

A further accident at Lichfield was reported in the *Lichfield Mercury* of Friday 8th June, 1900:

FATAL ACCIDENT AT LICHFIELD
A Guard Killed

On Wednesday afternoon an accident occurred near the Lichfield City Station, whereby a goods guard named Harry Cliff lost his life. It appears that a goods train, travelling to Walsall, stopped at Hammerwich, the engine being detached for shunting purposes. While Cliff was engaged in the van, the wagons started to run down the incline towards Lichfield. The officials at Hammerwich immediately forwarded a telegraphic message to Lichfield, but the deceased does not seem to have realised any danger, as he had not applied the brake when passing the signalbox on the Birmingham Road. Fog signals were laid at Lichfield in consequence of the message which had been received, but unfortunately it was too late. The wagons, which had attained great speed, were turned into the stop block siding between the Lichfield City Station and Cherry Orchard Bridge, and they dashed with terrific violence into a number of empty cattle wagons. Several wagons were piled one upon another, and the guard's van was completely buried in the wreckage. The guard was found in the debris quite dead, and his body was removed to the Anglesey Arms to await the inquest, which will be held today. The unfortunate man, who was about forty years of age, belonged to Stafford, although he was attached to the locomotive department at Walsall.

The *Lichfield Mercury* a week later included a lengthy article on the inquest, which confirmed the identity of the guard, who was living at 2 Bridgman Place, Walsall and had been in the service of the LNWR for 25 years. The train involved was the 12.55 pm Wichnor to Bescot goods, which had left Lichfield City at about 3.55 pm, comprising 21 loaded and 9 empty wagons. Whilst at Lichfield City, the guard mentioned to the driver that one wagon (nearest to the engine) was due to be detached at Hammerwich, and in view of the length of the train, asked him to uncouple this wagon when Hammerwich was reached (even though this was the guard's duty). This was not an unusual practice and the driver agreed. When they reached Hammerwich, the driver received a hand signal from the guard for him to proceed. After doing so, and in the course of shunting this wagon, he noticed the train starting to move away, but could do nothing about it. He gave evidence that the guard must have released his brake, as the train was initially quite stable. Various other witnesses confirmed that the brake was not applied as the runaway passed them, eventually reaching an estimated 50 miles per hour on the 1 in 145 downgrade. Lichfield was 3¼ miles from Hammerwich. The verdict was 'accidental death', and no conclusion could be reached as to why the guard had not performed his duty.

The *Walsall Advertiser* of 8th April, 1911 reported a particularly spectacular incident:

RAILWAY SMASH
WALSALL DRIVER AND FIREMAN INJURED IN WEDNESBURY ACCIDENT

A serious railway collision, in which two Walsall men were injured, one severely, occurred near Wednesbury Station (LNWR), about four o'clock on Wednesday morning [*5th April*] near the spot where about a year ago, a signal box was demolished and a man killed. Considerable shunting operations take place hereabouts, and it appears that for some reason or other ten waggons had been left foul of the main line, and a goods train, which was proceeding from Great Bridge in the direction of Walsall, had been given the 'line clear' signal. A violent collision occurred, the force of which sent the trucks against the brickwork of the bridge which spans the line. The railway engine was nearly turned round, the front of the engine lying more in the direction from which the train came, and with the wreckage lying about in all directions and twisted rails, the scene presented a remarkable spectacle.

The driver of the engine, Harry Cater (55), of 151, Whitehall-road, Walsall, and the fireman, Robert Souster, of 81, Dora-street, Walsall, who it is stated jumped from the engine on realising that a collision was imminent, were both injured, and removed to the Walsall Hospital. Here it was found that Cater was in a serious condition, suffering from several injuries to the head, but Souster was not so badly hurt, and after being attended to proceeded home.

Mr. Morcomb (the district superintendent), Mr. Guest (assistant superintendent, of Birmingham), Inspector Cooper (of the Permanent Way Department, Walsall), Inspector Blakemore, and Mr. Stevens (the Wednesbury stationmaster) were early on the scene of the accident. The passenger service had to be worked on the up line, but traffic was resumed on the down line during the day. Large numbers of people visited the scene.

Clearly, the cause was human error on the part of the shunter(s) and signalmen.

Moving to more modern times, on 6th February, 1963 Rushall level crossing was the scene of an accident involving a car and a 34 wagon freight train. The brakes of the car, driven by a Mr Robert Wright (52) had failed, and it smashed through the crossing gates and became stuck across both of the running lines. The freight train reduced the car to scrap, but fortunately both the car driver and the engine driver escaped injury. Apparently, the signalman, seeing the incident unfold in front of him, and fearing that the lorry would derail the freight train, took the only course open to him, and threw himself out of the rear window of the signal box!

The aftermath of the accident at Wednesbury LNWR station on 5th April, 1911 as described in the text. The locomotive appears to be a Webb 2-4-2T or an 0-6-2 'Coal Tank', most probably the latter in view of the goods wagons, the first of which seems to belong to the MR. From the track layout, the exact location is likely to have been beneath the bridge carrying the GWR Birmingham to Wolverhampton line.   *Bill Mayo Collection*

The next three photographs show the result of the accident on 5th July, 1963 at Rushall Crossing when a two-car Derby Lightweight dmu travelling from Burton to Wolverhampton collided with a lorry carrying coke. Remarkably, there were no serious injuries to anyone on the train, or to the lorry driver.
R. Selvey

Shortly after, on Friday 5th July, 1963 another accident occurred at this place, as reported in the *Walsall Observer* a week later :

On Friday night the passengers of a Wolverhampton bound diesel train on the Walsall-Lichfield line had miraculous escapes when it smashed into a lorry on the Rushall level crossing.

The lorry, which was completely wrecked, was carried fifty yards along the line, crashing into a gate on the Walsall side, and strewing its 15 ton load of coke on to the tracks.

Seconds before, the driver of the lorry, James Tracey (37) of The Gables, Poplar Street, Norton Canes, leapt to safety as the lorry's brakes failed on approaching the gates, with the train only 500 yards away.

Mr. Tracey and only one train passenger, Mrs. Margaret Hawkesworth, of Osborne Court, Calais Road, Burton on Trent, were taken to hospital. Mrs. Hawkesworth was treated for a slight leg injury. No one else was hurt.

The train driver, Mr. J.W. Jones (64) of The Broadway, Codsall, escaped with a cut finger.

Rails were buckled for 75 yards and sleepers ripped up as the leading coach left the rails. The driver's cab was torn open, and windows along one side were ripped open.

Such incidents continue to this day, and although in these cases the road user can hardly be blamed if his brakes failed, there are still many occurrences of road users ignoring the warning signs or lights at level crossings - not only to their own peril, but also to that of the railwaymen involved.

Venerable Johnson '1282' class 2-4-0 LMS No. 157 moving off from Ryecroft shed in August 1936. It was the first of the class, MR No. 1282, and was built by Dübs & Co of Glasgow (Works No. 910) and had 6 ft 6 in. driving wheels. It was renumbered by Deeley as No. 157 in 1907, which it retained as shown here. Its LMS number 20157 was applied shortly afterwards, but it was withdrawn in December 1939.   *E. Talbot Collection*

Johnson MR '483' class 4-4-0 No. 40364 arrives in Lichfield City station with a local passenger train composed of LMS non-corridor stock from the Walsall direction on 16th April, 1956. Lichfield City No. 1 signal box is at the end of the well-tended platform. This engine was built at Derby in 1924 under Fowler to replace an earlier engine, and was withdrawn two months after the photograph.   *Author's Collection*

Chapter Nine

Midland Railway Influences

That the MR was interested in the area served by the SSR is illustrated by its shareholding in the original SSR company, and its representation on the Board of Directors. But following the lease of the line, it did not actually obtain any running rights over the SSR system until the subsequent LNWR years. These were given in three parts. Firstly, having conceded to the LNWR the running powers over MR tracks to Burton (and eventually Derby) in 1861, reciprocal rights were given to the MR for goods trains to run from Wichnor to Dudley, although this did not occur until 1st September, 1867. To service these workings the MR built its own four-road goods shed at Dudley and a further structure alongside the Walsall Canal wharf at Great Bridge. This was sited just south of the original SSR goods shed, on the north side of the Tipton Road bridge, and was used right up until BR days. A further goods shed was built at Walsall at this time, but curiously was a much smaller single-road structure, sited on the east side of the station, and subsequently taken over by the LNWR.

Secondly, the Wolverhampton & Walsall Railway opened from Wolverhampton High Level to Walsall via Wednesfield and Ryecroft Junction on 1st November, 1872. Unusually, it was worked by the LNWR and MR individually for the first month, and then from 1st December by the LNWR alone, although the MR retained running powers. However, on 1st July, 1875 this railway was vested in the LNWR, who thereafter worked the line. But this only lasted for one year, as on 1st July, 1876 it was sold to the MR, who started running the trains from the beginning of the following month. So the MR had finally gained another foothold at Walsall. In the original Act for this line, running powers were also given to the GWR to run goods services from Wolverhampton (using the spur from Low Level to Heath Town Junction) to Walsall. These powers were used from the outset, and a review of Working Timetables disclosed that the service consisted of two trains each way per weekday, one in the morning around 6.00 am and one in the late afternoon, around 5.00 pm, although times did vary somewhat. A third service was introduced in 1883, running as required around midday. By May 1920 the morning train continued, but the afternoon working ran only on Tuesdays, Thursdays and Fridays, with the conditional working being discontinued. Each of these gave a layover at Walsall of between 30 minutes and one hour, so allowing for shunting there was presumably no time to visit either shed for locomotive servicing. It is believed that the locomotives used were the Dean 0-6-0STs and later 0-6-0PTs by Churchward and Collett. The service is believed to have ceased during World War II, although no firm date has been traced.

Thirdly, a line from Castle Bromwich to Walsall, via Sutton Park, was promoted by the MR as the Wolverhampton, Walsall & Midland Junction Railway. This line opened for goods traffic on 1st January, 1879 and passenger traffic on the following 1st July. This gave the MR its third set of running powers into Walsall, again from Ryecroft. The initial service consisted of four trains each way from Water Orton, and eight from New Street station, rivalling the LNWR service. A direct line between these two railways, avoiding Walsall, and running from Walsall North Junction to Lichfield Road Junction was opened at the same time.

By the 1870s, as we have already seen, Walsall station was becoming overcrowded with rail traffic. The remedy was a series of major engineering and structural works that were to last from 1879 until 1883. Those relating to the MR were included in the MR Act of 1877 (Vict. 40 & 41, cap. 44) wherein Section 4 authorized the construction of the MR goods depot, carriage sidings and engine sheds. Section 38 of the same Act extended the time for the completion of the north-facing junction at Water Orton to 6th August, 1878, thus creating a triangular junction with the MR Birmingham to Derby line.

In 1875 at Walsall, the MR purchased the former racecourse situated a little to the south of the station, on the up side. This area was used for the construction of a new goods yard and a large goods shed with but a single road passing through, which opened on 1st July, 1879. In anticipation of these events, the MR had withdrawn its goods services from Wichnor to Walsall as from 19th May of that year, thereafter running from Walsall to Dudley. The goods depot remained in use until the area alongside Midland Road was redeveloped for the new goods depot in 1962.

The MR laid its own independent lines from the goods yard for about ½ mile further south to just short of the Corporation Street overbridge, where it created its own three-road engine shed, with a standard MR wooden coaling plant approached by a lengthy ramp for the coaling trucks, and turntable in the yard of 50 ft diameter. It was generally known as Pleck shed, but locally it was also often referred to as New Mills. The building measured 220 ft by 48 ft, and was constructed of red brick, with single gable-ended slated roof. All three roads terminated inside the building, although one was originally planned to pass through. Alongside, and next to the main running lines were three carriage sidings. The shed was constructed to hold 12 engines of the time, but the initial complement was only nine, comprising six 0-4-4Ts, an 0-6-0T (No. 1417), and two 2-4-0s (Nos. 86 and 120). By 1892 there were still only six passenger tanks, by then accompanied by four 0-6-0s. The parent depot for the shed was Saltley, and so Pleck was coded 3B in MR days. As might be expected, following the Grouping much rationalization took place, and the shed closed on 2nd September, 1925, its allocation moving to the former LNWR depot at Ryecroft. However, that was not the end for the building, which was thereafter used for carriage storage and maintenance, lasting well into BR days in this role. Eventually it became redundant, and was left empty for several years whilst a further use or potential lessee could be found. However, it caught fire in 1984, and was subsequently demolished as being in a dangerous condition. The site remains unused.

In 1881 the LNWR had opened the Pleck curve and a new curve linking the former GJR route at Portobello to the WWR route at Heath Town, thus providing a faster route between Walsall and Wolverhampton. We have already seen that this resulted in a gradual reduction, and finally elimination of Walsall to Wolverhampton services travelling via Wednesbury and the Princes

End branch. This had the additional benefit of reducing some of the traffic over the congested Stour Valley route south of Wolverhampton. But this also meant that it was further in competition with the MR for traffic between these towns.

From 1st January, 1909 the MR and LNWR invoked an agreement for the rationalization of duplicate services. It had been realised that some competitive lines simply produced losses for both competitors, whereas a sharing of routes could eliminate such wasteful practices. This agreement involved the sharing of the two routes between Wolverhampton and Walsall, such that trains from both companies were likely to appear on each other's routes. This had the additional benefit that trains could travel into Walsall by one route, and return by the other, thus eliminating the need for reversal. The level of services offered at this time is covered in Chapter Seven. This practice lasted until 5th January, 1931 when the passenger service over the WWR line to Wolverhampton was finally withdrawn.

Goods traffic was immensely important to the MR, as indicated by the erection of goods sheds at Walsall, Great Bridge and Dudley. A review of the Working Timetables shows a substantial pattern of goods workings, as follows:

Between	*November 1885*		*July 1898*	
	Up	Down	Up	Down
Weekdays				
Walsall and Wednesbury	1	2	0	1
Walsall and Great Bridge	2	2 MO	1	2
Walsall and Dudley	1	2	4	4
Dudley and Wednesbury	2	1	1	0
Dudley and Water Orton	3	2	1	1
Great Bridge and Water Orton	1 MO	1	0	0
Great Bridge and Wednesbury	1 + 1 MO	0	0	0
Sundays				
Walsall and Great Bridge	1	1	0	0
Walsall and Dudley	0	0	1	1

MO = Mondays only.

The rationalization agreement of January 1909 also extended to goods services, and meant that the MR goods services from Walsall to Dudley were withdrawn. As a result, any MR goods traffic still arriving at Walsall and intended for the Dudley line, was handed over to the LNWR for onward movement.

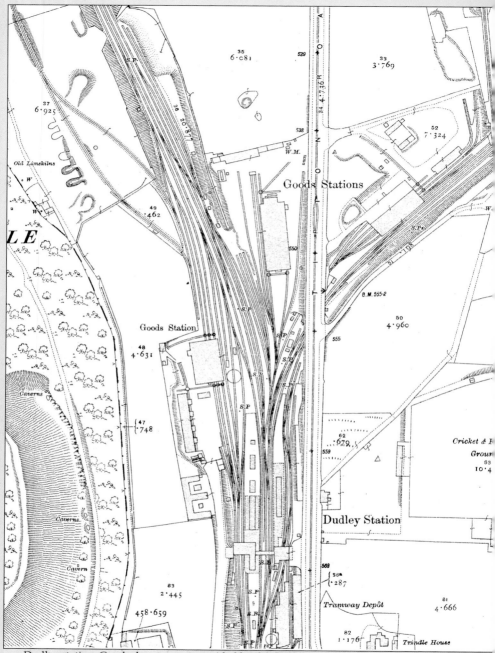

Dudley station. Goods depots were provided by the GWR (*centre left*), LNWR (*centre upper*), MR (*centre right*), with the small building to the right of the latter being the original SSR structure. The first and second SSR passenger stations were sited almost opposite this goods shed.

Reproduced from the 25", 1919 Ordnance Survey map

Chapter Ten

Description of the Line

Dudley was an enclave of Worcestershire, an island in the sea of Staffordshire until the boundary changes of the 1970s, when it became part of the new county of the West Midlands. The town's history is closely related to the castle, whose remains, some dating from the 14th century, dominate the skyline as it is approached from the south and the west. The castle became a favourite place for working class families to relax during the Victorian times, and was further enhanced by the opening of Dudley Zoo in 1937. As we have already seen these twin attractions proved to be worthwhile destinations for thousands of visitors from across the East and West Midlands, as well as further afield, arriving in special excursion trains for many years. Doubtless, first time visitors would have wondered where they were going as they approached the town through the heavily industrialized area: iron and steel works, foundries, heavy machine shops, ribbons of canals and other railway lines. For Dudley was known as the 'Capital of the Black Country' - a title it still proudly proclaims.

The SSR was the first main line railway to arrive in Dudley, in 1849 as we have seen. The OWWR line, passing through on its way from Worcester, Kidderminster and Stourbridge to Wolverhampton did not arrive until 20th December, 1852. The temporary and permanent stations built in 1849, 1850, 1855 and 1859 are dealt within Chapter Six, along with a description of the disastrous fire of 1889, which resulted in the final station rebuilding. The location of the station was determined by the geography of the area, being located partly in a deep brick-lined cutting, provided intending visitors to the town centre with a stiff uphill walk. This meant that the entrance to the later SSR station was at a high level in Tipton Road, where the entrance also included a booking office and parcels office. The exterior was originally panelled in wood, but was reclad with corrugated asbestos sheet in the 1950s.This led to a lengthy footbridge of lattice iron construction, infilled with wood panelling, and glazed upper half, surmounted by a slated gabled roof, that connected to the GWR station. This also featured a short tower at the Tipton Road end, topped by a pitched tiled roof, that was strangely out of keeping with the rest of the buildings. A tall brick-built goods lift was positioned on the south side of the footbridge, and the passenger steps to the platform were given a wooden enclosure. Sometime in the 1930s the SSR (LNWR/LMS) booking office was closed, and the GWR booking hall at the opposite end of the footbridge was utilized for all tickets, with separate ticket windows for GWR and LMS passengers. The working arrangement within the booking hall was such that separate staff were employed for each of the windows, but certainly in LMS days they had to be familiar with each other's procedures to allow for interchangeability at certain times. For example by the late 1930s there was only one clerk on duty in the very early morning and after 6.00 pm. Nonetheless, the requisite tickets could only be issued from the appropriate company window, so it was not unusual for passengers to be asked to go to the next window, only to be met by the same

Ex-LNWR class '7F' 0-8-0 No. 49077 struggles through Dudley station with a southbound goods, as steam escapes from its leaking glands, on 18th October, 1952. *F.W. Shuttleworth*

Bowen-Cooke '7F' class 0-8-0 No. 49361 steams through Dudley station on 4th June, 1963. The sidings below the retaining wall in the background are on the site of the LNWR engine and carriage sheds, demolished during World War II. *M.A. King*

clerk! This procedure was eventually simplified with the outbreak of World War II, and under a new arrangement with the GWR the ticket office was manned entirely by LMS staff thereafter.

The SSR station comprised a single island platform, which whilst convenient for SSR trains, was operationally awkward for the GWR trains from Birmingham Snow Hill arriving over the BWDR route from Swan Village and Great Bridge South. For they had to discharge their passengers at the SSR platform, then run across several lines before returning to the GWR platform for their return journey. But the return journey required the train to be firstly reversed out of the platform in order to gain the down through line, and thus be able to reach the SSR line northwards. The SSR island platform featured brick-built staff rooms, waiting rooms and toilets, that were protected by a long overall canopy reaching almost the entire length of the platform, and incorporating the usual decorative edges. Four tall brick-built chimneys protruded through the canopy from the fires in the rooms below, where they had hopefully warmed the passengers and staff during the cold Winter months.

A portion of the original 1850 up platform survived at the north end, against the cutting wall, in use as a parcels platform until closure. At the southern end, the lines continued to a site firmly against the high brick-lined cutting, where a small locomotive shed was erected. On 8th August, 1865 John Ramsbottom (LNWR locomotive superintendent) was authorized to build 'a small shed for (2) engines ... with covering also for two trains of carriages'. The shed was an irregular-shaped building of three terminal roads, but by the 'Grouping' it seems that it was unusual for there to be more than one engine stabled there. This was normally the engine working the 'Dasher' to Dudley Port, which was cleaned and oiled by a cleaner from Ryecroft shed, who arrived on the last train of the day, and left on the first train the following morning. His duties also included knocking up the local driver and fireman, some of whom lived a good distance away. As there was no facility for coaling of the locomotive at Dudley, the engine from the 'Dasher' changed duties with the engine and stock from the Cannock line at Ryecroft during the afternoon, so that it could be coaled ready for its duties the following day. The shed closed as a wartime economy measure in 1941, and was demolished shortly afterwards. A turntable was located on the western side of the shed, and this too disappeared around the time the shed was closed. Afterwards, the sidings remained and were used for carriage and wagon storage.

The 1889 GWR station was of more generous dimensions, and entirely of brick construction, suspended over the three running lines on the western side. The entrance from Station Road was at a high level, as on the SSR/LNWR side, leading directly to the booking hall and footbridge. Once more, generous canopies were provided on the platform, and a small bay platform was included on the western side of the southern half of the platform. At the end of this platform a standard GWR signal box (Dudley South) protected the entrance to the tunnel. This closed in 1967 along with the other GWR signal box (Dudley North) and the LNWR No. 1 box (later Dudley East) by the Tipton Road bridge. These were replaced by a new box on the eastern side of the line next to the junction of the former SSR and OWWR lines, which opened on 16th July, 1967.

A view of the area once occupied by the LNWR engine and carriage sheds at Dudley. The GWR Dudley South signal box, situated at the south end of the former GWR station platform controlled all movements south towards Stourbridge.   *M.A. King*

Dudley South signal box viewed from the eastern side on 4th June, 1963 with the Castle Hill road bridge immediately behind, and the tunnel beneath the town in the background.   *M.A. King*

An earlier LNWR box (No. 2) had been located at the south end of the SSR platform, but closed on 13th January, 1935 and was replaced by a ground frame giving access to the engine shed sidings.

The original SSR goods shed, north of Tipton Road, was closed and demolished just after World War II, although its use by that time had become somewhat limited. The adjacent five-road, former MR goods depot was named 'Dudley Town' by the LMS, and continued to function, along with the later LNWR goods depot for some time into BR days, but that too succumbed, and the site was taken over by a scrap dealer. The LNWR goods depot (described in Chapter Six) then became known as 'Dudley Town', with the nearby WR goods depot becoming 'Dudley Castle' from 19th July, 1950. After the closure of Dudley station on 6th July, 1964 (the former WR section had closed on 15th June) the parcels facilities, formerly undertaken at the station with loading being performed on the remains of the 1850 platform, were gradually transferred to the newly named 'Dudley Town' goods depot. The station, along with the adjacent WR station and the former GWR goods depot were swept away in the redevelopment of the site for the new Freightliner Terminal in 1967 (*see Chapter Five*). The LMR goods depot continued to be used for parcels traffic, and remained intact at least until 1971, although by this date it had almost certainly been disused for some time.

As the line continued out of Dudley northwards, it passed the former MR and original SSR goods depots on the left. Near to this point a further running line was installed, on the up side, which ran the full distance to just south of the Stour Valley line overbridge at Dudley Port, a distance of just over a mile. The purpose was to provide refuge for slow moving goods trains travelling south, which were usually banked up the 1 in 60 gradient. This additional running line could accommodate three goods trains of up to 20 wagons, as well as providing access to the private sidings mentioned below, but was removed in the 1960s.

Next, the line passed beneath a narrow gauge tramway carried on a substantial bridge, the abutments for which remained in place long after the tramway had disappeared. This tramway linked the Castle Fields Limestone Pits of the Earl of Dudley (on the immediate right hand side of the line) to a wharf on the Birmingham Canal Navigation (BCN) at Tipton, close to the present day Black Country Museum, but had gone out of use by 1913. The line continued to descend, passing through an area of quiet desolation, where once there had been numerous shallow coal, iron and limestone workings. The Birmingham New Road was constructed through the middle of this derelict area between 1924 and 1927. So from that date the line crossed over this major highway on an underslung steel girder bridge, just to the north of Burnt Tree Island, a road landmark of some note for its frequent traffic jams.

Immediately on the other side of this bridge was the site of a triangular junction, where single lines had led to the complex of mines, ironworks and brickworks that formed yet more parts of the Earl of Dudley's industrial empire. These were linked between themselves and to the Castle Mill Ironworks further west by a network of narrow gauge tramways. The history of this hive of activity is indeed complex, but the works and lines in this area had generally gone out of use by 1928. The north-facing line of the original triangular connection to the SSR that had fed the Coneygre mines and furnaces

Stanier '8F' class 2-8-0 No. 48713 restarts a southbound freight from a signal check at Sedgeley Junction on a snowy day, 30th November, 1962. Evidently there had been some problem with the signals, perhaps caused by the snow fall, as the signalman has resorted to manual clearance, using a green flag from the signal box. *D. Wilson*

Two class '25' diesels, Nos. 25194 and 25261, approach Dudley Port Low Level from Dudley with an empty steel train on 5th November, 1980. The line to Dudley Port High Level from Sedgeley Junction passed from left to right in front of the houses in the top right corner of the picture. *R. Selvey*

was retained by the firm of Freakley & Sons, who cleared the site of reusable slag over a number of years. This line also led to the large industrial boiler works of Babcock & Wilcox Ltd, which utilized the rail connection until around 1962 using its own locomotive (*see Appendix Four*), and is still in business at this site today.

Now the line passed over the Wolverhampton Level of the BCN, the original canal link from Birmingham to Wolverhampton and the Black Country. On the left could be seen a large reservoir and pumping station belonging to the South Staffordshire Waterworks Company, one of the monuments to John Robinson McClean, whose career will be detailed in Volume Two. A short distance further we reach Sedgeley Junction (⅞ mile), where the famous Palethorpes' factory was located a short distance away on the left, alongside Park Lane West. The company was established by Henry Palethorpe in 1850, and this factory site was built specifically for his meat products, being known as the Model Sausage Factory, opening in 1896. The company siding was, somewhat inconveniently, situated on the opposite side of the line, necessitating movement by road vehicles from the factory. A loading platform was provided alongside the siding, complete with a wooden transhipment shed, approximately 60 feet long. The roof of the shed was cantilevered out to cover partially the rail vehicles and so give protection to the loaders and the goods. The factory continued in production until 1967, at which time a move was made to a new factory, costing £650,000, at Market Drayton (which by that date had no rail facilities). The familiar Palethorpes' railway vans then became just another memory. A substantial LMS-style signal box of brick lower half construction, and timber upper half, with 40 levers, was sited here on the up side, to control the junction, the two southbound loops and the northbound sidings, accessed via a crossover. The box had a gable end, and one of the familiar, and no doubt uncomfortable, outside toilets in a wooden 'sentry box' was located at the top of the stairs. The double track junction to Dudley Port High Level swept off across to the left, climbing through another area once left derelict, but eventually put to good use as allotments, and reached the LNWR Stour Valley Line. A little further north stood a tall distant signal on a lattice iron post that was a familiar sight, until replaced by a colour light signal around 1960. This whole area is now a housing estate.

Meanwhile, our line continued its now easterly direction, past the small Dudley Port Low Level signal box on the right, that guarded the entrance to the up goods loop and passed beneath the Stour Valley line to arrive at Dudley Port Low Level (1¼ miles). The station was located in a cutting and comprised one platform on each side of the line, but was not provided with any goods facilities, as its main function aside from serving the local population was to act as a passenger interchange to the High Level station. Actually the SSR arrived here first, the High Level station not opening until just over two years later, on 1st July, 1852. This in some ways accounts for the lack of cohesion in the two stations, with an unnecessarily complicated arrangement of footpaths and steps connecting the two. The main buildings of the SSR station were sited on the down (northbound) side, and comprised a two-storey brick building of an ornate style with elongated windows on the upper floor. Seven window apertures were included on the south side of the building, but each alternate

The Low Level station at Dudley Port seem from beneath the Stour Valley, and looking north, in the early 1950s. The wooden platform shelter on the up platform was due for replacement, but the remainder of the buildings appear in good order. The small upper sign on the main building on the left proclaims the station name 'Dudley Port', whilst the larger one beneath it reads 'Change here for stations on the Stour Valley line'. The large wooden sign fixed to the wall of the gents, further along the platform, reads 'Trains for Wednesbury and Walsall'. *D. Thompson*

The station buildings at Dudley Port, giving a clear view of the size, and ornate structure of the main building. Taken on 16th November, 1969 the station had been out of use for some four years by then, and is showing signs of its neglect. The replacement concrete footbridge can be seen to good effect, and also the relationship with the High Level station (*top left*) and the Dudley Port signal box (*top right*) for the Stour Valley line. *A. Perks*

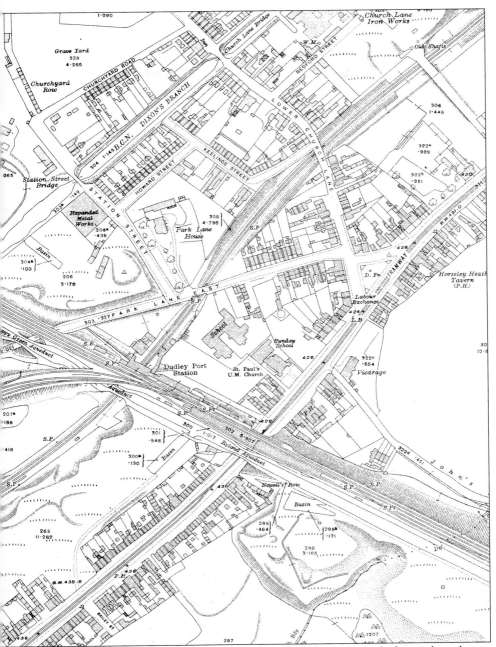

Dudley Port station. Lack of space for the Dudley branch platform, alongside the canal, can be appreciated.
Reproduced from the 25", 1919 Ordnance Survey map

The main station building at Dudley Port Low Level, on the down platform, on 26th May, 1962. The interesting architectural style of the building shows up well in this view, particularly of the windows on the upper floor, with the corresponding blind window recesses. The four chimneys placed one at each corner of the building can be seen protruding through the hipped slated roof. The later gents lavatory is on the right, and on the left is the pathway leading behind the rear of the station to Park Lane East. On the extreme left is the staircase leading to the footbridge and an alternative pedestrian exit.
Historical Model Railway Society/ESR

Stanier class '5' 4-6-0 No. 45385 heads through the cutting to the south of Great Bridge with a haul of coal. It has just passed Horseley Fields Junction, whose signal box can be seen to the left of the splitting signals for the former GWR line to Birmingham.
D. Wilson

one was bricked in. The roof was formed from square-hipped sections each side, giving a central point, and included four tall chimneys, one at each corner. This building included the booking hall, waiting rooms and station master's accommodation. Pedestrian access to the southbound platform was from a short Station Drive, which itself led from the nearby main road, Horseley Heath. However, the up platform contained only a smaller arc-roofed wooden waiting room, which was replaced after World War II by a more substantial building of brick, with a flat roof and containing an enclosed waiting room. A further wooden building also with a rounded roof, and possibly of corrugated iron, was also located on this platform, in use as a store room and lamp hut. Covered steps clad in wood and glass linked the south end of the platform to the northbound platform, and also to a path leading eastwards to the High Level station, and westwards to Park Lane, a few yards away from the station entrance. However, the covered footbridge was removed during the 1950s and replaced by an uncovered concrete structure. Later still, a 'portacabin' type of building provided the only waiting accommodation on the up platform. A sign was positioned on the down side cutting above the platform, which for many years proclaimed 'Dudley Zoo - Next Stop'.

Still in the cutting, the line continued to fall, now at 1 in 254, and moved slightly to face north-east. Immediately after passing beneath the Horseley Road bridge, rows of houses could be seen on the top of the cutting on the right. On the left, the line passed alongside the major engineering works of the world famous bridge builders, Horseley Bridge & Thomas Piggott Ltd (latterly NEI Clarke Chapman-John Thompson Ltd), established here in 1865. A steep single track line led from their works to the SSR just as it passed beneath the road bridge carrying New Road to Toll End. This was worked by their own locomotive from the establishment of the rail link in 1895 until around 1970, although one locomotive was retained for use on purely internal movements until 1982 (see *Appendix Four*). A further line led off this single track to a boat building works situated at the end of the BCN Dixon's branch. But before we reach that point, the GWR line for Great Bridge South, Swan Village and Birmingham Snow Hill swung off to the right at Horseley Fields Junction (1¾ miles), at which the line changed from being in a cutting to riding on an embankment. The signal box to control this junction was sited on the west side of the down line, opposite the junction and was quite unusual in design. It was built by Saxby & Farmer, and installed in 1866 coincidentally with the opening of the GWR line to Swan Village. It was virtually square in shape, with a brick base and vertical wooden boarding to the upper half, and a hipped slated roof. The entrance was positioned in the centre of the northern end of the box. Its situation halfway up the embankment meant that the operating wires and rods had to be inconveniently routed at an angle down to the track level. It was originally provided with an Saxby & Farmer lever frame, but this was replaced in 1886 by an LNWR tumbler frame comprising 18 levers, although this was later reduced to just 12. This ancient box managed to survive until the closure of the GWR line in June 1964.

Still falling, but now at 1 in 100, the line entered the busy confines of Great Bridge station (2⅛ miles), which was renamed Great Bridge North from 1st July,

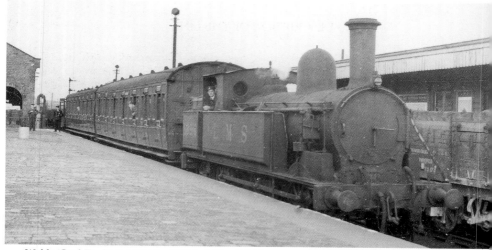

Webb 'Coal Tank' 0-6-2T No. 58916 at Great Bridge, propelling a two-coach motor train from Dudley to Walsall around 1948. The engine has been renumbered following nationalization, but still defiantly retains its LMS initials on the side tanks. It was withdrawn in 1950.

W.A. Camwell

A Webb 5 ft 6 in. 2-4-2T eases into Great Bridge North station in the early 1950s with an autotrain from Walsall to Dudley. At this date the station still retained its LMS yellow 'Great Bridge' nameboards, as affixed to the wooden waiting room on the down platform.

Historical Model Railway Association

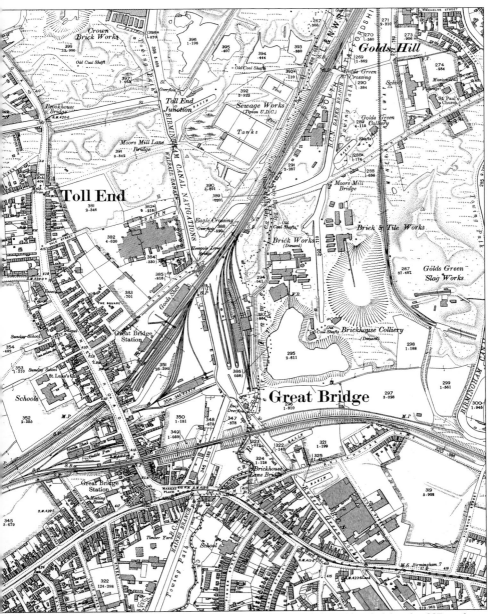

Great Bridge station. The goods yard to the left of the canal was provided by the SSR and enlarged by the LNWR. The goods yard and canal wharf to the right was constructed by the MR. The GWR line from Horseley Fields Junction to Swan Village runs from left to right.

Reproduced from the 25", 1904 Ordnance Survey map

Great Bridge North station in the early 1950s, looking north. Although the platform buildings appear shabby, the station staff were still making an effort with the flower beds on the platforms. The original LNWR goods shed is on the left, and a Fowler 3F 'Jinty' 0-6-0T can be seen in the up goods yard in the centre of the picture. The poster on the end of the waiting shelter advertises Lewis's 'permanent wave' kits for 17s. 6d.   *D. Thompson*

Looking southwards at the closed Great Bridge station in the late 1960s. The signal box in the distance remained in use, and the lattice iron footbridge was surprisingly still complete, along with the water tank and range of simple wooden buildings on the right.   *Lens of Sutton*

1950 to distinguish it from its WR near neighbour, which was also renamed (Great Bridge South) at the same time. An LNWR gable-ended signal box was sited at the south end of the up goods loop, containing a 25-lever tumbler frame. The main station building was a single-storey wooden-panelled structure, with gable-ended tiled roof. A water tank was mounted on a brick base that also saw duty as a store room, and was located near the lattice iron footbridge at the south end of the platform. The tank supplied the water cranes positioned at each end of the platforms. Three small wooden stores were positioned along the down platform, although a further brick-built structure was provided in LMS days and lasted until closure. The southbound platform was edged with a brick wall at the rear to separate it from the goods relief line that passed behind, and contained a solitary building. This was a brick-built waiting room, with wood panelling to the front, on which was mounted a flat roof that cantilevered forward as an awning over the platform to give some small protection to passengers, and finished with the usual feather edge vertical boards. Both platform surfaces were of brick, and were illuminated by a range of ornate gas lamps, as was the station approach lane. The whole station had an air of meanness about it, and by the time of closure in 1964 was especially uninviting.

At the north end of the down platform was a large brick-built goods shed, with one through road (originally two roads with a central internal loading platform). This was also originally served by two wagon turntables at the south end, which led at right angles across the two running lines to the up goods loop, where a further turntable was located. This very questionable and potentially dangerous arrangement lasted well into LNWR days, although hopefully the LNWR did their best not to use it! The bracket for the down starter was fixed to the side of the goods shed alongside the running line, instead of the signal being mounted on its own post. Behind the goods shed, to the west, a single siding led alongside Eagle Road. To the east of the up goods relief line lay a yard of some six terminal sidings, where engines could often be found stabled in between banking duties on the heavy coal trains from there to Dudley. A small engine shed was provided in this area, in use probably from around 1870 to 1910. Further eastwards three more loop sidings led to a headshunt, from which five further sidings led to a canal basin and the MR goods and transhipment shed.

Immediately to the north of the main goods shed, the line started a short ascent at 1 in 60 to cross the Walsall Canal of the BCN on a bridge carrying four running lines, then easing to 1 in 500 and eventually to 1 in 627 and then 1 in 3440. A 28-lever frame signal box , Eagle Crossing (2¾ miles), was located at this point to control access to another north-facing goods yard on the up side that contained up to 10 tracks around the various unloading bays, transhipment sheds, and alongside wharves on the other side of the Walsall Canal (of 1794) from the first-mentioned wharf. A massive Goliath crane was positioned in this yard, and one track passed beneath it. The original 28-lever box was replaced in 1970 by another of modern BR wooden square style with an overhanging flat roof to provide an overall awning. This new box also replaced the boxes at Horseley Fields Junction, Great Bridge, and Golds Hill Crossing, opening on 20th December of that year. In its turn, this box was closed as from 14th December, 1975 due to elimination of sidings connections. Just beyond the Eagle Crossing box, the line then crossed the

Former LNWR 0-8-0 No. 49126 plods along southwards at Eagle Crossing around 1962, with a local goods working to Dudley. *D. Wilson/R.S. Carpenter*

Ivatt class '2' 2-6-2T No. 41279 passes over Eagle Crossing, just north of Great Bridge, with a two-coach push-pull working from Walsall to Dudley on 25th May, 1951. The two goods loops on the right continued over the crossing, meaning that shunting there caused the gates to be closed to road traffic for lengthy periods. Fortunately, the road was not a major highway. *Historical Model Railway Society/ESR*

BR class '25' Bo-Bo diesel-electric No. 7630 shunting a local trip working at Eagle Crossing in the early 1970s. The signal box was a new construction here, opening on 20th December, 1970, replacing four local boxes.
D. Wilson/R.S. Carpenter

English Electric class '37' No. 37051 is seen at Eagle Crossing, near to Great Bridge, with a train of steel pipes on 25th June, 1991.
R. Selvey

Danks branch of the BCN (authorized by an Act of 1783), continuing as a stretch of quadruple track, passed a large sewage works on the left, and then recrossed the Danks branch, at which point the line became double once more. This canal has since been filled in. A short distance further on, a mineral line came in from the right, facing north. This had originally led to the Golds Green and Brickhouse collieries and Golds Green Furnaces and Golds Hill Ironworks of John Bagnall & Sons Ltd. However, when these were worked out by 1882, the slag heaps were taken over by John Freakley & Sons, for the reclamation of reusable materials, primarily for road building. Eventually the northern end of the line was used as the site for the scrapyard activities of John Cashmore Ltd, and became infamous as the last resting place for many former BR steam locomotives. It used its own locomotives for the shunting of incoming loads until well into the 1970s (*see Appendix Four*).

Now the line ran on the level for ¼ mile, crossing fairly flat and obviously overworked industrial landscape, reaching Golds Hill Crossing (2¾ miles), the site of a level crossing converted into a road underbridge, but retaining its signal box as a block post. This was another LNWR style gable-ended box with red brick base, with a wood and glazed upper half (20-lever tumbler frame), located on the up side, south of the crossing. Immediately after, the line crossed yet another canal, this time the Tame Valley Canal of the BCN and then continued on its straight north-east course on an embankment. The same rather desolate landscape is actually the result of being the original flood plain of the River Tame, and known locally as the Monway Fields which were sourced for clay used in the local earthenware industry. As the line passed over this small river, it started a gradual descent and turned further to the right to head in a more easterly direction. On the right a single siding from the up line led to the works of the Hill Top Foundry Co. Ltd, who used their own locomotive (*see Appendix Four*) purely for the positioning of wagons containing coke and pig iron for unloading. Almost immediately, the Princes End line (*see Chapter Three*)

Eagle level crossing and signal box, before the track was rationalized in this area, and the LMS box was replaced in 1970 with one on the opposite side of the line. Compare to photographs on the previous two pages.   *K. Hodgkins*

swung in from the left, followed in rapid succession by the chord and exchange sidings from the GWR route from Snow Hill to Wolverhampton. A lengthy lattice iron footbridge spanned these tracks, providing a right of way across the railway at this point. The GWR line passed over our line and the adjacent tracks leading to the exchange sidings, on two steel plate bridges, and is now the route of the Midland Metro. A large LNWR gable-ended signal box ('Wednesbury No. 1') with a 50-lever tappet frame was located on the northern side of the line between the GWR overline bridge and the Potters Lane level crossing, to control the junctions for the Princes End line and the exchange sidings, as well as the crossing. In front of the box, a further line was formed, which ran through the station as an independent line (the 'Middle Siding') between the two platform lines, and could be worked in either direction. The up goods loop, passing behind the up platform, continued well past the Princes End line junction. Thus, the level crossing was noticeably wide, having to span four running lines.

The first Wednesbury station (3½ miles), opening with the line, was positioned immediately adjacent to the Potters Lane crossing, so as to provide pedestrian access. However, the opening of the Darlaston loop (*see Chapter Three*), necessitated a remodelling of the track layout, and reconstruction of the station slightly further east, so as to provide platforms for that line. This later station, opening on 1st September, 1863 was renamed Wednesbury Town on 13th June, 1960. The main buildings were on the down platform, which formed a 'V' shape with the northbound Darlaston platform, and included the usual waiting rooms, toilets and staff rooms in a single-storey structure of red brick with cream stonework surrounds to the windows and doors, and hipped slated roofs. A footbridge led across the line to the southbound platform which contained a similar range of buildings in the same style, with a second storey capped by a slated hipped tower, where the footbridge entered at the upper level. The tower also contained a parcels lift, which gave access to the single-road parcels depot situated behind the platform wall. A further siding led from the up goods relief line to a large, black wooden store that was part of the timber merchant's premises belonging to C.W. Graham. The fully-enclosed footbridge was of lattice iron construction finished with wood panelling and half-glazed. It continued across the Darlaston lines to give access to the entrance from Ford Street. This entrance building actually comprised two hipped-roof buildings, incorporating the booking hall, a parcels office and other staff rooms. An attractive partly-glazed awning over the street entrance completed the ensemble. 'Wednesbury No. 2' box was of a somewhat squat shape, with a hipped slated roof. It was sited on the up side, between the up goods loop and the up platform line, opposite the Darlaston line junction, and contained a Webb 36-lever tumbler frame. This box controlled the arrivals and departures at the northern end of the station, and those for the Darlaston loop. Both of the signal boxes closed on 27th March, 1965.

The station was situated quite conveniently for the town centre, which rose above it, and was notable for the two churches of St Bartholomew (Anglican) and St Mary's (Roman Catholic) at the top of the hill (now Church Hill) which can still be seen from miles around. St Bartholomew's was first mentioned in 1201, and although the present church incorporates traces of 13th century

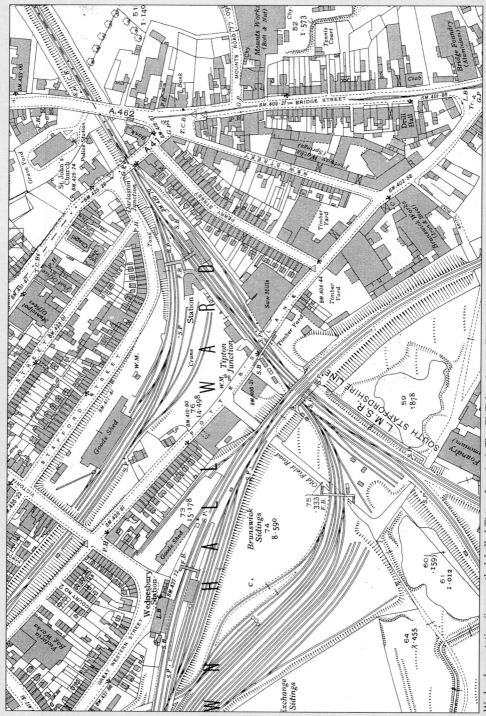

Wednesbury station (incorrectly labelled Tipton Junction). The GWR line (originally BWDR) from Wolverhampton to Birmingham crosses from left to lower

Wednesbury station in the early 1950s viewed from the northern end, clearly showing the branch line to Darlaston veering off to the right. The platform for this line seems to have been partly reduced to rubble even at this time. The up goods relief line passes to the left, behind the up platform, where an autotrain from Walsall to Dudley is taking on passengers. The full extent of the footbridge and range of the station buildings on the down platform can be appreciated in this view.   *D. Thompson*

Wednesbury Town station looking towards Dudley in the early 1960s. The No. 2 signal box is seen in the foreground, at the northern end of the up platform. Some of the architectural features of the buildings on this platform are shown.   *R.S. Carpenter Collection*

Wednesbury looking north, with the bridge carrying the GWR line from Birmingham Snow Hill to Wolverhampton Low Level framing former LNWR '7F' class 0-8-0 No. 49361, which is standing alongside Wednesbury No. 1 signal box.   *R.S. Carpenter*

Ivatt class '2' 2-6-2T No. 41223 stands at the platform at Wednesbury station with a push-pull working from Dudley to Walsall in the mid-1950s. The station buildings behind, and at street level in the background, seem to include rather a lot of chimneys.   *R.S. Carpenter*

English Electric Bo-Bo diesels Nos. 20177 and 20171 leave the loop line at Great Bridge with a mixed load of steel and coal, probably bound for the Round Oak steelworks, on 3rd June, 1980. The station platforms had been totally removed by this date. *R. Selvey*

architecture, it dates mainly from around 1500 and was largely restored in the 19th century. The Catholic church dates from 1872, replacing an earlier structure. The hill had been chosen by the early pagan settlers as a settlement, who gave it the name from 'Woden' (the Norse god) and 'Bury' (meaning 'fort'). Thus it is likely that the hill included a defended settlement, and probably a temple to Woden. The town was mentioned in the Domesday Book of 1086, and the medieval town centre grew around High Bullen to comprise the church, a manor house and a few dwellings. Pottery was made here from the 17th century, and brickmaking continued as a logical extension until the 20th century. The white clay from the Monway Fields was also used to make clay tobacco pipes. From medieval times coal mining also took place, which helped to give rise to nail making, from which the local industry for bolts, screws and fasteners developed, further diversifying into a whole range of metal products including edge tools and tubes. Canals had reached Wednesbury in 1785, and in succeeding years various other branches were opened, eventually being linked in 1794 to provide a route to Walsall known as the 'Walsall Canal'.

Just beyond the station the line passed beneath the Holyhead Road, which had been a turnpike road from 1766 on the main coaching route from London to Shrewsbury, but was rebuilt and straightened by Thomas Telford in the 1820s, thus avoiding the town centre. Beyond this bridge the line entered a deep cutting for nearly a mile, as it approached the area of Mesty Croft (4¼ miles) alternating between rising and falling gradients. Here an up goods loop and one siding was provided in 1917, just near to where the South Staffordshire Waterworks Company had sited the Crankall pumping station, on the left,

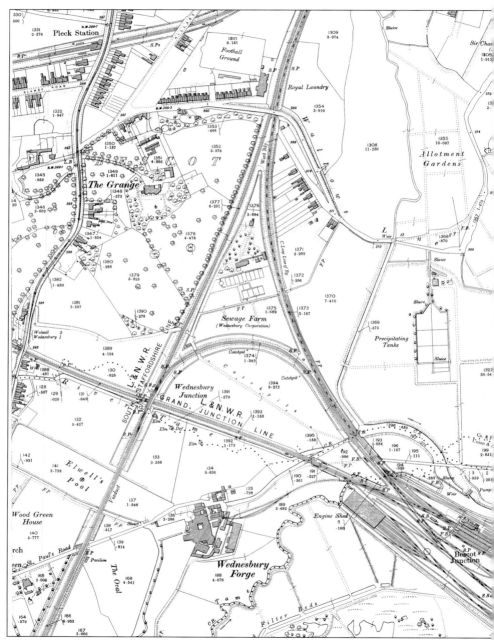

Pleck station (*top*) and Bescot curve (*centre*). Bescot LNWR locomotive shed is prominent at bottom right.

Reproduced from the 25″, 1901 Ordnance Survey map

together with rail access of one siding from the down line. These were controlled by a small signal box of LNWR design entirely in wood, containing a 10-lever Webb's tumbler frame, and located at the entrance to the up loop, on the eastern side of the line.

Continuing in a straight, north-easterly direction, the line left the cutting and ran on to an embankment as it approached the Wood Green area. To the right would be glimpsed the edge tool works of Edward Elwell, known as Wednesbury Forge, dating from around 1600, when Lord Comberford, Lord of the Manor of Wednesbury, first established a forge on the site. Next came the crossing of Elwell's Pool, on a 10-arch brick viaduct. This viaduct was originally constructed by the SSR of wood, but was rebuilt at a later date, and even the replacement displayed signs of strengthening over the years, as the result of movement in this rather marshy area. The pool was actually filled in shortly after World War I, and the bridge was subsequently replaced by a four-arch brick structure, still standing today. Just over a hundred yards later, the line crossed over the original GJR line from Birmingham to Manchester and Liverpool that had opened in 1837. The bridge over the GJR route was entirely replaced during the electrification works of the 1970s by a concrete and steel structure now carrying the mothballed double track SSR line. Immediately on the other side came the junction known as Bescot Curve, where a chord linked to the Walsall to Bescot line. Bescot Curve Junction box (5 miles), with a 20-lever Webb's tumbler frame was sited at the junction, on the down side, and was entirely of wooden construction, with a slated gable roof, and toilet outside at the top of the steps. The site of this junction is today directly beneath the elevated portion of the M6 motorway. In the centre of the triangle formed by these lines was a sewage works, one of many in this area. The view to the left of the line was much more pleasant, looking across the grounds of The Grange towards Bescot Hall, and the railway was lined with trees as a screen for the noble residents all the way to the road bridge at Wallows Lane. Immediately on the other side of this road bridge, on the left, was the original Walsall FC stadium.

Here the main line from Birmingham via Bescot came in on the right, running parallel for about ¼ mile until reaching Pleck Junction (5½ miles), where the chord connecting to the northern section of the original GJR route swept in on the left. The first two lines actually met at a ladder junction just before this second junction. The whole area was controlled from Pleck Junction signal box, on the right of the line in front of the overbridge carrying Wednesbury Road. This large signal box of LNWR design contained 64 levers in a Webb's tumbler frame, and apart from controlling the junction also controlled the lines leading to the MR engine shed and carriage sidings immediately to the north of the bridge, and the sidings on the opposite (left) side of the line. Two reception loops led via a headshunt to the Pleck gas works, where their locomotives could be seen fussing about with wagons of coal, coke and ash from around 1883 (although the works had actually opened in 1877) until rail traffic ceased in 1969 shortly after production had ceased; see *Appendix Four* for details of the locomotives. The reception sidings also led northwards to a group of lengthy sidings, curving round the western perimeter of the Queen Street cemetery, used by the LNWR and later BR Permanent Way Department for their

Construction of the M6 motorway on 15th October, 1964. The site is Bescot North Curve Junction, with the signal box of that name directly beneath the elevated motorway, and alongside the junction itself. This box was removed following the opening of the new Walsall power signal box at Pleck Junction in the following year.   *R. Shenton*

The Bescot Curve Junction became almost subterranean when the M6 was built, as shown in this view from 19th March, 1993. A class '37' diesel with a train of steel products has just traversed the curve from the Bescot yards to join the SSR route southwards, and is seen having just crossed the original GJR route, just beyond the overhead M6 viaduct.   *R. Selvey*

departmental vehicles, and included a stocking ground of permanent way materials. One line from these sidings continued across Rolling Mill Street for rail traffic to the Cyclops Iron Works and Alma Tube Works of John Russell & Co. Ltd, and was worked by horses from 1889 and then their own locomotives from 1902 until 1930. The permanent way sidings surrounded a large blue brick building with a slate gable-ended roof, with a complex of two- and three-storey buildings at the north end that had been specifically constructed to house the offices and workshops of the district engineer in LNWR days, probably from the 1883 enlargement. These buildings survived in use for their original purpose until the Summer of 2009, when they were demolished. New structures have since arisen on the same site for use by the Permanent Way Department of Network Rail and its associated contractors.

The responsibilities of the district engineer covered a wide area, varying considerably over the years, and necessitating a dedicated locomotive and inspection saloon. During LMS days these were logically based at the MR shed opposite, but previously were based at Ryecroft, to which they reverted with the closure of the MR shed in 1925, to move again, this time to Bescot in 1958. Locomotives known to have been allocated to these duties include the venerable outside-framed 2-4-0 bearing the LMS No. 20008, and kept in immaculate crimson lake livery as 'Engineer Walsall' from 1937 to June 1942 when it was eventually withdrawn. This engine had been built at Derby in June 1867 as a member of the '156' class carrying No. 106, but as early as June 1879 it was placed on the duplicate list as No. 106A, then rebuilt in May 1881 and returned to duty as No. 106. In June 1895 it was rebuilt again, with its 16½ in. cylinders being replaced by ones of 18'. In December 1907 it was renumbered to 8, and had replacement boilers in 1913, 1923 and 1926. It was 'reconditioned' in December 1933 and received its LMS number in the following May - some 10 years after the Grouping! After the war, one of the LMS-built 4-4-0s of MR design was allocated to this duty, and by the late 1950s, Bescot's Nos. 40646 and 40694 were reserved for the duties, being kept in pristine condition.

Continuing along a rising gradient of 1 in 500 the quadruple track , running here from left to right as the down slow, up slow, down fast and up fast, we passed beneath the Corporation Street West road bridge, and were surrounded by goods yards. On the left were the goods depots of the LNWR and GWR, and on the right further MR yards leading to their goods depots. The MR activities in Walsall were described in Chapter Nine, whilst the development of the other LNWR yards, depots and the station itself were covered in Chapter Five. In the centre of the sidings on the down side was Walsall No. 1 signal box, another typical LNWR style structure, with a gable roof, and containing a 48-lever Webb's tumbler frame. Some 565 yards further north was the imposing Walsall No. 2 box, with a 72-lever Webb's tumbler frame and controlling the yards and approaches at the southern end of the station. Walsall No. 3 box was virtually hidden beneath the reconstructed booking hall at the north end of Walsall station (6¼ miles), sited between the slow and fast lines, and contained a 50-lever Webb's tumbler frame. This, and the Walsall Nos. 1 and 2, and Pleck Junction boxes were all replaced by a new power-operated box at Pleck Junction (known as 'Walsall') as from 3rd April, 1965.

Walsall station. The original (temporary) SSR station was south of Bridgman Street, which itself originally crossed the railway on the level, causing

Walsall is located around a steep limestone hill, and is thought to have originated around the time of Earl Leofric, receiving its first charter in 1159. The church of St Matthew's is mounted on this hill, and although founded by the Normans, the present structure dates from the 13th century, but was mostly rebuilt in the 19th century. The town developed into a market town, but began specializing in the manufacture of saddlery and other leatherware, for which it is still well known. However, the presence of local limestone and coal deposits saw the area develop its metal industries, and the population grew rapidly from 25,674 in 1851, to 46,452 in 1871, and to 86,440 in 1905. Walsall is noted for two of its inhabitants - Sister Dora (who became famous for her unselfish devotion to the sick of the area), and Jerome K. Jerome (author of *Three Men In A Boat*).

As the running lines passed through Walsall station on level track, they were arranged so that the down slow fed into an independent through road (the 'down middle'), then ran into platform 1, from which the 'Cannock Bay' led, at the north end of the platform. The up slow ran through platform 2, and the down fast fed into the 'Middle (or Sutton) Bay' then ran into platform 3. The up fast divided at the north end of the station to run either side of the easternmost island platform, thus serving platforms 4 and 5, and then combined at the south end of the platforms. A double track crossover was provided north of the station, between the Park Street and St Paul's Street bridges. Here the quadruple track continued in a brick-lined cutting all the way to the next overbridge, for Littleton Street, on a short stretch falling at 1 in 65 followed by short climbs at 1 in 103 and 1 in 209. Beyond this, sidings led off to the left to a brewery, and to the right from the Hatherton Sidings to the Oak Tannery, a foundry and a saw mill. Passing beneath the North Street bridge, the large wooden-panelled LMS-style signal box at Ryecroft Junction (7 miles) was seen on the left, containing an LMS 75-lever frame, and controlling the four-way junction, as well as the entrance to the locomotive shed and yard. This box closed from 4th June, 1967 and its duties were taken over by enlargements to the new Walsall power box.

Firstly the line to Walsall North and Wolverhampton via the MR route diverged off to the left climbing steeply, followed by the Cannock and Rugeley line passing beneath the direct line linking the MR Wolverhampton route to its eastward path through Sutton Park to Water Orton. Then on the left was the large 12-road locomotive shed, with the yard containing the coaling plant, water tower, and turntable at the rear. The next divergence was to the right, and was the MR chord linking to the direct MR Water Orton route. This chord ran parallel with our route northwards for some ½ mile, as it climbed to meet the direct line, with both lines passing beneath Mill Lane, a fine vantage point for trains disappearing in different directions at Ryecroft. Finally our line passed beneath the direct line, and just on the other side could be seen the earthworks for a further chord, running from the direct line to join our line northwards, that was in fact never laid. Beyond these earthworks, on the left was the massive Ryecroft Cemetery, and a separate pedestrian entrance was provided at the southern corner, necessitating a lattice iron footbridge over the line, known locally as the 'Sixty Steps'. Ornamental trees were planted around the perimeter of the cemetery, and continued as a pleasant lineside screen as far as the level

A view of the Park Street entrance to Walsall station, dating from around 1912. The Grand Theatre, built in 1890, dominates this busy scene.   *Lens of Sutton*

Looking south in the cutting towards Walsall station on 3rd December, 1963 with the Park Street station entrance visible on the overbridge. The station platforms can be seen beyond the overbridge.   *R. Shenton*

Dramatic smoke effects as a northbound diverted express storms out of Walsall station and alongside Hatherton Road, hauled by an unrecorded rebuilt 'Patriot' 4-6-0 and piloted by Stanier class '5' 4-6-0 No. 44805. The date is believed to be around 1962.   *R. Selvey*

BR class '25/3' Bo-Bo diesel-electric No. 7557 heads northwards out of Walsall station with a rake of empty coal wagons returning to Burton on 28th January, 1971. The multi-storey car park leading to the newly opened Saddlers Centre straddles the line.   *R. Selvey*

Ryecroft Junction signal box in the 1920s. This important box controlled the divergence of four routes, plus the access to Ryecroft engine shed.   *LNWR Society*

In the evening sun, an unidentified Fowler '4F' class 0-6-0 powers a nine-coach excursion, probably returning from Dudley Zoo to the East Midlands, past the site of Ryecroft shed around 1962.   *R. Selvey*

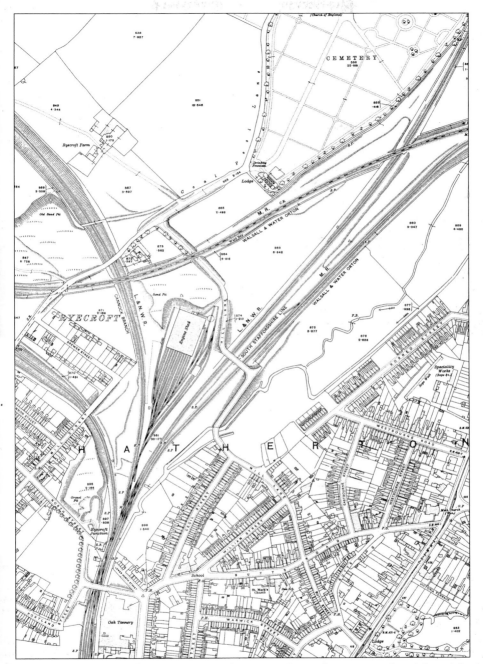

Ryecroft Junction. The MR line from Wolverhampton to Water Orton crosses from left to right here, with the connecting spurs being the lines at extreme left and right. The earthworks of a spur to join the SSR northwards runs just below the cemetery. The Cannock line runs off to the top left.

Reproduced from the 25", 1913 Ordnance Survey map

North of Walsall, the SSR route passed close to the Ryecroft Cemetery, whose margins were marked by a row of trees. A footpath led to the cemetery, passing over the railway by a footbridge which was locally known as the 'Sixty Steps'. This was the vantage point for the photographer as Stanier '5MT' class 4-6-0 No. 44805 passed southwards with a parcels train in 1964.	*R. Selvey*

Rushall Crossing signal box and level crossing looking north, on 4th August, 1975. The station here, closed in 1909, was located on the far side of the level crossing.	*R. Selvey*

crossing at Cartbridge Lane. This was protected by gates operated by a crossing keeper, whose cottage was sited alongside the up line, just south of the crossing.

The line then ran on a gradual climb into a fairly open area, with the Ford Brook over on the right, and into Rushall station (8⅛ miles) where level track was once again reached. This was sited to the north of the level crossing over Coalpool Lane, which was later renamed Station Road, but the station lasted only until 1st March, 1909 closing as another victim of the competition from local tramways and omnibuses. There is scant information on the station itself, but it was popular for visitors to the local pleasure grounds. A signal box was situated on the up side, immediately south of the level crossing, which was under its control, and containing a 20-lever LNWR tumbler frame. This box survived in its role supervising the crossing until the complete closure of the line on 18th March, 1984.

The line continued more or less level in a northerly direction on an embankment, crossing the Ford Brook by way of a culvert, then passing beneath the Walsall to Hednesford road (now B4154) and arriving at Leighswood Sidings (9 miles). There were two reception sidings on the up side, from which the line to Leighs Wood colliery ran (*see Chapter Three*). Directly opposite, on the down side stood the signal box controlling these sidings, which closed in August 1965.

Continuing through quite pleasant countryside, the line crossed Fordbrook Lane on an ornately-panelled wrought-iron bridge to enter Pelsall station (9¾ miles). This comprised one platform on each side of the line, with the station master's accommodation of a two-storey gable-ended brick building on the down platform at right angles to the line. The decorative gable ends were unusually slightly proud of the roof line. A single-storey range of buildings

The view from inside Rushall Crossing signal box as a 'Peak' class diesel heads north with empty steel bogies. The wheel for operating the level crossing gates dominates the foreground. *R. Selvey*

At Leighswood sidings on the SSR route to Brownhills, a footpath crossed the route by way of this attractive and rather ornate cast-iron footbridge. The line to Leighswood veered off to the right. *R. Selvey*

Bowen Cooke 'Super D' 0-8-0 No. 48950 plods through Pelsall station on 16th April, 1954 with a southbound loose-coupled haul of coal. The varied styles of wooden wagons, with a few obviously brand new steel wagons as evidence of modernization, elevates this train above the anonymity of today's uniform fleet freights. *T.J. Edgington*

extended southwards containing the booking office and waiting room. A decorative string course ran under the roof line, and there were three rather tall chimneys, but no platform canopy was provided for waiting passengers. Slightly apart, and further south, a small wooden gents urinal completed the ensemble. A wooden fence to the rear of the platform was later replaced by concrete posts threaded by wires. The up platform was connected by a wrought-iron lattice girder footbridge at the north end of the platforms, which continued from the down platform directly into Station Road, as it also formed part of a public right of way to High Heath. The up platform was furnished with a substantial brick-built waiting room with slated gable roof and decorative ridge tiles, finished with a canopy cantilevered out from the shelter and trimmed with decorative wooden edging. There were large windows in each end, and the ornate brick chimney was topped with a spindly tall chimney pot.

Local opinion of the station facilities was not always complimentary, as a Pelsall Vestry meeting on 31st January, 1890 recorded that the present waiting rooms were 'little better than barns and totally inadequate for the requirements of the place'. A deputation was organized to petition the LNWR district superintendent, Mr Sutton, for the required improvements: installation of a footbridge, improvements to the Heath End crossing, and repairs to the road beneath the railway bridge at Fordbrook. The petition evidently had some effect, as the footbridge was certainly installed, and had been wanting since several fatalities had occurred at this crossing (*see Chapter Eight*).

The goods yard north of the station on the down side consisted of just two north-facing sidings connected by a crossover to the up line, and finishing in a sizeable, but single-road brick good shed, the rear of which almost abutted to the station master's house. The crossover was removed prior to the closing of the signal box in November 1951 so that goods wagons could only gain access to the shed when travelling northwards. After closure to passengers in 1965 the station was demolished during 1976/1977, but as goods services still operated the footbridge remained until complete closure and was finally removed 'suddenly one Sunday morning' shortly after 22nd April, 1984.

The village of Pelsall was recorded in Wulfrun's Charter of AD 994 as 'Peolshale' as being one of 11 places given by Lady Wulfrun to the monks of Hamtune (Wolverhampton), and later was mentioned in the Domesday Book. By 1300 Pelsall was officially 'disafforested' from the Cannock Forest and thus its lands were freed from forest laws. Coal mining had been taking place in the area from medieval times, and in 1806 W. Gilpin constructed an arm of the Wyrley & Essington Canal from near Ryder's Hayes to Pelsall Common and onwards to a network of hand- and horse-worked tramways linking his pits. The mining activities, and later ironworks, contributed to the growth of the population which rose from 721 in 1831 to 1,132 in 1851, then to around 2,400 by 1885 and 3,626 in 1900. The centre of the town is today unusually laid out with the main road crossing two sections of attractive common land, today appearing more like park land, and it is difficult to envisage how this looked 150 years ago with railways and tramways crossing, and an overall smoke laden atmosphere.

Northwards the line passed on the left a single private siding, then ran on to an embankment and through the middle of Rails Wood to Ryders Hayes, where

Pelsall station looking north on Christmas Eve 1962. The frost on the sleepers gives only a small clue as to the heavy snowfall that was to blanket the country during the following days and remain for many weeks. The footbridge can be seen to disappear behind the main station building, on the left, as it formed part of a public right of way as well as a crossing point for passengers. *R. Shenton*

Ivatt class '2' 2-6-2T No. 41279 calls at Pelsall station with a Lichfield to Walsall push-pull train in the 1950s. The station platforms were still well tended at this time. *Bill Mayo Collection*

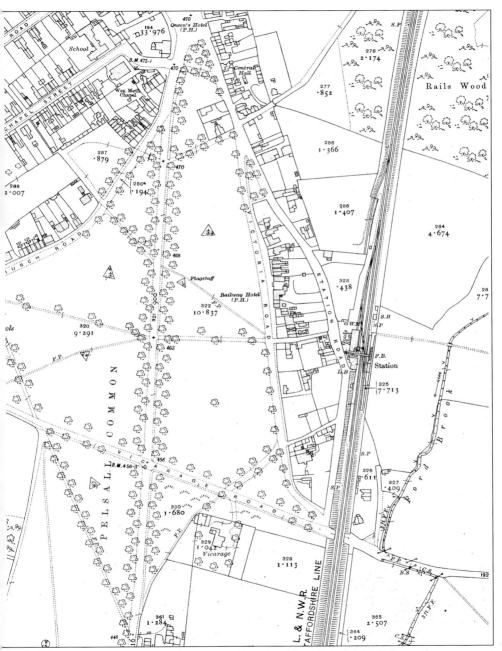

Pelsall station.

Reproduced from the 25", 1919 Ordnance Survey map

Ryders Hayes signal box on 8th August, 1953. This unusual design of box is believed to date from shortly after the opening of the SSR line.   *F.W. Shuttleworth*

The marshalling yard at Norton Junction, looking from the Norton branch southwards towards the SSR line on 19th June, 1965. A class '08' diesel is doing duty as the yard pilot in the centre of the picture.   *R. Shenton*

a station had opened with the line in 1849, but was closed in May 1858. It is almost certain that it was sited to the south of the ungated crossing, but it has not been possible to determine the extent of any buildings provided. The crossing was protected by an unusual signal box of brick construction with rather small windows in its upper wooden section, and surmounted by a hipped slated roof. It contained a 45-lever tumbler frame, and controlled access to the Ryder's Hay Sidings (*see below*), but was closed in September 1953. This curious structure may have been an original SSR structure, and was derelict by 1981. A large water tank was situated opposite, on the down side, south of the crossing. There are alternative spellings for this location - the word 'Hay' denoting a division of the Forest of Cannock, and present in many other villages of the area.

Just north of this point lay the Ryder's Hay Sidings, comprising a group of three through sidings, from which at their southern end a single line ran to the ironworks, furnaces and collieries of the Pelsall Coal & Iron Co. Ltd. This line, completed in 1865, was taken across Pelsall Common and then crossed the Wyrley & Essington Canal by an iron bridge, serving the company's Nos. 8, 9, 10, and 11 mines, and later to the furnaces and ironworks. In 1882 the lines were extended to the No. 12 or Ebenezer mine, west of the ironworks, and by 1884 the internal system was complete. However, the company ran into difficulties during the depression years of the late 1880s, and was wound up in August 1891. A sale in September 1892 only managed to find a buyer for the No. 12 mine (the local Walsall Wood Colliery Company), and so the entire remaining plant was dismantled during October and November 1892. The locomotives used on this system are detailed in *Appendix Four*. The new owners of the No. 12 mine continued to use the connection to the Ryder's Hay Sidings until they closed the mine in 1903. Two of these sidings were then extended alongside the down line of the Norton branch, which had opened on 1st February, 1858. By 1904 five further south-facing sidings had been added on the up side of the Norton branch. Later still, an extensive marshalling yard was developed here, and this will be covered in Volume Two. On the up side of the Lichfield line, two loops ('Nos. 1 and 2 Dudley Sidings') were located, with the Norton Junction No. 1 box (10¼ miles) at the northern end of these. This box contained a 45-lever LNWR tumbler frame, and was of the usual gable-ended brick and wood construction. A down goods loop led to a reception siding on the Norton or East Cannock branch, alongside which was a group of 12 single-ended sidings, controlled by the No. 2 box and facing towards the branch. Passing the junction, a further group of 16 sidings, of which 14 were double-ended, fed on to an extension of the down goods loop, and were controlled by the No. 3 box, again sited on the branch, just beyond the long road bridge known as High Bridge. The sidings were eventually taken out of use in December, 1966 but not lifted immediately. Further details of the working of the Norton branch will be contained in Volume Two.

On the opposite side, a single line was laid by the LNWR in 1882 to the Walsall Wood Colliery, and continued in use until 1964 when the colliery closed. This line was covered in Chapter Three.

The line had been climbing at fairly easy rates from Pelsall, and now started to move towards the north-east once more, as it passed through a fairly open area,

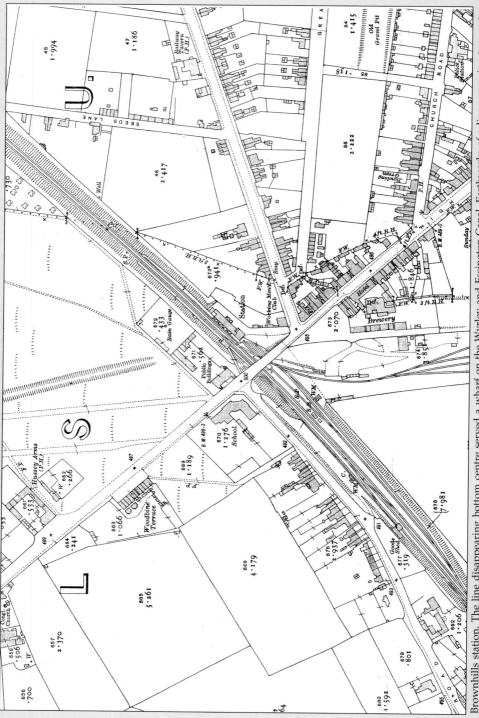

Brownhills station. The line disappearing bottom centre served a wharf on the Wyrley and Essington Canal. Earthworks of a line appearing top centre belonged to a former colliery tramway.

now infilled with housing, and was crossed by the double track MR Walsall Wood Extension, which ran from Aldridge to Conduit Colliery. As the line approached Brownhills station (11½ miles) a lengthy loop on the down side passed through a single-road brick-built goods shed, and alongside a side-loading deck. On the right, there were two up goods loops, passing behind the LNWR-style gable-ended signal box. At the north end of these sidings, a line led directly southwards to spread into four sidings, one on each side of the two wharves of the Wyrley & Essington Canal basin situated at the back of the town centre. One of the wharves has survived today, to become used by pleasure craft enjoying the benefits offered by the local canal network. Before the line reached the wharves it passed, on the north side, the depot where the first LNWR omnibuses had been garaged in 1912. The area between the canal basin and the up loops was later to become the site of a permanent way depot, with storage for materials and a mess room. The line passed beneath the High Street, which almost formed a crossroads at this point, and which in recent years has been modified to become a large traffic roundabout directly over the trackbed, in the centre of which a 30 ft stainless steel sculpture of a miner was erected in 2006.

The station was sited immediately on the northern side of this bridge, in a cutting, with pedestrian access from both sides, but the main approach road was on the up side. The station was another built to the designs of Edward Adams, and on the up side the main buildings included a two-storey station master's house with the gable end at right angles to the platform. From this, a range of single-storey brick buildings continued northwards, having a highly pitched roof line, and on which two further gable ends faced the platform. This range incorporated the porters' room, ladies waiting room, general waiting room, booking office, first class waiting room, gentlemen's toilets and lamp room respectively. A generous canopy was cantilevered from the main building over most of the length of the station buildings along the platform, with its own hipped roof and decorative pierced edgings. No footbridge was provided as the nearby road bridge permitted crossing of the line without using the boarded crossing at the north end of the platforms - a common practice in the years before 1900, but this was somewhat inconveniently sited. A footpath led from the road bridge to the down platform, which was provided with a simple wooden waiting shelter, whose flat roof continued outward as a cantilever to form a protective canopy, again with decorative piercing for the edging boards. Another gents lavatory was situated a little way further up the platform. Thus it can be seen that the station was extensively provided for, as befitted one of the larger communities on the line.

The reason for the lack of a boarded crossing at the south end of the platform, which would have been more useful for both staff and passengers, is that the line leading to the goods relief loops and the canal wharves, started abruptly at the up platform end in order to make the angle necessary to reach the wharves. Thus any crossing would have interfered with the operation of the pointwork. From the plans of the trackwork, it is assumed that this line was put in at a later date, as it certainly seems to have been an afterthought.

The station at Brownhills was at first simply named 'Brownhills', but following the 1923 Grouping the LMS then had the additional former MR

A *circa* 1912 view of a Webb 'Coal Tank' 0-6-2T arriving at Brownhills with a Walsall train. The station is particularly busy with the passengers from both trains mingling on the platforms
.
R.S. Carpenter/Lens of Sutton

Brownhills station viewed from the High Street overbridge and looking towards Lichfield, during the late 1950s. The neat platform awning on the up side is cantilevered out from the main station building. The crossover between the running lines also led to the goods yard and canal wharf, and necessitated a shortening of the up platform in order to pass beneath an arch of the overbridge.
Bill Mayo Collection

station of 'Brownhills'. To avoid confusion, the former MR station was renamed 'Brownhills Watling Street', and the former LNWR station renamed 'Brownhills High Street' as from 2nd June, 1924. However, matters did not rest there, as the former MR line lost its passenger service as from 31st March, 1930 and the Watling Street station closed. As a result, the former LNWR station reverted to its original simple title of 'Brownhills' on 1st August of that year.

It is some measure of the extent of the goods traffic at Brownhills that around 1914 there were six drays in use for the delivery and collection of goods by the LNWR. Brownhills was actually a comparatively modern town, having been first recorded in the 18th century and owing its subsequent enlargement to the proliferation of coal mining in the area during the 19th century. The nearby parish of Ogley Hay is much older, dating back over 4,000 years. It was one of the parishes, like Pelsall, given by Earl Leofric in AD 994 to the monks of Wolverhampton, being known at that time as Ocgingtun (meaning 'Ocga's town'). The High Street was actually part of an alternative route from London to Chester laid out in the 17th century, and thus provided a suitable stopping place for the horse transport of the times. On 29th September, 1877 Brownhills was created as a local government district by the formation of parts of the parishes of Norton Canes and Shenstone, the manor of Ogley Hay, the township of Walsall Foreign and the chapelry of Hammerwich. The Station Hotel in the High Street became a well known venue for music hall variety acts, and was part of what became a sizeable estate of 26 licensed houses belonging to one William Roberts. His visiting music hall acts along with their props would often be transported from the station to the Station Hotel in the horse and cab of the local greengrocer, a Mr Jones. Interestingly, in his early working life he obtained work on the construction of the SSR, later moving to other areas as a 'railway navvy' including the Standege tunnel for the Huddersfield & Manchester Railway, and then other construction projects. On his return from several years working away he took over the small Station Hotel, trebled its size, and opened a brewery at the rear. He had considerable other brewery interests in Ireland and Lichfield, and became a large landowner and farmer, and was active in local government as well as being a magistrate. It is worth recalling that in this latter role, he would often pay the fines of miscreants if he thought the charge was unfair. There were many other acts of local generosity.

The station area here is now the site of a large 'Beefeater' pub/restaurant named 'Smithy's Forge'. It is regrettable that a more appropriate name, perhaps acknowledging the railway connections, could not have been found.

Leaving Brownhills where the line had reached a second 'summit' on the route, it starts to fall all the way to Wichnor, firstly continuing in the cutting, which deepens and allows the line to pass beneath the Anglesey branch of the Wyrley & Essington Canal, then almost immediately beneath the crossroads of Watling Street (A5 trunk road) and the Brownhills to Chasetown road. The 1½ mile canal branch was installed in 1797 as a feeder channel for water to the main canal from a reservoir created at Norton Bog, and now known as Chasewater. The construction of this reservoir was a rushed job, causing several initial problems on the main canal due to loss of water. Furthermore, in June 1799 the eastern dam of the reservoir burst, sending millions of gallons of water down the valley as far

Fowler LMS '4F' class 0-6-0 No. 44439 is seen nearing Anglesea Sidings on 28th December, 1957 with a lengthy unfitted freight, consisting mostly of empty mineral wagons. The middle portion of this train is passing a point that is nowadays bridged over the M6 toll road.

R. Shenton

BR class '25' Bo-Bo diesel No. 25211 pauses at Anglesea Sidings with a permanent way train on 28th February, 1977. Another locomotive is shunting oil tankers into Charrington's oil depot from the down line. The signal box controlling access to these sidings is visible in the distance on the down side.   *R. Selvey*

as Shenstone, washing away roads and bridges, flooding fields, and killing sheep and cattle. But by March 1800 the reservoir had been rebuilt and was in use once again. As the Marquis of Anglesey developed his coal mines in the immediate area, this channel was considered as a suitable means of transport for the coal, and so it was converted, opening as a canal in 1850. This conversion was carried out at the same time that the SSR was under construction, with the aqueduct carrying the canal over the railway being built in 1848.

At the other side of the road bridge, were the Anglesea Sidings (12¼ miles), which was the junction for a mineral line leading to the Marquis of Anglesey's mines - note the different spellings. These mines were eventually leased by McClean, and that aspect of them will be covered in Volume Two. The line to these mines was opened in 1852, also serving a wharf beside the Anglesey Branch Canal to the north of the SSR. Exchange sidings were placed alongside the SSR line here, and continued in use by the Cannock Chase Colliery Co. Ltd and its successor the National Coal Board, but were removed in 1960, predating the closure of the last mines in this area in 1962. Locomotives used on this line will be detailed in Volume Two. A 30-lever signal box was sited on the down side opposite the entrance to the sidings, which comprised six south-facing and two north-facing sidings, with a single set-back siding on the up side. At a later date, the exchange sidings were taken over by Messrs Charrington Ltd and the site redeveloped as a rail-served oil and petroleum storage depot. Trains of oil tankers were delivered here at least twice each week by BR, whose locomotives performed any necessary shunting at the depot. In fact, these trains were the sole reason that the northern section from this point to Lichfield remained open after the complete closure of the southern section in 1984. At this time, the signal box was closed, any movements thereafter being controlled from a ground

Two class '37s', Nos. 37047 and 37167, in Mainline freight livery, stand in the yard at Charrington's oil depot at Anglesea Sidings, on 20th February, 1997. The original SSR route lies straight ahead towards Brownhills, but by this time was severed just out of sight. *R. Selvey*

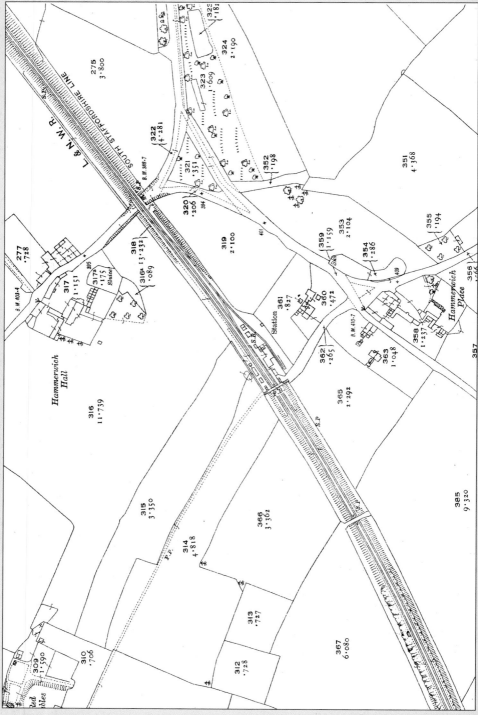

Hammerwich station. Even today the rural nature of this location has hardly changed. Reproduced from the 25″ 1923 Ordnance Survey map.

frame. However, the depot closed in 2001, and has since been converted into a road transport yard, although some of the trackwork beyond their perimeter fence remains *in situ*, as does one of the running lines all the way to Lichfield, and a second, unconnected line to just past Hammerwich.

From here, the line runs on to an embankment giving fine views across the first truly agricultural area that the line has traversed since leaving Dudley. Now it starts a significant decline at 1 in 145 for four miles to the outskirts of Lichfield, and over to the left can be seen Chasetown, whilst to the right the northern end of Brownhills is still visible. Today the line now crosses the M6 Toll Road on a fine new steel girder bridge, then entering a cutting it is facing eastwards as it snakes slightly at the approach to Hammerwich (13½ miles). The station here comprised the usual two platforms, latterly connected by a plate steel footbridge, which is still extant. The main station buildings were on the up side at the end of a lane. These comprised a two-storey station master's house, with its gable ends at right angles to the platform. The gable end walls were actually higher then the roof line, as at Pelsall. This building contained the booking office and waiting room, and was flanked by a small brick gentlemen's toilet and two small gabled wooden buildings, which were painted maroon on the lower halves and cream on the upper parts during BR days. The opposite, down platform contained a large brick-built waiting room, similar to the one on the up platform at Pelsall, but without a canopy, plus a wooden structure, possibly a store or lamp room. The signal box was sited at the eastern end of the up platform, controlling an adjacent single siding with headshunt that terminated behind the box, and a crossover from the down line. The station was reduced to the status of an unstaffed halt in 1959, although the signal box remained open until October 1964. Most of the station buildings and platforms were afterwards removed, but the station master's house remains, now as a private residence and almost out of recognition as a former railway building. The footbridge remains, as it forms part of a pedestrian right of way. Beyond the down platform to the north, the outlook is across fields to the Hall, St John the Baptist's Church and the centre of the village of Hammerwich, on top of a hill.

The line continues in a north-easterly direction, on an embankment and through pleasant rolling agricultural countryside, interspersed with copses, until it passes beneath the course of the original Fosse Way (now the A461 Walsall to Lichfield road), where it plunges into a grass-lined cutting. It finally emerges from this cutting just before it crosses a minor lane at a level crossing protected by the rather incorrectly named Fossway Road Crossing signal box, sited just north of the crossing on the up side. This small 10-lever box was closed on 16th December, 1973 and the crossing thereafter protected by automatic half-barriers. However, since the cessation of rail traffic in 2001, the barriers have been removed, although the box curiously remains complete, although boarded against the inevitable attentions of mindless hooligans. Now the line runs on an embankment, totally unobstructed by vegetation, and gently curving to a more northerly direction. Proceeding along this embankment there are fine views to the west of rolling hills and the edge of Cannock Chase, whilst to the north the city of Lichfield is recognisable by the tall stately spires of its cathedral towering over the skyline.

The station at Hammerwich viewed from the fields to the west of the station. The signal box can be seen on the extreme left, with the range of small buildings on the down platform next, and the main station building behind. The footbridge leads to the footpath in the foreground that ran up to the village on the hill behind the photographer. This view is believed to date from around 1910.   *R.S. Carpenter/Lens of Sutton*

The station master at Hammerwich was proud of the floral enhancements to his platforms, and went so far as to provide an ornamental pool and small fountain for the delight of passengers. This evidently also attracted the local children, seen here admiring the station master's work on the down platform around 1960.   *Bill Mayo Collection*

A view from the north of Hammerwich station on 4th April, 1964. Even though the station was only to remain open for another seven months, it is remarkably tidy and weed free.

R. Shenton

Hammerwich station, viewed from the south on 4th April, 1964. The sidings had been removed by this date, and the signal box was usually switched out, no longer being regularly used as a block post. Although ostensibly available for passengers crossing from one platform to another, the footbridge also formed part of a public right of way. As a result, extensions to the steps were provided on each side, as may be seen. *R. Shenton*

Stanier class '4' 2-6-4T No. 42586 runs into Hammerwich with a Walsall-bound stopping train in the early 1950s. The usual formation for such trains was three coaches of non-corridor stock.

Bill Mayo Collection

A Metropolitan-Cammell dmu leaving Hammerwich with a Lichfield to Walsall stopping service on 2nd December, 1963. The low level of the up platform necessitated the use of steps for passengers joining or leaving trains, as can be seen from the small lightweight steps remaining on the edge of the platform. The footbridge has been elevated since the 1950s view.

Bill Mayo Collection

The line northwards from Hammerwich passed beneath the Walsall to Lichfield road at this point, then headed over the Fossway Road Crossing, seen in the distance. Former 'Pacer' two-car dmu, now in use as a departmental vehicle, number DB 999601 traverses this line on a sunny day, 21st July, 1997. *R. Selvey*

Stanier '8F' class 2-8-0 No. 48101 working hard on the 1 in 145 southwards away from Fossway Road Crossing, visible in the background, on 27th February, 1965. *R. Shenton*

Lichfield City No. 1 signal box at the southern end of Lichfield City station in the low light of a snowy winter's day in the early 1960s.   *D. Wittamore/Kidderminster Railway Museum*

The gable-ended Lichfield City No. 2 signal box at the north end of Lichfield City station on a snowy, crisp day in the 1960s. The spire of St Michael's church stands on the horizon.
          D. Wittamore/Kidderminster Railway Museum

Members of the Chasetown detachment of the Royal Army Medical Service seen assembled outside the entrance to Lichfield City station on 26th October, 1914 on their way to active service in World War I. The canopy over the entrance to the station was still in position at that date.   *Bill Mayo Collection*

And so the line from Sutton Coldfield is reached, still on the embankment as we roll into Lichfield City station (17 miles), passing the Sandfield pumping station of the South Staffordshire Waterworks Company on the right near to the junction. The line passes over several road bridges, the last one before the City station actually being two bridges side by side and of an ornate plate construction. This bridge, over St John's Street, is attractively adorned with various armorial devices on the brick abutments facing the road beneath. Lichfield City No. 1 signal box (50 levers, LNWR tumbler frame) was first reached, at the end of the island platform, and controlling the double junction, plus crossovers, where the two sets of lines became four through the station (down main, down platform, up platform, up main) - although today only the up and down platform lines remain. At the north end of the station, Lichfield City No. 2 box (60 levers, LNW tumbler frame) controlled the loops and sidings to the goods shed on the left, and to Peaches Maltings on the right. From these latter, a reverse siding reached a loading dock and cattle sidings, which were an important part of the rail traffic. Both of the signal boxes were removed in the 1988 modernization of the line from New Street via Sutton Coldfield, and their function taken over by an extended and updated power box at Duddeston ('Saltley'). However, the goods shed dating from the 1884 reconstruction is still extant, although now in other commercial uses. Once again, further description and the development of the stations here are included in Chapters Five and Ten.

The line carried on through a deep sandstone cutting until it reached the level crossing over Burton Old Road, controlled by a crossing keeper with manually-operated gates. Today, this road has been terminated each side of the railway, and the crossing reduced to one for pedestrians only, the gates operated by users of the crossing. Just after, the line emerges on to an embankment to cross what is today an arterial road (Cappers Lane), then into Lichfield Trent Valley High Level (18 miles).

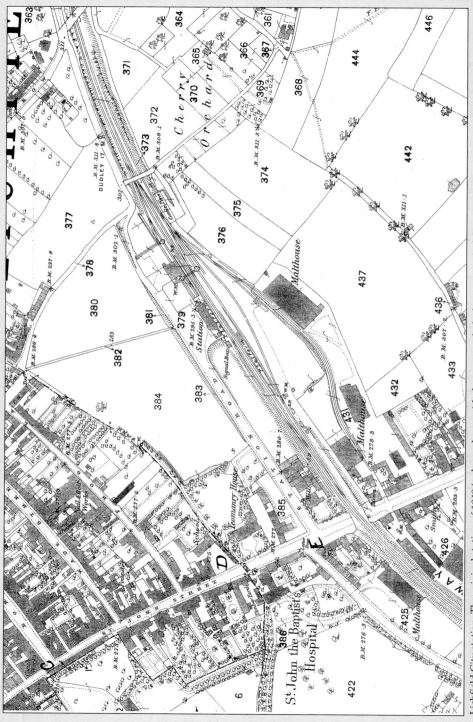

Lichfield City station. The original station of 1849 is shown here, with the staggered platforms typical of the period. The line from Sutton Coldfield had not yet opened, and work had not then started on the new City station. *Reproduced from the 25" 1887 Ordnance Survey.*

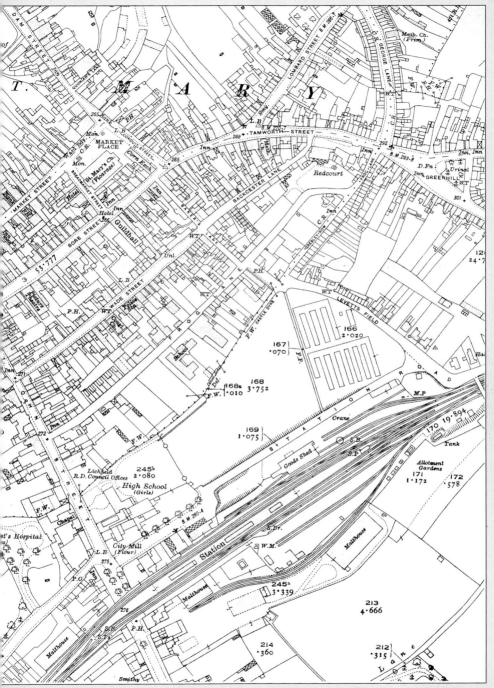

The new Lichfield City station, with a second set of double track running lines to accommodate
traffic from the Sutton Coldfield line. *Reproduced from the 25", 1923 Ordnance Survey map*

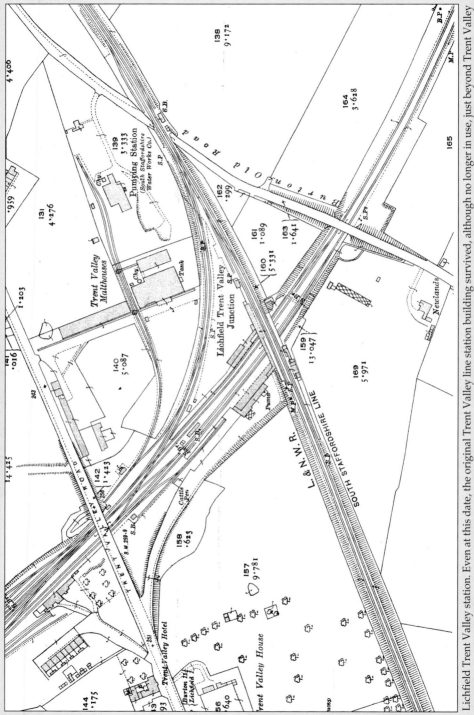

Lichfield Trent Valley station. Even at this date, the original Trent Valley line station building survived, although no longer in use, just beyond Trent Valley Road. Burton Old Road level crossing had been converted into an underline bridge, but today is truncated on either side of the line.

An unidentified 'Royal Scot' 4-6-0 in its original parallel boiler form rushes through Lichfield Trent Valley Low Level station, sometime in the 1930s, with a northbound express. This view illustrates well the northern side of the High Level station, and just how it was incorporated into the station as a whole. *M. Whitehouse Collection*

Today, both up and down trains use only the down track into the station, by way of a crossover almost on the bridge just mentioned. Again the station has been described in Chapter Six, so we move on quickly, past the trailing junction for the 47 chain (½ mile) chord from the LNWR Trent Valley line and reach Lichfield Trent Valley Junction box on the up side, still operational to control the junction and the aforementioned crossover. This operates as a fringe box to the power signal box at Saltley. The up track from this junction to the crossover is only used by through trains, which seldom use this line. Originally this box worked a 45-lever LNWR tumbler frame, with sidings on both sides of the line, one serving yet another South Staffordshire Waterworks Company pumping station, and the other a local maltings. The level crossing has been closed, with the two ends of the lane terminating at either side of the railway, and again only pedestrian use is permitted.

A short distance further on was the ungated Streethay crossing, which has been changed to a gated crossing for pedestrians and road users, who are responsible for operating the gates. A telephone is located here to contact the signalman at Trent Valley Junction in case of emergency. This site is now almost under the upgraded A38 trunk road (Birmingham to Derby), which the line now passes beneath. On emerging the other side it passes over the Coventry Canal and starts its journey across the flat flood plain of the River Trent, at this point some 1½ miles to the east. Running on another embankment the line is right alongside a loop formed by the Coventry Canal, and then passes over the Brookhay level crossing. This was originally protected by a crossing keeper, who had charge of a 12-lever frame in a small box situated south of the crossing on the up side, and manual control of the gates. His cottage was located on the other (northern) side of the crossing. This arrangement was converted to automatic half-barriers on 15th May, 1966 which are still operational.

Brookhay Crossing, north of Lichfield, in September 1964 with a Stanier class '8F' class 2-8-0 passing with a coal train. The substantial level crossing keeper's cottage is on the left, and the hipped-roof signal box controlling the crossing is on the right. Both structures have long since been demolished, and the crossing is now protected by automatic half-barriers.   *C. Shepherd*

Alrewas station looking north around 1912. The wooden goods shed is on the left of this view of a well proportioned, but simple country station.   *Lens of Sutton*

Heading in a straight line north-eastwards, we come to two more level crossings over minor lanes. The first is Fine Lane Crossing, with double wooden gates under the control of crossing keepers, who are responsible to the Alrewas signal box. Next is Roddige Crossing, also manned by crossing keepers, but having only single wooden gates, and also responsible to Alrewas. Now the line passes beneath a new bridge carrying the A513 from Rugeley to Tamworth, which originally crossed the line at Riggetts Crossing, and was another formerly supervised by a crossing keeper.

Alrewas station (22 miles) was positioned just south of the level crossing for the road from the village to Tamworth, with its controlling signal box (25-lever frame) on the down side at the far end of the crossing. At the south end of the station there was a lengthy up goods refuge, accessed by Annett's Key C from the box. On the down line, a loop gave access to the goods yard containing three sidings leading to a mileage siding, cattle pens, a substantial single-road wooden goods shed, and a loading dock adjacent to the platform. A headshunt was provided at the south end of the yard. The main station buildings were located on the down side, consisting of a two-storey station master's house, with its gable end at right angles to the platform. Again, the end gables were higher than the roof line, and a small brick building next to this probably contained a waiting room, with a wooden stores/staff room next to that. The rear of the platform was fenced with wooden upright palings. On the up platform a simple brick-built waiting shelter was provided. Platform canopies were not provided on either platform. The level crossing was replaced with lifting barriers operated from the signal box in the 1970s, and the previously double track line today becomes single just beyond the box.

Alrewas station looking north from the down platform on a very rainy 22nd February, 1958. Although the varied styles of buildings on the left do not represent a unified appearance, the neatness of the modest structures on the up platform will be appreciated.

M. Whitehouse Collection

Alrewas station.

Reproduced from the 25", 1923 Ordnance Survey map

A fine cottage was originally provided for the level crossing keeper at Alrewas, and this structure was still in excellent order when photographed on 29th March, 1965.   *C. Shepherd*

After the demolition of the wooden goods shed at Alrewas, the goods storage facilities comprised a small shed and three grounded box vans, as seen here. Just beyond is visible the cattle loading dock, which was an important feature at this rural location. The date is 29th March, 1965.   *C. Shepherd*

An unidentified 'Peak' class diesel runs through Alrewas station with a northbound express, diverted from the former MR Derby-Birmingham route in May 1963.   *P. Waterfield*

Metro-Cammell units Nos. M51180 and M56343 depart from Alrewas with the 10.45 Saturdays-only Wolverhampton to Burton on 9th May, 1964, passing over the level crossing at the north end of the station.   *C. Shepherd*

Now the line swings into a more easterly direction and on to another embankment as it prepares to cross the River Trent, this time on a lengthy but low viaduct, consisting of 22 piers over the marshy flood plain then a plate girder bridge over the river, followed by a further low viaduct of nine piers. The bridge decking was completely renewed in concrete during the 1970s, but the brick piers appear to be original. Since Lichfield City the line has continued to descend on fairly easy grades, alternating with a couple of spots of level track, and carries on for a short distance further through this flat land, punctuated by what today appear to be a group of lakes, but are actually flooded gravel pits, before arriving at Wichnor (23¾ miles). A group of up to eight sidings (the number varied over the years) was sited on the right, in the fork of the SSR line and the MR Birmingham to Derby line. Alongside, a 100 ft-long three-road engine shed had been erected around 1854, the contract being awarded to an unnamed person for £1,782 18s. 4d. A turntable was positioned at the rear of the shed. However, the shed had gone out of use after the running powers to Burton had been settled, but was not removed until late 1896 or early 1897. An LNWR minute dated 12th December, 1896 recorded that 'the Steam Shed at Wichnor having been closed, there will be no man available for working the pumping engine at night; he (Webb) therefore recommends that the water tank be made a plate deeper ... Approved'. This indicated that locomotives were still expected to be serviced there, and indeed this continued, along with the turntable, which remained in use up to LMS days. A row of six cottages for railwaymen was also erected here, south of the engine shed, but these have long since disappeared.

This was a rather remote area, and although unlikely to attract many passengers, it had one claim to fame in that the village had the distinction, along with Dunmow in Essex, of a charming medieval manorial custom. This was the awarding to newly-married couples of a flitch of bacon, providing they had completed their first 12 months of conjugal happiness without an argument. A local public house, 'The Flitch of Bacon' was named in honour of this custom.

The station had opened with the line in 1849, but closed on 1st November, 1877. No descriptions or photographs of the station or its precise position have been traced, but it is thought unlikely that it was of any substance, being simply a transfer point to MR trains. So it was probably sited at the northern extremity of the site, near to the lane leading to Catholme, as the MR trains would have to call to collect or set down passengers. In this area, further sidings were added at a later date, and numerous goods workings were remarshalled here. This was actually the point at which the SSR and MR lines made a junction. Today, the whole area is empty, with the former SSR line joining the MR route at a simple ladder junction further south. The area nearby is dominated by sand and gravel workings, and a short distance further north is the Bombardier Central Rivers depot servicing the Voyager dmus used on their cross-country routes.

A closing comment concerning the remains of the line today, for those wishing to visit any portions of the line. The route of the line can easily be traced, with most of the over- and under-line bridges in place, and almost all cuttings and embankments on the closed sections easily recognized. However, only three of the railway buildings survive - Wednesbury goods shed (1863) and Lichfield City station and goods shed (both 1884). Although Lichfield City station remains substantially complete, it lost its porte-cochère at a relatively early date, possibly before World War I. Also the present booking office on the left in the entrance hall was originally the parcels office. The original booking office was on the right, now a refreshment room and shop. All of the other railway buildings have been demolished, or in the case of Walsall station totally redeveloped.

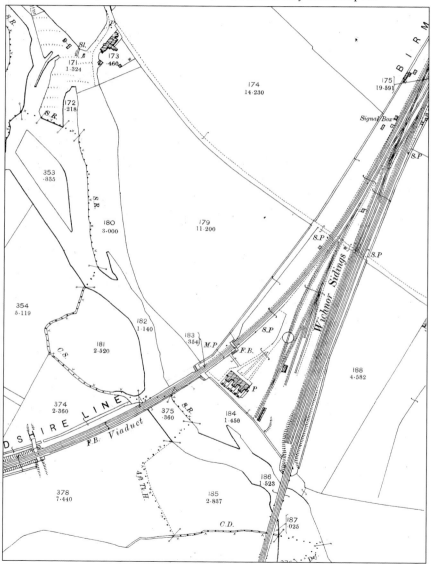

Wichnor.   *Reproduced from the 25", 1901 Ordnance Survey map*

Chapter Eleven

Modern Times - 1965 to Today

We begin this period with no passenger traffic on any part of the SSR, with the exception of trains from Birmingham New Street to Walsall, which of course only passed over the SSR from Bescot Junction to Walsall, and those entering Lichfield City from the Sutton Coldfield line. The remaining sections continued with the important freight work, but the gradual closure of mines in the Cannock Chase area were having a noticeable effect on these traffic levels. In fact, the only remaining pits were those in the Cannock and Hednesford area, whose traffic was taken over the Cannock to Walsall line. As a result the line from Norton Junction to East Cannock Junction (on the Cannock line) had closed on 25th May, 1964. Thus the yards at Norton Junction were initially no longer required, but did have a renaissance, as we shall see in Volume Two. The Working Timetable for the period 3rd October, 1966 to 5th March, 1967 reveals that the following freight duties were being worked over some or all of the SSR main line:

Aston Goods-Scunthorpe	Bescot-Tinsley (Sheffield)
Stourbridge-Branston (Burton)	Ocker Hill-Swadlincote
Littleton Colliery sidings-Lawley St	Mollington (Cheshire)-Coleshill
Spring Vale (Bilston)-Corby	Pensnett-Lea Hall Colliery/Burton
Great Bridge-Aldwarke (Rotherham)	Wolverhampton New Steel Terminal-Scunthorpe
Stoke-Washwood Heath sidings	Corby-Oldbury & Langley Green
Tinsley-Kingswinford/Bescot	Whitemoor (March)-Curzon Street
Branston-East Usk Junction (Newport)	Duddeston Sidings-Pensnett
Chaddesden (Derby)-Bescot	Lamport Ironstone sidings-Spring Vale
Bescot-Bilston West	Tees Yard (Gateshead)-Bescot
Water Orton-Crewe	Nottingham-Swansea

Thus it will be appreciated that the former MR Sutton Park route was performing a vital task in the routeing of trains to the yards and depots in the north-east of Birmingham, as well as feeding on to lines for the south-west and Wales. At Lichfield, the daily goods service over the Sutton Coldfield line from Aston was extended to run twice daily to Branston and return, with a further trip from Branston on Wednesdays only.

As from 1st January, 1968 the short WR line from Swan Village to Horseley Fields Junction was closed completely, and the track removed very shortly afterwards. The only station on the line, Great Bridge South, had already been demolished following the withdrawal of passenger services in 1964 - although that would not have taken much effort as it was in a shocking state by then. It is unlikely that any goods workings had passed over the line since 1964, as there had never been much goods traffic even at the height of this line's career.

By 1970, there was a further shift to long distance through workings, as this summary of the Working Timetable for 4th May to 4th October, 1970 reveals:

BR 'Peak' class 1Co-Co1 diesel-electric No. D69 passes through Wednesbury with a full load of
iron ore, destined for Bilston steel works in the late 1960s. It has just passed over the Potters Lane
level crossing, controlled by Wednesbury No.1 signal box, seen on the left.

D. Wilson/R.S. Carpenter

BR Sulzer Bo-Bo No. D7523 tackles the 1 in 60 climb near Dudley with a loaded coal train on
22nd August 1969, necessitating the assistance in the rear of a similar locomotive. The up goods
relief line, formerly to the right of the engine had been removed by this time.   *D. Wilson*

Via Sutton Park route

Penzance-Sheffield (perishables)   Oldbury-Sheffield Freight Terminal
Crewe-Washwood Heath   Carlisle-Bristol
Trentham (Stoke)-Hams Hall (Coleshill)   Crewe-Stoke Gifford (Bristol)
Dudley Freightliner-Wensum (Norwich)   Johnstone (Glasgow)-Kings Norton
Fratton (Portsmouth)-Bolton   Washwood Heath-Manchester London Rd
Dee Marsh (Chester)-Washwood Heath (via Wednesbury WR)
Tipton Gas Sidings-West Thurrock, Fawley and Ripple Lane
Ince & Elton-Carmarthen, Bridgwater, Andover, Plymouth, Gillingham, and Gloucester

Via Wichnor

Langley Green-Normanby Park   Norton Junction-Scunthorpe
Wednesfield-Scunthorpe   *   Tees Yard-Brierley Hill
Tees Yard-Great Bridge   Newstead (Nottingham)-Brierley Hill
Spring Vale-Manton (Leicester)   Spring Vale-Chaddesden
Wolverhampton Steel Terminal-Scunthorpe, Corby, and Tinsley

Via Dudley

Waterston (Milford Haven)-Albion (Oldbury)

Via Lichfield Trent Valley curve

Overseal - Rugby   Cotgrave Colliery (Notts)-Rugby

Terminating

Severn Tunnel Junction-Bescot   Carlisle-Bescot
Severn Beach-Bescot   Winsford Junction (Cheshire)-Bescot
Immingham-Anglesea Mobil Oil Terminal, Brownhills
Peterborough-Walsall, parcels

The workings to and from Tipton Gas sidings, Albion and the Anglesea Terminal were all block oil trains bringing oil to the region's main terminals.

In addition, there were 31 light engine movements to/from Bescot, three to/from Spring Vale, eight to/from Saltley, four to/from Burton, two from Great Bridge, and one to Dudley. Although these movements were in addition to the freight workings mentioned above, they were almost all made as the result of travelling from the nearest traction maintenance depot to take up the out going workings, or in reverse on incoming workings. There were few occasions where the locomotive was able to take up a new working directly it arrived at its destination.

Goods workings from the Sutton Coldfield line comprised just three weekday trains: 12.40 pm Aston Goods to Burton, 09.45 Saturdays-only (SO) or 09.50 Saturdays-excepted (SX) Branston to Aston Windsor Street, and 17.10 return. In the following year this was reduced to just one working each way on weekdays, although these were timed differently on Saturdays.

Two locomotives were still required for shunting and local trip work at Wednesbury in 1971. Bescot's No. 5 duty was for a class '08' locomotive from 06.15 Mondays-excepted (MX) (06.55 MO) until 20.00 SX (1200 SO), and rather than return to Bescot, it was immobilised at Wednesbury when not required. The second duty was No. 77, again for an '08' locomotive, this time working mainly on the former GWR lines. It was to be operational from 06.05 MX (06.25 MO) until 21.00 SX (13.30 SO). On weekdays it was to shunt private sidings in the Bilston area

Brush A1A-A1A diesel-electric No. 5844 passes through the closed Wednesbury Town station around 1970 with a fully-loaded coal train, probably bound for Bilston steel works. The up platform seems to have been removed, but the down platform, along with some of the buildings, remains.   *D. Wilson/R.S. Carpenter*

An unidentified 'Peak' class diesel-electric running light engine and approaching Eagle Crossing from the Walsall direction around 1972. The track formation has been considerably reduced from that shown in the photographs on pages 216 and 217.   *K. Hodgkins*

as required, with further shunting at Swan Village on Monday, Wednesday and Friday. Again, it was immobilised at Wednesbury in between duties. At Walsall goods depot, a class '08' was scheduled for attendance as Bescot Duty No. 18 (Walsall downside shunt and trip) from 11.00 until 18.00 SX, and another as Duty No. 19 (Walsall goods depot shunt) continuously from 0600 MO until 1100 SO.

Assistance was still sometimes required to southbound goods workings towards Dudley at this time, and Bescot's No. 6 duty for a class '25' locomotive included this along with shunting at Great Bridge, where the yards still attracted quite a large amount of steel traffic. This duty was from 05.00 to 13.30 Monday to Saturday. Any trains requiring assistance from there to Dudley would be notified by Control, who would also arrange for the locomotive at Great Bridge to be ready. This duty also included providing assistance to trains working between Wednesbury and Princes End, again as notified by Control; class '31s' were also noted on this duty occasionally.

During 1970, the remaining sidings at Norton Junction were temporarily reopened to serve as sorting sidings for wagons from the various steel industry users, due to a lack of space at Bescot yard. This new facility was given the wholly inappropriate designation of 'Bescot Down Empty Wagon Sidings', but lasted for only around a year.

The aforementioned general level of traffic continued throughout the 1980s, with an increasing amount of company-sponsored block trains in addition to the steel and oil trains, such as scrap metal from Handsworth to Aldwarke, and transport of cars and vans from Washwood Heath to Garston (Liverpool) and Purfleet (Essex), and from Southampton to Crewe Gresty Lane. Into the new century, the transport of nuclear flasks became regular traffic from Berkeley Road and Bridgwater to Crewe. With the closure of Lea Hall Colliery in December 1990 supplies for Rugeley Power Station came from a variety of sources, some from UK pits at Daw Mill and Welbeck travelling via the Trent Valley curve at Lichfield, but increasingly imported coal from the docks at Hunterston (Ayr), Avonmouth and Carlisle. To avoid too many reversals, these often travel inwards from the Trent Valley line at Rugeley, then after discharge, empties continue through Walsall to Bescot. Further details on these workings will be found in Volume Two of this work. Almost all of the later BR diesel types could be seen during this period, of the classes '20', '25', '31', '37', '40', '45', '46', '47', '56', '58', '60', '66' and at least on one occasion a class '50'.

Despite the withdrawal of passenger services north of Walsall, the line continued to be visited by diversions, just as the Sutton Coldfield line was used, when engineering works required possession of parts of the Birmingham to Derby MR route. Even HSTs traversed the line, as well as the more familiar class '47s'. The last known passenger train to run on the Lichfield to Walsall section was a returning football excursion from Rotherham to Hamstead, hauled by 'Peak' No. 45065 on 18th January, 1984.

The middle part of the northern section of the line, from Anglesea Sidings southwards through Norton Junction to Ryecroft closed from 19th March, 1984 and the rails were removed soon after. The trackbed remains unobstructed, although there has been some fairly close development at Brownhills, and the southern part from Pelsall to the outskirts of Walsall has been converted into a footpath and cycleway. Meanwhile, the section northwards from Anglesea

An unrecorded English Electric class '37' Co-Co diesel electric approaches the level crossing at Rushall Crossing around 1975 with a southbound freight working. The signalman appears to be more interested in the photographer than the approaching train.   *R. Selvey*

Brush A1A-A1A diesel-electric No. 31155 passes Rushall Crossing signal box with a northbound working of bogie steel wagons around 1975.   *R. Selvey*

'Peak' diesel No. 44004 (originally named *Great Gable*) has just passed beneath the former MR direct line from Water Orton to Wolverhampton at Walsall, with a mixed southbound freight train. Included in the consist is a class '08' 0-6-0 diesel shunter travelling 'dead'.   *R. Selvey*

A diverted northbound HST passes Mill Lane, Walsall on Sunday 12th June, 1977 with power car No. 253026 at the rear. Doubtless the reason for the diversion was weekend engineering work on the MR Birmingham-Derby route.   *R. Selvey*

Two class '20s', Nos. 20054 and 20049 running south through the remains of Wednesbury Town station on 5th July, 1977. The independent through line has been taken up, and a crossover installed, which the train has passed over in order to run 'wrong line' to reach Tipton via the Prince's End branch. *R. Selvey*

BR 'Peak' class 1Co-Co1 diesel No. 45043 heads southwards on 8th March, 1978 from beneath the M6 at Bescot on the SSR route, with a train of oil tankers probably bound for the oil storage depot at Albion. *R. Selvey*

Sidings to Lichfield was saved by the regular oil trains (at least two per week) from the Lindsay refinery in Lincolnshire to the depot there, latterly operated by Messrs Charrington. Regrettably this too closed (in 2001) and the site was converted into a road transport depot, although the track remains *in situ* outside their perimeter fence, and one line of rails is still in place all the way to Lichfield. (A second set of rails lies alongside, from Anglesea to north of Hammerwich, but is unconnected.) However, this section was breached during 2008 for the construction of the Lichfield southern by-pass road, involving removal of part of the embankment south of Lichfield. The track panels were removed and stored nearby until such time as a bridge could be constructed across the new road.

Initial Freightliner services from Dudley served Glasgow, Newcastle, Stockton and Swansea, although the destinations did vary over the years. However, its closure in September 1986 eliminated one source of traffic over the Dudley to Pleck section, and the subsequent gradual run down of manufacturing at Round Oak steelworks severely reduced another source of traffic. The steel terminal at Wednesbury closed soon after, as the manufacture of steel in the area dwindled to virtually nothing. The expected outcome was that the line from Pleck Junction to Dudley including the Bescot curve was closed as from 19th March, 1993. The track initially remained *in situ*, and although it has since disappeared in most places, the trackbed remains complete. The intention is eventually to use this as part of an expanded Midland Metro system with a line from Walsall to the retail park at Merry Hill on the southern side of Dudley. Currently no firm decision has been made regarding funding of the proposed link, but a recent (2006) promise from central government seems to suggest that a line will be put in at an unspecified date, from an interchange with the Wolverhampton to Birmingham route at Wednesbury southwards to Merry Hill. Once again, the good people of Walsall are waiting for their transport link.

Floods continued to affect Walsall station and the immediate area during January 1977 when the water level rose to platform level, and exactly one year later when the flood level reached five feet. More concerted efforts were made to eliminate the persistent flooding, and works known as the 'Walsall Flood Relief Scheme' were begun shortly after, lasting through 1979 and 1980. The work was undertaken by Leonard Fairclough Ltd, with sites at Corporation Street (Caldmore), Littleton Street, Broadway and Upper Rushall Street. Further work was carried out by J.J. Gallagher & Co. Ltd from March 1980 through 1981 with tunnel sites in Corporation Street and Midland Street. All this work seems to have paid off, as there have been no floods since that time.

Passenger services resumed between Lichfield City and Lichfield Trent Valley High Level as from 28th November, 1988 at last recognising the importance of this link with the West Coast Main Line. Services were finally upgraded with the electrification of the 'Cross City' line to Redditch via Sutton Coldfield, starting from 30th November, 1992. The level of services is currently unparalled for the city, but it really exists only because of the traffic arising at the intermediate stations elsewhere on the route, and the spreading area of 'commuter belt' for Birmingham. A little over half of the trains now run through to Trent Valley station, but this is still a very satisfactory level. The present services are as follows:

The much-rebuilt Dudley Port High Level station viewed from across the Birmingham Canal in the 1970s, after the introduction of overhead catenary on the main line. This view emphasises the difficulty of installing the line from Dudley in the small space between the station and the canal.   *Revd J. Algar/Kidderminster Railway Museum*

An unidentified class '47' heads a permanent way train southwards towards Dudley, having just passed beneath the Stour Valley main line at Dudley Port in the 1980s. The chord linking the SSR at Sedgeley Junction to the Stour Valley line passed in front of the houses, upper right in the photograph.   *K. Hodgkins*

BR class '47' Co-Co No. 47356 heads a southbound steel train away from Great Bridge in 1986, passing the works of the Horseley Bridge & Thos Piggott on the left. *K. Hodgkins*

A view of the northern end of the platform at Lichfield City in July 1988 with a class '101' waiting for departure to Longbridge. Whilst the waiting rooms had been recently redecorated, the area in the foreground, not expected to be used by the travelling public, was clearly not subject to the same degree of tidiness. *R. Webster*

A detailed study of the waiting rooms on the island platform at Lichfield city station in 1988. The substantial wrought-iron canopy supports can be seen to advantage. Also the buildings may be seen to be of a pleasingly ornate design, albeit executed in wood. *R. Webster*

Services to/from Lichfield	Monday to Friday	Saturday	Sunday
Trent Valley up	32	32	26
Trent Valley down	36	32	24
City up	56	57	26
City down	60	57	24

One final note is fairly symptomatic of our times, and that is the report in the *Lichfield Post* of 10th September, 1992 that the kiosk on Lichfield City station was forced to close, after the owners had experienced nine burglaries in the preceding four years.

Efforts were being made around this time to get the passenger services reinstated on the line from Lichfield or Brownhills to Walsall. The Railway Development Society added its weight to the proposals being made by the communities in Brownhills and Pelsall in 1988, 1990, 1997, 2000 and 2008 but so far there have been no signs of success.

The passenger services across Cannock Chase were reinstated from 10th April, 1989 as far as Hednesford, then from 2nd June, 1997 to Rugeley Town. From the latter date, this gave a weekday service of 13 trains from Rugeley Town and four from Hednesford to Birmingham. From 25th May, 1998 the service was extended from Rugeley through to Stafford, with the same frequency. However, improvements were gradually made and by 2006 this had reached 10 from Stafford, one from Rugeley Trent Valley, four from Rugeley Town and nine from Hednesford to Birmingham. All these services were operated by Centro, using dmus of classes '150', '153' or '158'. When London Midland took over operations from 12th December, 2008, the Stafford services were terminated at Rugeley Trent Valley, since when Stafford passengers must await a connecting service on the Trent Valley line. However, the frequency has improved, with a total of 31 trains in each direction (of which four originate at Hednesford) on weekdays and 14 on Sundays. Class '170' dmus are now normally rostered.

At Walsall, the weekday Birmingham service changed in March 1967 from an average frequency of one per hour throughout the day, to two per hour. The introduction of electric-multiple-units (emus) in May 1977 allowed an improved service of around 32 emus operating solely between Walsall and New Street. The current (2010) level of service now gives around two per hour, plus a similar rate from the Rugeley services, for at total of 60 trains each way on weekdays and 30 on Sundays. The emus from Walsall call at all stations via Aston, whereas the dmus from the Rugeley line call at Tame Bridge Parkway and/or Hamstead and Bescot Stadium, then travel via the Soho loop line to enter New Street station from the opposite direction to the emus. The first emus were of classes '312' and '313' cascaded from other areas of BR, but the current units are of classes '321', '322' and '323', as also used on the Lichfield to New Street and Redditch 'Cross City' route. Both the Lichfield to Wichnor Junction, and the Cannock line continue to see diverted trains, particularly at weekends, due to engineering work elsewhere.

During 2005 a new rail-served cement distribution depot comprising two silos was installed at the northern end of the original MR carriage sidings at Pleck, directly opposite the Civil Engineering Depot (now part of Network Rail). This depot is run by a company with the name of Dalkia, and evidently

A Birmingham Railway Carriage & Wagon Company class '101' dmu departs from the south end of Lichfield city station in July 1988 for Longbridge. At that time, Longbridge (reopened in 1978) was the southernmost destination for the Birmingham 'Cross-City' services from Lichfield.

R. Webster

Two-car dmu No. 150202 runs into Pleck Junction from Bescot with a Birmingham New Street to Walsall local train around 1997. It is running on the very first stretch of the SSR, opened on 1st November, 1847 from Walsall to Bescot. On the right, the former SSR main line to Wednesbury and Dudley is still *in situ*, although overgrown.

R. Selvey

Looking down at the site of Great Bridge station from the 'Black Country Route' on 30th December, 1999. The view is southwards, and although no trace remains of the station, which would have been located in the centre of the photograph, the bridge over the Walsall Canal fixes the location. The modern houses in the centre are standing on the site of the goods shed.

R. Selvey

Walsall station in February 2006 with Centro dmu No. 150125 waiting to leave platform 3 with a service to Birmingham New Street. The Saddlers retail development and associated car park completely overshadow the rather basic three-platform station. Platforms 1 and 2 are not equipped with overhead catenary, thus denying access to the emus normally used on the Birmingham services.

Author

The present day site of Ryecroft Junction, with the Cannock line running off to the left, and the former MR line to Sutton Park to the right. The site of Ryecroft locomotive shed and the line to Lichfield are completely overgrown by the trees in the centre of the photograph.   *Author*

Lichfield City station from the eastern side in February 2006. The track layout is nowadays very much simplified, but the 1884 goods shed remains intact, although used for non-railway commercial purposes, and can be seen on the right-hand side.   *Author*

The exterior of the 1884 Lichfield City station in February 2006. Still remarkably complete, the only change has been the loss of the canopy over the station entrance. *Author*

Alrewas signal box and level crossing in February 2006. The crossing gates have been converted to lifting barriers operated from the adjacent box, which retains its standard LMS gable-ended structure. *Author*

Lichfield Trent Valley Junction looking south showing the High Level platform in the centre, and the chord connecting to the West Coast Main Line on the right. The overhead catenary on the SSR route finishes at this point.   *Author*

The remains of Hammerwich station on 4th April, 2006. The main station building on the left, is in use as a private residence, and the footbridge is still in use.   *Author*

The signal box at Fossway Road Crossing is still *in situ*, as seen here on 15th April, 2006. However, the crossing gates were converted to automatic half-barriers, being removed after the line closed in 2001. *Author*

serves Buxton Cement amongst others, whose JGA bogie tank wagons may be seen discharging at this point.

A little further south are the remnants of the Bescot Chord, which ran from Bescot West Junction (on the Bescot to Walsall line) to Bescot Curve Junction (on the now closed Pleck to Wednesbury SSR line). The rails were still in place in 2007, although not connected at either end to the former running lines.

The Walsall to Wolverhampton service was axed from 1st January, 2008. Local fury at being denied this service had no effect, with the so-called 'consultation process' being a complete sham. However, Walsall to Birmingham New Street services now operated by London Midland continue onwards in a northwards loop from Birmingham to Wolverhampton. The result is that the journey from Walsall to Wolverhampton now takes around one hour instead of 15 minutes previously.

Lichfield Trent Valley station on 10th May, 2006 with two class '323' 3-car emus standing at the High Level platform. The low level platforms serving the West Coast Main Line are directly beneath. *Author*

SSR Rolling Stock at 1st January, 1851

No. of vehicles	Description
8	First Class carriages
4	Composite carriages
12	Second Class carriages
24	Third Class carriages
10	Passenger luggage vans
6	Horse boxes
6	Carriage trucks
31	Low sided waggons
20	Ballast waggons
74	Iron coal waggons
31	Cattle waggons
6	Goods break [sic] vans
130	Low sided waggons
10	Timber trucks
126	Coal waggons
31	High sided waggons
200	Coal waggons
300	Coal waggons
100	Hanson's Patent covered waggons

Total value £64,196 - signed by Joseph Beattie.

Appendix Two

Locomotives of the
South Staffordshire Railway

No. 1 *Dudley*
2-2-2 built by W. Fairbairn & Sons in February 1849.
Cost £2,070. Outside sandwich frames. Driving wheels 5 ft 9 in. Cylinders 16 in. x 20 in. (increased to 16 in. x 21 in. at Wolverton *c*.1860).
In July 1859 numbered in LNWR Southern Division as No. 297. From 1859 worked the Peterborough branch. In April 1862 renumbered as LNWR No. 897. Rebuilt with Ramsbottom boiler in December 1864 after boiler explosion at Overton. January 1867 to LNWR duplicate list as No. 1122, renumbered 1921 in December 1871, scrapped 12th March, 1881.

No. 2 *Walsall*
2-2-2 built by W. Fairbairn & Sons in March 1849.
Cost £2,070. Outside sandwich frames. Driving wheels 5 ft 9 in. Cylinders 16 in. x 20 in. (increased to 16 in. x 21 in. at Wolverton *c*.1860).
Repaired at Wolverton after collision at Vauxhall, Birmingham. In July 1859 numbered in LNWR Southern Division as No. 298. In April 1862 renumbered as LNWR No. 898. Renumbered as No. 1124 on duplicate list in January 1867, and rebuilt in 1869 with Ramsbottom boiler. Renumbered as 1919 in December 1871 and scrapped 30th April, 1878.

No. 3 *Wednesbury*
2-2-2 built by W. Fairbairn & Sons in April 1849.
Cost £2,070. Outside sandwich frames. Driving wheels 5 ft 9 in. Cylinders 16 in. x 20 in. Worked on the St Albans branch between 1858 and 1860. In July 1859 numbered in LNWR Southern Division as No. 299. In April 1862 renumbered as LNWR No. 899. January 1867 to duplicate list as No. 1248, and rebuilt in December 1867 with Ramsbottom boiler. Renumbered as 1920 in December 1871 and scrapped in August 1881.

No. 4 *Lichfield*
2-2-2 built by W. Fairbairn & Sons in 1849.
Cost £2,070. Outside sandwich frames. Driving wheels 5 ft 9 in. Cylinders 16 in. x 20 in. In July 1859 numbered in LNWR Southern Division as No. 300. Rebuilt in 1860, and renumbered as LNWR No. 900 in April 1862. To duplicate list as No. 1249 in January 1867, renumbered as 1922 in December 1871, and scrapped in April 1874.

No. 5 *Burton*
2-2-2 built by Sharp Brothers, on 19th May, 1849, possibly Works No. 581.
Cost £1,500 plus £389 for tender. Driving wheels 5 ft 6 in. Cylinders 15 in. x 20 in. In July 1859 numbered in LNWR Southern Division as No. 53. Renumbered as LNWR No. 653 in April 1862, and rebuilt in May 1869 as a saddle tank. During much of the early 1870s it worked on the Nuneaton-Leicester line. To duplicate list as No. 1887 in January 1875, and scrapped 26th March, 1877.

No. 6 *Stafford*
2-2-2 built by Sharp Brothers, in May 1849, possibly Works No. 584.
Cost £1,500 plus £389 for tender. Driving wheels 5 ft 6 in. Cylinders 15 in. x 20 in. In July 1849 numbered in LNWR Southern Division as No. 84. Rebuilt in 1859 and renumbered as LNWR No. 684 in April 1862. In May 1871 rebuilt as a saddle tank. Worked on Nuneaton-Leicester line during 1870s. To duplicate list as No. 1913 in January 1875, and scrapped 20th January, 1879.

No. 7 *Bescot*
2-2-2 built by Sharp Brothers, in June 1849, possibly Works No. 585.
Driving wheels 5 ft 6 in. Cylinders 15 in. x 20 in.
In July 1859 numbered in LNWR Southern Division as No. 116. Renumbered as LNWR
No. 716 in April 1862, and rebuilt in September 1869 as a saddle tank. Worked on
Nuneaton-Leicester line during 1870s. To duplicate list as No. 1924 in January 1875, and
scrapped 4th April, 1879.

No. 8 *Birmingham*
0-6-0 built by W. Fairbairn & Sons, as a Sharp Brothers 'Sphynx' type in 1849. Cost £2,240
including tender. Driving wheels 5 ft 0 in. Cylinders 18 in. x 24 in.
In July 1859 numbered in LNWR Southern Division as No. 307. Renumbered as LNWR
No. 907 in April 1862. To duplicate list in May 1866 as No. 1165. Rebuilt as a saddle tank
around 1868 and restored to capital list as No. 1156 in December 1871. To duplicate list
again, in May 1877 as No. 1935, and scrapped 30th April, 1880.

No. 9 *Wolverhampton*
0-6-0 built by W. Fairbairn & Sons, as a Sharp Brothers 'Sphynx' type in 1849.
Cost £2,240 including tender. Driving wheels 5 ft 0 in. Cylinders 18 in. x 24 in.
In July 1859 numbered in LNWR Southern Division as No. 308. Renumbered as LNWR
No. 908 in April 1852. To duplicate list as No. 1173 in May 1866. Rebuilt as a saddle tank
around 1868, and restored to capital list as No. 1157 in December 1871. Sold in August
1875 to Richard Evans & Co., Haydock Colliery, Lancashire for £1,295, where it became
their *Newton*, and was still running in the early 1880s.

No. 10 *Belvidere*
0-4-2 built by W.J. & J. Garforth & Co., Dukinfield Foundry, Lancashire, in 1850. Inside
frames. Driving wheels 5 ft 0 in. Cylinders 16 in. x 22 in.
Never allocated a LNWR Southern Division number. Probably scrapped *c*.1859.

No. 11 *Angerstein*
0-4-2 built by W.J. & J. Garforth & Co., Dukinfield Foundry, Lancashire, in 1850. Inside
frames. Driving wheels 5 ft 0 in. Cylinders 16 in. x 22 in.
In July 1859 numbered in LNW Southern Division as No. 221. Renumbered as LNWR No.
821 in April 1862. To duplicate list as No. 1179 in May 1863. Renumbered as 1865 in
December 1871, and scrapped at Crewe 10th February, 1876.

No. 12 *Pelsall*
0-6-0 built by Robert Stephenson & Co. in January 1851, probably Works No. 632.
Driving wheels 5 ft 0 in. Cylinders 18 in. x 24 in.
In July 1859 numbered in LNWR Southern Division as No. 309. Renumbered as LNWR
No. 909 in April 1862. In January 1865 rebuilt as an 0-6-0ST, and to duplicate list as No.
1188 in February 1867. Renumbered as 1806 in December 1871. On 10th February, 1874
sold for £1,100 to Wrexham, Mold & Connah's Quay Railway as their No. 7, being
renumbered to No. 3 in 1876. In 1882 rebuilt as an 0-6-2ST and withdrawn in 1899. Many
parts were used in the construction of a 2-6-0T in 1901 that became GCR No. 400B in
January 1905, and was scrapped in June 1907.

No. 13 *Alrewas*
0-6-0 built by Robert Stephenson & Co. in January 1851, probably Works No. 634
Driving wheels 5 ft 0 in. Cylinders 18 in. x 24 in.
In July 1859 numbered in LNW Southern Division as No. 310. Renumbered as LNWR No.
910 in April 1862. To duplicate list as No. 1143 in May 1866. Renumbered as 1801 in

December 1871. Rebuilt as an 0-6-0ST in 1868. Sold for £1,065 to Barber Walker & Co., Eastwood, Nottingham on 13th April, 1875 where it became their No. 7. Final disposition in period 1892-1901, details unknown.

No. 14 *Sylph*
2-4-0T built 1852 by Sharp Brothers, Works No. 675.
Cost £1,720. Outside sandwich frames. Driving wheels 5 ft 0 in. Cylinders 16 in. x 20 in.
In July 1859 numbered in LNWR Southern Division as No. 111. Renumbered as LNWR No. 711 in April 1862. To duplicate list as No. 1208 in October 1863. Given 16 in. x 22 in. cylinders by 1867. Renumbered as 1831 in December 1871. Sold for £700 to Northampton & Banbury Junction Railway in April 1873, probably scrapped 1875 or 1876.

No. 15 *Safety*
2-4-0T built 1852 by Sharp Brothers, Works No. 676.
Cost £1,720. Outside sandwich frames. Driving wheels 5 ft 0 in. Cylinders 16 in. x 20 in.
In July 1859 numbered in LNW Southern Division as No. 112. Renumbered as LNWR No. 712 in April 1862. To duplicate list as No. 1209 in September 1863. Given 16 in. x 22 in. cylinders by 1867. Renumbered as 1830 in December 1871. On 9th August, 1873 sold for £900 to contractors Scott & Edwards of Chester. Used firstly on a contract in Cardiff, then on the Lancashire & Yorkshire Railway Lytham connecting line contract from1873 to 1876, and advertised for sale on 14th January, 1876. Final disposal not known. This may have been their *Lady Cornewall*, hired to the Golden Valley Railway around 1887. This engine worked on the Nottingham suburban Railway, and was advertised for sale in 1890 as 'Lady Cornwall, 16 inch, by LNWR'.

No. 16 *Viper*
0-6-0 built by E.B. Wilson & Co. in December 1852.
Outside sandwich frames. Driving wheels 5 ft 0 in. Cylinders 16 in. x 24 in.
In July 1859 numbered in LNW Southern Division as No. 301. Renumbered as LNWR No. 901 in April 1862. Replaced in 1864, and possibly given duplicate list No. 1166 (*see Further Comments, below*).

No. 17 *Stag*
0-6-0 built by E.B. Wilson & Co. in January 1853.
Outside sandwich frames. Driving wheels 5 ft 0 in. Cylinders 16 in. x 24 in.
In July 1859 numbered in LNWR Southern Division as No. 302. Renumbered as LNWR No. 902 in April 1862. Replaced in 1864, and possibly given duplicate list No. 1170 (*see Further Comments, below*).

No. 18 *Esk*
2-4-0 built by E.B. Wilson & Co. in May 1853.
Outside frames. Driving wheels 5 ft 9 in. Cylinders 16 in. x 20 in. (may have been built with 6 ft 6 in. driving wheels and 16 in. x 22 in. cylinders).
In July 1859 numbered in LNW Southern Division as No. 160. Renumbered as LNWR No. 760 in April 1862. At Bushbury shed in 1863, with regular duty as Wolverhampton station pilot. To duplicate list as No. 1205 in October 1863. New boiler in 1867. Renumbered as 1935 in December 1871, and scrapped in April 1876.

No. 19 *Justin*
2-4-0 built by E.B. Wilson & Co. in May 1853.
Outside frames. Driving wheels 5 ft 9 in. Cylinders 16 in. x 20 in. (may have been built with 6 ft 6 in. driving wheels and 16 in. x 22 in. cylinders).

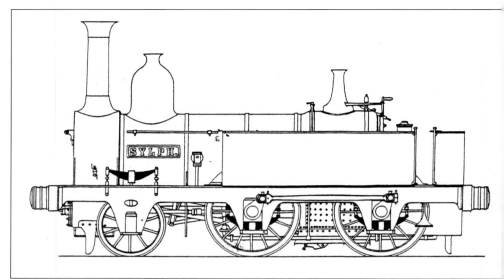

One of only two 2-4-0Ts, both built by Sharp Brothers of Manchester in 1851, No. 14 *Sylph* became LNWR Southern Division No. 111 and was sold out of service in March 1873.
Courtesy Harry Jack

No. 16 *Viper* was one of two 16 in. 0-6-0s with 5 ft driving wheels and sandwich frames produced by E.B. Wilson of Leeds in 1853, and became LNWR Southern Division No. 301. Both of these engines were sold out of service in 1864, but the individual identities are not known, so the individual purchasers cannot be confirmed. *Courtesy Harry Jack*

In July 1859 numbered in LNW Southern Division as No. 181. Renumbered as LNWR No. 781 in April 1862. To duplicate list as No. 1207 in October 1863. Renumbered as 1936 in December 1871, and scrapped in October 1874.

No. 20 *Priam*
0-6-0 built by Vulcan Foundry in April 1855, Works No. 381.
Double-framed. Driving wheels 5 ft 0 in. Cylinders 17 in. x 24 in.
Originally ordered for Shrewsbury & Hereford Railway, but order diverted to SSR. In July 1859 numbered in LNWR Southern Division as No. 305. Renumbered as LNWR No. 905 in April 1862. Given 5 ft 6 in. Driving wheels at Wolverton by 1863. To duplicate list as No. 1226 in February 1866, and withdrawn in 1867.

No. 21 *Ajax*
0-6-0 built by Vulcan Foundry in April 1855, Works No. 382.
Double-framed. Driving wheels 5 ft 0 in. Cylinders 17 in. x 24 in.
Originally ordered for Shrewsbury & Hereford Railway, but order diverted to SSR. In July 1859 numbered in LNWR Southern Division as No. 306. Renumbered as LNWR No. 906 in April 1862. Given 5 ft 6 in. driving wheels at Wolverton by 1863. To duplicate list as No. 1227 in February 1866. Renumbered as 1827 in December 1871. Sold for £700 to Northampton & Banbury Junction Railway in June 1872. Probably scrapped in 1875 or 1876.

No. 22 *Bilston*
0-4-2 built by Beyer, Peacock & Co. in July 1856, Works No. 29.
Cost £2,750. Inside frames. Driving wheels 5 ft 0 in. Cylinders 16 in. x 24 in.
In July 1859 numbered in LNWR Southern Division as No. 304. Renumbered as LNWR No. 904 in April 1862. To duplicate list as No. 1269 in December 1867. Restored to capital list as 1177 in December 1871. Scrapped as 'cut up No. 1984' 26th March, 1877.

No. 23 *Derby*
0-4-2 built by Beyer, Peacock & Co. in July 1856, Works No. 30.
Cost £2,750. Inside frames. Driving wheels 5 ft 0 in. Cylinders 16 in. x 24 in.
In July 1859 numbered in LNWR Southern Division as No. 303. Renumbered as LNWR No. 903 in April 1862. To duplicate list as No. 1268 in December 1867. Restored to capital list as 1176 in December 1871, and at Bangor shed in the early 1870s. Scrapped as 'cut up No. 1986' 14th July, 1877.

No. 24 *Cannock*
0-6-0 built March 1858 by W. Fairbairn & Sons.
Cost £2,950. Inside frames. Driving wheels 5 ft 0 in. Cylinders 18 in. x 24 in.
Fell into Elwell's Pool, Wednesbury after the wooden bridge collapsed in June 1859. The recovery and repair cost £110 17s. 7 ½d. which was recharged by the LNWR to the SSR. In July 1859 numbered in LNWR Southern Division as No. 311. Renumbered as LNWR No. 911 in April 1862. Rebuilt in 1865 and to duplicate list as No. 1982 in July 1877. Scrapped 30th July, 1879.

No. 25 *Bloxwich*
0-6-0 built March 1858 by W. Fairbairn & Sons.
Cost £2,950. Inside frames. Driving wheels 5 ft 0 in. Cylinders 18 in. x 24 in.
In July 1859 numbered in LNWR Southern Division as No. 312. Renumbered as LNWR No. 912 in April 1862. Rebuilt in 1865 and to duplicate list as No. 1808 in April 1878. Scrapped 1st December, 1879.

E.B. Wilson also provided two 2-4-0s in 1853 for passenger work, this one being No. 19 *Justin*. It became LNWR Southern Division No. 181 in the 1859 renumbering, and No. 782 in the 1862 renumbering. It was scrapped in April 1874.   *Courtesy Harry Jack*

The Vulcan Foundry of Newton-le-Willows built this 17 in. 0-6-0 No. 21 *Ajax* as one of a pair in 1855. It was renumbered as No. 306 under the LNWR Southern Division in 1859, and was sold out of service in 1872.   *Courtesy Harry Jack*

No. 26 *McConnell*
0-6-0 built April 1858 by W. Fairbairn & Sons.
Cost £2,950. Inside frames. Driving wheels 5 ft 0 in. Cylinders 18 in. x 24 in.
In July 1859 numbered in LNWR Southern Division as No. 313. Renumbered as LNWR No. 913 in April 1862. Rebuilt in 1865 and to duplicate list as No. 1809 in April 1878. Scrapped 12th March, 1881.

No. 27 *Vauxhall*
0-6-0 built May 1858 by W. Fairbairn & Sons.
Cost £2,950. Inside frames. Driving wheels 5 ft 0 in. Cylinders 18 in. x 24 in.
In July 1859 numbered in LNWR Southern Division as No. 314. Renumbered as LNWR No. 914 in April 1862. Rebuilt in 1865 and to duplicate list as No. 1829 in April 1878. Scrapped 14th January, 1881.

No. 28 *Aston*
0-6-0 built May 1858 by W. Fairbairn & Sons.
Cost £2,950. Inside frames. Driving wheels 5 ft 0 in. Cylinders 18 in. x 24 in.
In July 1859 numbered in LNW Southern Division as No. 315. Renumbered as LNWR No. 915 in April 1862. Rebuilt in December 1863 and to duplicate list as No. 1871 in May 1878. Scrapped 17th October, 1878.

No. 29 *Tipton*
0-6-0 built June 1858 by W. Fairbairn & Sons.
Cost £2,950. Inside frames. Driving wheels 5 ft 0 in. Cylinders 18 in. x 24 in.
In July 1859 numbered in LNWR Southern Division as No. 31. Renumbered as LNWR No. 916 in April 1862. Rebuilt in 1868 and to duplicate list as No. 1879 in May 1878. Scrapped 26th August, 1878.

Further comments

All locomotives had inside cylinders.

Nos. 10 and 11 probably originate with John Brogden, who was awarded the contract for the construction of the South Eastern Railway's line from the Grand Surrey Canal to Erith, and from Gravesend to Rochester in 1847. In February 1849 a 22 ton locomotive was hauled from London to Charlton by 38 horses, and put on to temporary rails at Woolwich. This was probably one of two locomotives advertised in *The Times* of 30th August, 1849 for sale on the following day at Blackheath, upon completion of the construction contract. They were stated to have been built new for this job, and to have only worked for six months. However, although they were said to have been built by Garforth of Duckenfield [*sic*], they were further described as 12 in. x 16 in tender engines. Baxter's list of SSR locomotives (*see Bibliography*) gives *Belvidere* and *Angerstein* as built in 1850 and having cylinders of 16 in. x 24 in. and 16 in. x 22 in. respectively. Despite the discrepancies, the North Kent names ascribed to the SSR locomotives, and the obvious connection to John Brogden, an associate of John Robinson McClean, gives credence to this being their origin.

One of the 0-6-0s built by E.B. Wilson, No. 16, was possibly sold to the Grand Trunk Railway of Canada on 1st July, 1864 for £700. On arrival it was rebuilt as a 4-4-0 with 5 ft 6 in. driving wheels and 16 in. x 24 in. cylinders, and there after worked on the Port Huron to Detroit section of the line in the USA, until it was scrapped around 1889.

The other Wilson 0-6-0, No. 17, was possibly sold for £600 on 2nd August, 1864 to Eckersley & Bayliss, contractors on the MR extension from Rowsley to Buxton.

In G.P. Neele's *Railway Reminiscences*, mention is made of two LNWR Northern Division locomotives at Walsall in 1859 - *Saracen* and *Stork*, which were presumably on loan.

The locomotive line drawings are reproduced from *Locomotives of the LNWR Southern Division* (RCTS, 2001) with the kind permission of the author, Harry Jack.

Webb 5 ft 6 in. 2-4-2T in LMS red livery as No. 6707 on the turntable at the rear of Ryecroft shed around 1924-1928. This engine was built in June 1894 and withdrawn in January 1936. The northlight pattern of the original shed roof is clearly evident.   *R.S. Carpenter/Lens of Sutton*

Walsall's Ryecroft shed in its heyday, on 7th July, 1935 with Webb 5 ft 6 in. 2-4-2T LMS No. 6685 on the easternmost shed road. This engine was built in September 1893 as LNWR No. 2216, and withdrawn in August 1947.   *A.N.H. Glover/A. Wycherley/Kidderminster Railway Museum*

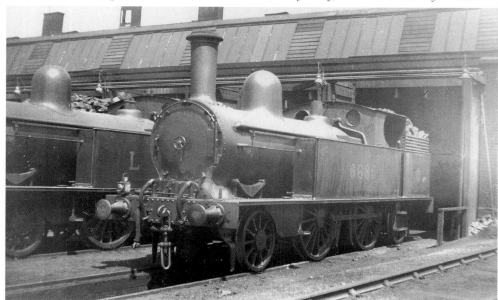

Appendix Three

Walsall (Ryecroft) Shed Allocations

Allocation as at March 1939 - 64 locomotives

LMS Fowler '3MT' 2-6-2T	9, 11, 16, 17, 18, 19, 45, 50, 54, 69
LMS Stanier '3MT' 2-6-2T	110, 143, 144, 154
LMS Fowler '4MT' 2-6-4T	2351, 2390
MR Johnson '3F' 0-6-0	3410, 3502
LMS Fowler '4F' 0-6-0	4068, 4069, 4339, 4506, 4507, 4508, 4512
LMS Stanier '5MT' 4-6-0	5417, 5418
LNWR Webb 5 ft 6 in. 2-4-2T	6637, 6643, 6661, 6679, 6685, 6689, 6741, 6742, 6743, 6755
LNWR Webb '17 in.' 0-6-0	8246, 8247, 8251, 8289, 8308, 8313, 28088, 28105
LNWR Webb 'Cauliflower' 0-6-0	8594, 8597
LNWR '7F' 0-8-0	8913, 8943, 9015, 9032, 9081, 9173, 9174, 9189, 9195, 9222, 9230, 9283, 9309, 9375
MR Kirtley double-framed 2-4-0	20008
MR Johnson 2-4-0	20157
MR Johnson '2F' 0-6-0	22907

1945 allocation list - 52 locomotives

LMS Fowler '3MT' 2-6-2T	9, 11, 17, 18, 19, 45, 69
MR Johnson '2P' 4-4-0	462, 501
LMS Stanier '4MT' 2-6-4T	2448, 2466, 2562, 2627
MR Johnson '3F' 0-6-0	3410, 3502, 3786
LMS Fowler '4F' 0-6-0	4068, 4069, 4115, 4339, 4441, 4454, 4488, 4506, 4507, 4512
LNWR Webb '5 ft 6 in.' 2-4-2T	6661, 6679, 6685, 6689
LNWR '7F' 0-8-0	8902, 9015, 9040, 9048, 9174, 9222, 9232, 9248, 9266, 9283, 9325, 9364
LNWR Webb '17 in.' 0-6-0	28088, 28093, 28105, 28246, 28247, 28251, 28289, 28313
LNWR Webb 'Cauliflower' 0-6-0	28594, 28597

Allocation as at 22nd May, 1958 - 39 locomotives

LMS Stanier '3MT' 2-6-2T	40080, 40173
LMS Fowler '2P' 4-4-0	40673, 40692
LMS Ivatt '2MT' 2-6-2T	41213, 41223, 41234, 41279
LMS Stanier '4MT' 2-6-4T	42482, 42560, 42586, 42604, 42627
LMS Fowler '4F' 0-6-0	44078, 44115, 44444, 44448, 44512
LMS Stanier '5MT' 4-6-0	45344, 45395, 45419
LMS Fowler '3F' 0-6-0T	47296
LNWR '7F' 0-8-0	48905, 48943, 49020, 49114, 49249, 49278, 49301, 49343, 49373
MR Johnson '2F' 0-6-0	58122, 58169, 58174, 58181
MR Johnson '3F' 0-6-0	58283
LMS 0-6-0 diesel-electric shunter	12056
BR 0-6-0 diesel-electric shunters:	D3021, D3091

April 1965 allocation - 2 locomotives

BR 0-6-0 diesel-electric shunters:	D3021, D3091

Several former MR types found themselves at Ryecroft shed after the closure of the MR shed at Pleck, including this Johnson '1102' class half-cab 0-6-0T LMS No. 1690. It had been built in 1879 as MR No. 1420 and was finally withdrawn in June 1951 but never received its BR-allocated number 41690. The LNWR water tank and 'coal hole' is prominent in the background, and the date is 8th September, 1929.   *L.W. Perkins/A. Wycherley/Kidderminster Railway Museum*

Ryecroft shed had a number of the unfortunate Fowler 2-6-2Ts on its allocation over the years, including this one, LMS No. 69. It is seen at Ryecroft shed on 15th April, 1939 with the LNWR water tank and coal stage in the background, along with the 1937 mechanical coaling plant. These locomotives could be seen on all of the local passenger duties emanating from Walsall, until replaced by newer Stanier and Fairburn class '4' engines.

L.W. Perkins/A. Wycherley/Kidderminster Railway Museum

Ryecroft shed's Stanier 'Black Five' 4-6-0 LMS No. 5417 having its tender filled at the coaling plant installed in 1937. The original LNWR 'coal hole' with water tank mounted above is immediately behind. In the background a Webb 2-4-2T stands on one of the shed roads. This photograph was taken during 1940 from the ash handling plant. *R. Selvey*

Ex-Midland Railway Johnson '2F' class 0-6-0 No. 58277 on Ryecroft shed *circa* 1950. Locomotives of this type were used on the local lightly-laid colliery lines, such as the Leighswood branch *P. Wilson*

Appendix Four

Industrial Locomotives

Locomotives known to have worked on the industrial standard gauge lines in the area are listed below. To identify the type of locomotive the wheel arrangement has been shown in the usual fashion for steam locomotives. Locomotives whose driving wheels are connected by rods are shown as 0-4-0D, etc. Those whose wheels are driven by chains or motors are shown as 4w (4-wheel). These abbreviations for type have also been used:

DE	Diesel-electric
DH	Diesel-hydraulic
DM	Diesel-mechanical
ST	Saddle tank
T	Tank engine
VBTG	Vertical boilered tank engine with geared transmission

The following abbreviations for locomotive builders have been used:

AB	Andrew Barclay, Sons & Co. Ltd, Kilmarnock
AE	Avonside Engine Co. Ltd, Bristol
BD	Baguley-Drewry Ltd, Burton-on-Trent
Bg	E.E. Baguley Ltd, Burton-on-Trent
BP	Beyer, Peacock & Co. Ltd, Manchester
Crewe	LNWR, Crewe Works
Derby	BR, Derby Works
FE	Falcon Engine & Car Works Ltd, Loughborough
FH	F.C. Hibberd & Co. Ltd, Park Royal, London
JF	John Fowler & Co. (Leeds) Ltd, Hunslet, Leeds.
HC	Hudswell, Clarke & Co. Ltd, Leeds
HE	Hunslet Engine Co. Ltd, Leeds
HL	R. & W. Hawthorn, Leslie & Co. Ltd, Newcastle-upon-Tyne
JS	John Smith, Coven, Staffs
K	Kitson & Co. Ltd, Leeds
LF	Lloyds Foster & Co. Ltd, Wednesbury
Lill	Lilleshall Co. Ltd, Oakengates, Shropshire
MW	Manning, Wardle & Co. Ltd, Leeds
P	Peckett & Sons Ltd, Bristol
RH	Ruston & Hornsby Ltd, Lincoln
RS	Robert Stephenson & Co. Ltd, Newcastle-upon-Tyne
S	Sentinel Waggon Works Ltd, Shrewsbury
WB	W.G. Bagnall Ltd, Stafford

FROM DUDLEY TO WICHNOR

Engine	Type	Cylinders	Builder	Works No.	Dates on site
Babcock & Wilcox Ltd, Dudley Port Works					
No. 12	4wDM		RH	3049/1945	1945-1963

A second RH diesel locomotive is believed to have worked here at some point, identity and duration unknown.

Engine	Type	Cylinders	Builder	Works No.	Dates on site

Horseley Bridge and Thomas Piggott Ltd, Atlas Iron Works, Dudley Port

Engine	Type	Cylinders	Builder	Works No.	Dates on site
River	0-4-0ST	Outside	?	?	11.1918-1933
Pioneer	0-4-0ST	Outside	MW	1368/1897	7.1915-1928
J.T. Daly	0-4-0ST	Outside	WB	2450/1931	4.1931-7.1969
Noel	0-4-0ST	Outside	P	1172/1912	15.8.1946-21.11.1946
	0-4-0DM		AB	351/1941	By 3.1962-*c.*2.1969
	4wDM		RH	408496/1957	30.12.1968-15.1.1983

The sidings were originally worked by horses or capstans from their opening in 1865. Unknown locomotives may have been used prior to the first one recorded here in 1918. *J.T. Daly* (WB 2450) and RH 408496 have both been subsequently preserved.

J. Cashmore Ltd, Great Bridge Scrapyard

Engine	Type	Cylinders	Builder	Works No.	Dates on site
12077	0-6-0DE		Derby	/1950	10/1971-1979
AMW 150	0-4-0DM		JF	22498/1939	1973-Not known
AMW 213	0-4-0DM		JF	22960/1941	1973-Not known

12077 has been subsequently preserved. Many former BR locomotives were scrapped here, but they were not used for shunting the yard, as were these listed here.

Hill Top Foundry Co. Ltd, Wednesbury

Engine	Type	Cylinders	Builder	Works No.	Dates on site
	4wDM		Bg	2107/1937	12.1957-*c.*4.1972

Rail traffic had actually ceased by 1970. The locomotive was sold to nearby R.A. Giblin Ltd, see below.

Walsall Corporation, later West Midlands Gas Board, Walsall Gasworks, Pleck

Engine	Type	Cylinders	Builder	Works No.	Dates on site
Economy	0-4-0ST	Outside	FE	/1883	1883-*c.*1908
597	0-4-0ST	Outside	P	597/1895	*c.*12.1896-*c.*5.1970
Marchnant	0-6-0ST	Inside	HE	687/1898	11/1907 – 1936
	0-4-0ST	Outside	P	1897/1936	7.1936-*c.*5.1970
	4wVBTG	Vertical	S	9632/1957	1957-12.1970

Gas production ceased August 1968, but rail traffic continued into 1969. Sentinel 9632 has been subsequently preserved.

John Russell & Co. Ltd, Cyclops Ironworks and Alma Tubeworks, Pleck

Engine	Type	Cylinders	Builder	Works No.	Dates on site
	4wVBTG	Vertical	S	7299/1928	1928-1930

Sidings at first worked by horses, but a locomotive was used from December 1902. Details are not known, but there may have been two Aveling Porter 4-wheel locomotives in use, possibly converted from road locomotives.

Leighswood Colliery Co. Ltd, Leighswood, near Aldridge

Engine	Type	Cylinders	Builder	Works No.	Dates on site
Leighswood	0-6-0ST	Inside	BP	1829/1878	11.1878-15.6.1881

This Bagnall 0-4-0ST *J.T. Daly* (2450/1931) shunted the works of the Horseley Bridge & Thos Piggott Ltd at Dudley Port from its delivery in April 1931 until July 1969. It is seen here on 2nd March, 1967, shortly before its retirement, when it was preserved, and at present can be found on the island of Jersey.   *A.N.H. Glover/F.A. Wycherley*

This Peckett 'R4' class 0-4-0ST (1897/1936) never received a running number or name, during its life, which was spent entirely at Walsall gas works. In this undated view, it has evidently received some fire damage to its paintwork. It was eventually cut up at Cashmore's scrapyard at Great Bridge around 1970.   *J. Tarrant/Kidderminster Railway Museum*

Engine	Type	Cylinders	Builder	Works No.	Dates on site

Pelsall Coal & Iron Co. Ltd, Pelsall Ironworks, Furnaces and Collieries

Engine	Type	Cylinders	Builder	Works No.	Dates on site
(Fame)	2-4-0T	Outside	Crewe	/1848	8/1859-not known
	0-6-0ST	Inside	RS	628/1848	1864-not known
Victor	0-6-0T		JS	/c.1865	1865-c.1920
Pelsall	0-6-0T		JS	/c.1865	1865-1893
	0-6-0ST		JS		Not known
Countess of Essex	0-4-0ST	Outside	BP	1148/1872	c.1894-not known
	0-4-0ST	Outside	AB	658/1889	c.1903-not known
No. 135 Enterprise	0-4-0ST				c.1903-not known

The LNWR also hired in two locomotives for short periods; one in December 1869, and one in October 1873. The No. 12 pit was taken over by Walsall Wood Colliery Co. Ltd and worked until c.1903. Slag at the site was reprocessed by John Freakley from around 1903 to 1920, using *Victor* plus the last two locomotives.

Walsall Wood Colliery Co. Ltd (later National Coal Board), Walsall Wood Colliery

Engine	Type	Cylinders	Builder	Works No.	Dates on site
Countess of Essex	0-4-0ST	Outside	BP	1148/1872	c.1881-By 1894
Cannock Wood	0-6-0ST	Inside	Lill	160/1870	1882-not known
Pelsall	0-6-0T		JS	/c.1865	By 1893-c.1918
5 Lord Kitchener	0-6-0ST	Inside	K	5158/1915	8.1915-4.1965
6 Lord French	0-6-0ST	Inside	K	5171/1916	11.1916-1948
Victor	0-6-0T		JS	/c.1865	By 1920-not known
Nuttall	0-6-0ST	Outside	HE	1685/1931	7.1948-6.1950, then 8.1955-8.1956
No. 3 Hanbury	0-6-0ST	Inside	P	567/1894	7.1949-c.1953
Aynho	0-6-0ST	Inside	MW	1722/1909	c.4/1950-1951
Griffin	0-6-0ST	Inside	K	5036/1913	1953-3.1962
Tony	0-6-0ST	Outside	HL	3460/1921	2.1959-5.1965
	0-4-0ST	Outside	AB	2247/1948	5.1964-9.1964 then 3.1965-5.1965

Colliery closed October 1964.

FROM WEDNESBURY TO PRINCES END

Central Electricity Authority (later Central Electricity Generating Board), Ocker Hill Power Station, Wednesbury

Engine	Type	Builder	Works No.	Dates on site
No. 1	4wDM	RH	245036/1947	5.1948-c.8.1978
2	4wDM	RH	394014/1956	1956-17.7.1978

Rail traffic ceased in March 1977 when the station was converted to oil burning.

John Bagnall & Sons Ltd, Leabrook Ironworks, Wednesbury

Engine	Type	Builder	Works No.	Dates on site
	0-4-0DM	HE	2372/1941	1941-2.1966
	4wDM	RH	218045/1942	5.1965-10.1970
	4wDM	RH	269603/1949	1969-c.1982
24	4wDM	RH	398611/1957	c.9.1971-5.1984
53	4wDM	FH	4016/1964	22.4.1970-5.1984

Most of RH 218045 was scrapped in October 1970, but the frames were retained for use as a carrier wagon until around December 1976. The siding connection to the Princes End line was taken out during 1980, but locomotives continued to shunt internal traffic until the works closed on 4th May, 1984.

Walsall Wood Colliery used this large outside-cylinder Hawthorn Leslie 0-6-0ST *Tony* (3460/1921) from February 1959 until May 1965 when it was scrapped on site. In this photograph dated 6th March, 1965 it is awaiting its fate.

L.W. Perkins/A. Wycherley/Kidderminster Railway Museum

The Patent Shaft & Axletree Co. Ltd had a sizeable internal railway system linking their Brunswick, Monway, and Old Park works at Wednesbury, and thus required a sizeable fleet of locomotives. Here are two examples, posed at the Old Park Works: Hawthorn Leslie 0-4-0ST *Shifter II* (2603/1905) on the left, and Andrew Barclay 0-4-0ST No. 8 (1064/1908) on the right.

A.N.H. Glover/A. Wycherley/Kidderminster Railway Museum

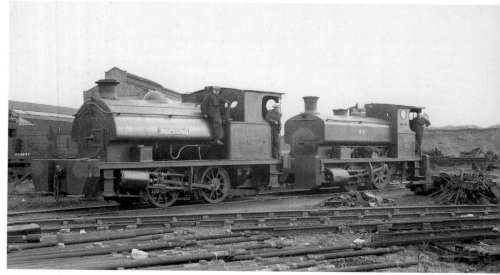

Engine	Type	Cylinders	Builder	Works No.	Dates on site

FROM THE DARLASTON LOOP

R.A. Gilbin Ltd (later Charles B. Pugh Ltd), Stafford Street Works, Wednesbury

Engine	Type	Cylinders	Builder	Works No.	Dates on site
	4wDM		Bg	2107/1937	c.4.1972-1991
L14	4wDM		RH	235515/1945	5.1972-c.1994
(L8)	4wDM		RH	349038/1954	5.1972-c.1994

All three locomotives have been preserved: the last two left this location sometime between 13th October, 1993 and 20th April, 1996.

Patent Shaft & Axletree Co. Ltd (later Patent Shaft Steel Works Ltd), Brunswick, Monway & Old Park Works, Wednesbury (production stopped in 1976 and rail traffic ceased in June 1980)

Engine	Type	Cylinders	Builder	Works No.	Dates on site
	0-4-0T		LF?		1867-not known
	0-4-0T		LF?		1867-not known
Britannia	0-4-0ST	Outside	LF?		1867-1900
Old Park	0-4-0ST	Outside	MW	855/1882	Not known
Monway	0-4-0ST	Outside	HL	2170/1889	1889-not known
Shifter	0-4-0ST	Outside	HL	2403/1898	1898-1911
5 Brunswick	0-4-0ST	Outside	AE	1409/1900	1900-c.3.1951
7 Century	0-4-0ST	Outside	AE	1414/1900	1900-c.1939
Shifter II	0-4-0ST	Outside	HL	2603/1905	1905-1949, then 1956-10.1957
6	0-4-0ST	Outside	HL	2624/1905	1905-1946
7	0-4-0ST	Outside	HL	2636/1906	1906-not known
No. 8	0-4-0ST	Outside	AB	1064/1906	1906-1949
No. 9	0-4-0ST	Outside	HL	2782/1909	1909-1911, then 1916-c.1963
No. 10	0-4-0ST	Outside	HL	2889/1911	1911-1916, then 1917-10.1957
1	0-4-0ST	Outside	AE	1766/1917	1917-1960
8	0-4-0ST	Outside	AE	1767/1917	1917-12.1917, then 21.1.1927-11.1958
2	0-4-0ST	Outside	AE	1781/1917	1917-3.1962
3	0-4-0ST	Outside	AE	1794/1917	1917-9.1966
Basic	0-4-0ST	Outside	AE	1549/1909	23.9.1925-1939
William	0-4-0DM		RH	408297/1957	1957-28.10.1980
Desmond	0-4-0DM		RH	414302/1957	1957-1979
Alan	0-4-0DM		RH	414304/1957	1957-22.10.1980
Harold	0-4-0DM		RH	418788/1957	1957-c.7.1974
Archibald	0-4-0DM		RH	418789/1957	1964-1.11.1980
Arnold	0-4-0DM		RH	421701/1958	1958-c.7.1974
Christopher	0-4-0DM		RH	437364/1961	1961-10.1980
	0-4-0DM		RH	281268/1950	1.1972-c.7.1974
	0-4-0DE		RH	418596/1957	9.3.1973-29.10.1980
Harvey	0-4-0DH		HE	7261/1972	1972-8.1980
Colin	0-4-0DH		HE	7346/1973	1973-12.1980
Brian	0-4-0DH		HE	7406/1977	1977-c.21.10.1980
Peter	0-4-0DH		HE	7424/1978	1978-28.10.1980

The first three locomotives came from Lloyds Foster & Co. Ltd when that works was acquired in 1867. That company is known to have built some locomotives, and so one or all three may have been built by them.

Engine	Type	Cylinders	Builder	Works No.	Dates on site
Bradley & Foster Ltd, Darlaston Green Furnaces					
	0-4-0ST	Outside	HL	2441/1899	Not known
Caponfield	0-4-0ST	Outside	WB	1649/1901	c.1922-1949
Solent	0-4-0ST	Outside	AE	2036/1931	10.1933-c.5.1960
Daisy	0-4-0ST	Outside	HC	691/1904	4.1935-c.1960
	0-4-0ST	Outside	HL	2739/1908	c.1938-not known
Brafos No. 1	0-4-0ST	Outside	WB	2663/1942	1942-7.1961
	4wDM		RH	441938/1960	1960-1972

Although the company and its predecessors on this site had been rail connected since 1863, this was worked by LNWR locomotives until 1910 when the internal system was enlarged and the company's own locomotives were then used. Rail traffic ceased on the standard gauge system ceased in 1972 and the connection was removed. A 3 ft gauge internal system in the ironworks used the following locomotives:

4wDM	RH	210495/1942	1942-c.1981
4wDM	RH	466582/1961	c.1969-c.1981
4wDM	BD	3750/1979	1979-3.1986

A further small 2ft gauge tramway used a 4wBE loco built by S. H. Hayward, but was disposed of around 1969 and the tramway replaced by a conveyor.

Bradley & Foster Ltd used a number of engines at its Darlaston Green Furnaces, including this Hudswell, Clarke 0-4-0ST *Daisy* (691/1904). In this view from 11th January, 1947 it is hard at work, but it was scrapped around 1960.

L.W. Perkins/A. Wycherley/Kidderminster Railway Museum

Appendix Five

Chronological List of Important Events

1845   Incorporation of OWWR (4th August).
1846   Formation of the LNWR (16th July).
       Incorporation of the SSJR (3rd August).
       Incorporation of the TVMGJR (3rd August).
       Incorporation of the BWDR (3rd August).
       Merger of the SSJR and TVGJMR to form the SSR (6th October).
1847   Contract for Walsall to Wichnor line awarded to Thomas Earle (17th May).
       Contract for Walsall to Dudley line awarded to Hoof & Hill (17th May).
       Act passes to confirm new status of the SSR (9th July).
       BoT inspection requested for Walsall to Bescot line (14th October).
       Walsall to Bescot line opened for passenger traffic (1st November).
1848   BoT inspector approves Walsall to Lichfield line (1st March).
       BoT inspector approves Lichfield to Wichnor line (4th April).
1849   Walsall to Wichnor line opens for all traffic (9th April).
       New Walsall station in Station Street opened (9th April)
       First train runs to Dudley, temporary station opened (1st November).
1850   Bescot Bridge station closed.
       Walsall to Dudley opens for goods traffic (1st March).
       BoT inspection passed Walsall to Dudley line (11th April).
       Walsall to Dudley opens for passengers, second Dudley station opened (1st May).
1850   Lease of SSR to John Robinson McClean starts (1st July).
1851   Sedgeley Junction to Dudley Port High Level line authorized (24th July).
1852   LNWR station at Dudley Port High Level opened (1st July).
       John Robinson McClean sub-contracts running of trains to LNWR (5th July).
       Permanent station at Dudley opened (20th December).
       OWWR opened to Dudley (20th December).
1853   Dudley to Dudley Port services commence (14th October).
1854   Birmingham to Kidderminster services via Dudley Port commenced (2nd January).
       All SSR line trains run from New Street station on its opening (1st June).
       Act passed authorizing Cannock and Norton branches (2nd June).
       Engine shed erected at Wichnor Junction.
1855   New island platform constructed at Dudley.
       Act passed authorizing Wyrley, Darlaston, Tipton and Leighswood branches (23rd July).
1856   Ryder's Hays station opened (April).
       LNWR Southern division takes over supply of locomotives and men to SSR.
1857   Contract issued for erection of engine shed at Walsall (5th June).
1858   Walsall to Cannock line opened for passenger traffic (1st February).
       Ryder's Hays station closed (May).
1859   Dual gauge spur from GWR to SSR at Wednesbury opened (1st June).
       New 'joint' station opened at Dudley.
       Act passed authorizing Darlaston loop, and Tipton branch (13th August).
1860   Wichnor engine shed opened.
       McClean surrenders lease; new lease of SSR granted to LNWR (1st February).
1861   LNWR starts regular passenger services from Birmingham to Burton (1st December).
       LNWR starts goods services from SSR line over MR to Burton (4th December).

1863	Darlaston loop line, Tipton branch and new Wednesbury station opened (14th September).
1864	Ocker Hill station opened (1st July).
1866	GWR starts passenger services from Birmingham Snow Hill to Dudley via SSR (1st September).
1867	Birmingham to Kidderminster services cut back to Dudley.
	SSR vested in the LNWR (15th July).
1871	SSR Lichfield Trent Valley Junction station closed (3rd July).
	TVR Lichfield Trent Valley station closed (3rd July).
	Lichfield Trent Valley High and Low Level stations opened (3rd July).
1872	Serious flood at Walsall station (23rd July).
	WWR opened from Wolverhampton to Walsall (1st November).
1872	Darlaston loop line doubled and opened (22nd December).
1875	WWR vested in the LNWR (1st July).
	Serious flood at Walsall station (20th July).
1876	WWR sold by the LNWR to the MR (1st July).
1877	Act passed authorising Leighswood branch, and Pleck and Portobello curves (28th June).
	Wichnor Junction station closed (1st November).
1878	Leighswood branch opened (14th November).
1879	MR Birmingham to Walsall goods services via Sutton Park commenced (1st January).
	MR goods services from Wichnor to Walsall curtailed (19th May).
	MR Birmingham to Walsall passenger services via Sutton Park commenced (1st July).
	New MR goods depot opened at Walsall (1st July).
1880	Ryecroft locomotive shed opened.
	Act passed authorizing Walsall Wood branch (6th August).
	Stechford to Aston LNWR line opened for goods traffic (7th September).
1881	Bescot Bridge station reopened and renamed Wood Green (Old Bescot), (1st February).
	Pleck-James Bridge and Portobello-Heath Town curves opened (1st March).
1882	Walsall Wood branch opened.
	Stechford to Aston LNWR line opened for passenger traffic (1st March).
1883	South-facing curve at Tipton Junction opened (1st January).
1884	New Walsall station at Park Street opened (1st January).
	Sutton Coldfield to Lichfield line opened for goods traffic (1st September).
	New station at Lichfield City opened, and old one closed (3rd November).
	Sutton Coldfield to Lichfield line opened for passenger traffic (5th December).
1885	Birmingham to Derby through trains via Sutton Coldfield, Lichfield commenced (1st May).
1886	Serious flood at Walsall station (13-14th May).
1887	Darlaston loop line passenger services withdrawn (1st November).
1889	Serious fire destroys GWR station and part of LNWR station at Dudley (6th January).
1890	Tipton branch services withdrawn (1st November).
1895	Tipton branch services recommenced (1st July).
1896	Wichnor Junction engine shed closed.
1909	Route sharing agreement between MR and LNWR starts (1st January).
	Rushall station closed (1st March).
1912	LNWR omnibus services from Brownhills commenced (1st October).
1915	LNWR omnibus services from Brownhills withdrawn (17th April).
	GWR Snow Hill-Dudley passenger services suspended (29th November).

1916   Tipton branch passenger services withdrawn (1st January).
       Major fire at Walsall station ; Park Street entrance closed (1st April).
1917   New up goods loop and siding installed at Mesty Croft.
       Pleck station closed (1st January).
1920   GWR Snow Hill-Dudley passenger services restored (5th January).
1923   MR and LNWR absorbed into the new LMSR (1st January).
       Walsall station reconstructed after 1916 fire finally reopened (4th November).
1924   Pleck station reopened (1st May).
       Brownhills LNWR station renamed 'Brownhills High Street' (2nd June).
1925   MR engine shed at Pleck closed (2nd September).
1927   'Pines Express' commenced, calling at Walsall three times per week (Summer).
1930   Brownhills High Street station renamed 'Brownhills' (1st August).
1931   MR passenger services on WWR line withdrawn (5th January).
1939   'Pines Express' suspended (11th September).
1941   Birmingham New Street to Dudley via Dudley Port services withdrawn.
       Wood Green station closed (5th May, 1941).
1946   'Pines Express' reintroduced (May).
1947   'Pines Express' suspended due to severe weather (January), restarted (Easter).
1948   LMSR vested in the nationalized BR (1st January).
1950   Great Bridge station renamed 'Great Bridge North' (1st July).
       Dudley WR and LMR goods depots renamed as 'Castle' and 'Town' (19th July).
1956   DMUs introduced on Birmingham to Lichfield route, via Sutton Coldfield (March).
1958   DMUs introduced on Birmingham to Walsall route (June).
       Steam locomotives removed from Ryecroft depot (9th June).
       'Motorail' service, Sutton Coldfield to Stirling commenced (Summer).
       Pleck station closed (17th November).
1959   Hammerwich station reduced to unstaffed halt.
1962   'Pines Express' rerouted away from Walsall (10th September).
       New goods depot opened at Walsall (7th October).
1963   Darlaston Junction to Fallings Heath closed completely (24th December).
1964   Passenger services withdrawn and intermediate stations closed (18th January):
           Lichfield City to Wichnor Junction
           Walsall to Lichfield City
           Walsall to Water Orton, via Sutton Park
           Walsall to Wolverhampton, via Pleck
           Walsall to Rugeley
       New power box opened at Pleck Junction ('Walsall') replacing four manual boxes
       (3rd April).
       Norton Junction to East Cannock Junction line closed (25th May).
       Dudley to Dudley Port services withdrawn (15th June).
       Swan Village to Dudley passenger services withdrawn and Dudley WR closed
       (15th June).
       Walsall to Dudley passenger services withdrawn and Dudley LMR closed (6th July).
       Leighswood branch officially closed (August).
       Walsall Wood branch closed (October).
       Ryecroft diesel depot closed.
1967   Dudley WR and LMR stations, and WR goods depots demolished.
       Ryecroft Junction box closed, replaced by enlargements at Walsall PSB (4th June).
       Dudley Freightliner depot comes into use (July).
       Dudley Freightliner depot officially opened (6th November).
1968   Fallings Heath to Patent Shaft sidings, Wednesbury closed completely (1st January).
       WR line from Swan Village to Horseley Bridge Junction closed completely (1st
       January).

1972 'Motorail' service from Sutton Coldfield withdrawn (17th September).
1977 Electrified services commenced from Walsall to Birmingham (May).
Serious flood at Walsall station (28th January).
1978 Demolition of Walsall station for redevelopment commenced (January).
Serious flood at Walsall station (28th January).
Demolition of Walsall station completed (1st October).
1979 Remaining short section of Darlaston loop closed completely.
1980 New Walsall station opened (Summer).
1981 Tipton branch closed completely (6th April).
1984 Anglesea sidings to Ryecroft closed completely (19th March).
1986 Last train leaves Dudley Freightliner depot (29th September).
1987 Wednesbury Steel Terminal closed.
1988 Lichfield Trent Valley High Level rebuilt and reopened (28th November).
1992 Electrified services began from Lichfield TV High Level to Redditch (30th November).
1993 Pleck Junction to Dudley closed completely (19th March).
2001 Charrington's Oil Depot at Anglesea, and line northwards to Lichfield, closed.

Bibliography and Acknowledgements

Primary documentation has been accessed at the following locations:

The National Archives, Kew - Minutes and records of the South Staffordshire Junction Railway, the South Staffordshire Railway, the Trent Valley Midlands & Grand Junction Railway, the London, Worcester & South Staffordshire Railway, and selected records of the London & North Western Railway, and the Oxford, Worcester & Wolverhampton Railway.

Staffordshire County Archives, Stafford and Lichfield – Deposited plans, Parliamentary Acts, the records of the Manchester, Lichfield & Birmingham Railway, Ordnance Survey maps, *Lichfield Mercury, Lichfield Post*, photographic collections.

Dudley Archive Services, Coseley – *Wolverhampton Chronicle*, photographic collections

Sandwell History Centre, Smethwick – *Midland Advertiser, Wednesbury Herald*, photographic collections.

Stafford Library – *Staffordshire Advertiser*.

Walsall Local History Centre – Ordnance Survey maps, *Walsall Advertiser, Walsall Observer & South Staffordshire Chronicle*.

William Salt Library, Stafford – *Staffordshire Advertiser*, Parliamentary Acts.

Wolverhampton Archives – Ordnance survey and other maps, *Express & Star, Wolverhampton Chronicle*.

London & North Western Railway Society – Working timetables, gradient schedules.

Author's collection – Photographs, public timetables, working timetables and sectional appendices.

The following secondary sources of information have been consulted:

The History of Walsall Station by B.J. Adshead (privately published, 1980)
Portrait of the Pines Express by S. Austin (Ian Allan,1998)
Cross City Connections by J. Bassett (Brewin Books, 1990)
British Locomotive Catalogue 1825-1923, Volumes 2A and 2B, LNWR and its constituent companies by B. Baxter (Moorland, 1978 and 1979)
British Locomotive Catalogue 1825-1923, Volume 3A, Midland Railway and its constituent companies by B. Baxter (Moorland, 1982)

Ocker Hill (100 years) by Revd F. Brighton (E. Blocksidge, 1949)

Rails Across the City by J. Boynton (Mid England Books)

Celebration of Steam - West Midlands by J.B. Bucknall (Ian Allan, 1994)

The GWR at Stourbridge and the Black Country, The Life, The Times, The Men, Volumes One & Two by C. Butcher (Oakwood Press, 2004 and 2005)

The Directory of Railway Stations by R.V.J. Butt (Patrick Stephens, 1995)

Staffordshire Railways by P.L. Clark (University of London Institute of Historical Research, 1967)

Track Layout Diagrams of the GWR and BR/WR, Section 31, West Midlands by R.A. Cooke

A Regional History of the Railways of Great Britain Volume 7, The West Midlands by R. Christiansen (David & Charles, 1983)

Railways of the West Midlands, A Chronology, 1808-1954 by C.R. Clinker (Stephenson Locomotive Society, 1954)

Darlaston Community History Project, Darlaston Community, 1994

Memories of Walsall - A Pictorial Record by A. Douglas (Birmingham Post & Mail, 1989)

Birmingham New Street - The story of a great station (parts 1,2,3) by R. Foster (Wild Swan, 1990)

A Pictorial Record of LNWR Signalling by R.D. Foster (Oxford Publishing Company, 1982)

It Ay Ere Our Kid by A. French (Walsall Local History Centre, 2000)

Mark Huish and the London & North Western Railway - A Study of Management by T.R.Gourvish (Leicester University Press, 1972)

History of Tipton by F. Hackwood (Brewin Books, 2001)

Railway Reminiscences by J. Haddock (Walsall Museum & Library Service, 1984)

Walsall Remembered by J. Haddock & R. Vyse (Tempus Publishing, 2004)

The Canals of the West Midlands by C. Hadfield (David & Charles, 1969)

LMS Engine Sheds Volume One, The LNWR by C. Hawkins and G. Reeve (Wild Swan, 1981)

LMS Engine Sheds Volume Two, The Midland Railway by C. Hawkins and G. Reeve (Wild Swan, 1981)

The Story of Bloxwich by E.J. Homeshaw (Walsall Local History Centre, 1988)

Locomotives of the LNWR Southern Division by H. Jack (RCTS, 2001)

'Locomotive Sheds, Part One: the LNWR' by 'Perseus' (L.W. Jones), *SLS Journal Vol. XXXIV, No. 395, May 1958*

West Midlands Branchline Album by A.J. Lambert (Ian Allan, 1978)

The South Staffordshire Railway 1846-1867 by J.T. Leach (Staffordshire County Council, 1992)

A Picture Tour of Shelfield, Pelsall and Rushall by W. Mayo and J. Sale (published privately)

Railway Reminiscences by G.P.Neele (McCorquodale, 1904, reprinted by E.P. Publishing, 1974)

War Record of the London & North Western Railway by Edwin A. Pratt (Selwyn & Blount Ltd, 1922, reprinted by the LNWR Society, 2007)

A Gazeteer of the Railway Contractors and Engineers of Central England 1830-1914 by L. Popplewell (Melledgen Press, 1986)

The North Western at Work by Dr R. Preston Hendry and R. Powell Hendry (Patrick Stephens, 1990)

The Oxford, Worcester & Wolverhampton Railway by S.C. Jenkins and H.I. Quayle (Oakwood Press, 1977)

Freightmaster, No. 23 Autumn 2001 by M. Rawlinson (Freightmaster Publications, 2001)

Brownhills, A Walk Into History by G. Reece (Walsall Local History Centre, 1996)

Crewe Locomotive Works and Its Men by B. Reed (David & Charles, 1982)

The London & North Western Railway, A History by M.C. Reed (Atlantic Transport Publishing, 1996)

The Brewery Railways of Burton on Trent by C. Shepherd (Industrial Railway Society, 1996)

Industrial Archaeology of Staffordshire by R. Sherlock (David & Charles, 1976)

Industrial Locomotives of the West Midlands by R.A. Shill (Industrial Railway Society, 1992)

Industrial Locomotives of South Staffordshire by R.A. Shill (Industrial Railway Society, 1993)

British Railways Layout Plans of the 1950s, Volume 11: LNW lines in the West Midlands, Signalling Record Society (1998)

British Railways Layout Plans of the 1950s,Volume 16: Ex-MR lines Derby to Barnt Green, Burton to Leicester and Branches, Signalling Record Society (2003)

West Midland Railway History by D. Spencer (privately published)

The History of the London & North Western Railway by W.L. Steel (1914)

An Illustrated History of LNWR Engines by E. Talbot (Oxford Publishing Co., 1985)

Pelsall, A Thousand Years of Village Life by A. Tomkinson & A. Galbraith (Walsall Local History Centre, 1994)

Britain in Old Photographs, Around Pelsall and Brownhills by D.F. Vodden (Sutton Publishing, 1998)

Britain in Old Photographs, Around Bloxwich by D.F. Vodden (Sutton Publishing, 1998)

A Short History of Rushall - anon - (Walsall Library & Museum Services, June 1982)

Pregrouping in the West Midlands by P.B. Whitehouse (Oxford Publishing Co., 1984)

Railways of the Black Country, Volume 1 - The Byways by Ned Williams (Uralia Press, 1984)

Black Country Folk at Werk by N. Williams (Uralia Press, 1989)

I Remember Pelsall by V. Woolridge (Walsall Local History Centre, 2002)

'The Junction That Moved' by C.R. Potts, *The Signalling Record* (SRS, 2002)

Contemporary traffic reports from various issues of *Railway Magazine, Trains Illustrated, Modern Railways* and *Railway Observer.*

Several articles appearing in *The Blackcountryman* (the journal of the Black Country Society) have also been consulted, as follows:

'Days of the "Dudley Dasher"' by J. Haddock (Spring 1976 (Vol. 9, No. 2)

'The Saga of Sedgeley Junction, Part One' by M. Hale (Summer 1977, Vol. 10, No. 3)

'The Saga of Sedgeley Junction, Part Two' by M. Hale (Summer 1977, Vol. 10, No. 4)

'The South Staffordshire Railway, Part One' by C.J.L. Elwell (Autumn 1977, Vol. 10, No. 4)

'The South Staffordshire Railway, Part Two' by C.J.L. Elwell (Winter 1978, Vol. 11, No. 1)

'The South Staffordshire Railway, Part Three' by C.J.L. Elwell (Autumn 1993, Vol. 26, No. 4)

'Sedgeley Signal Box' by J.H. Lloyd (Winter 1978, Vol. 11, No. 1)

'A Glimpse of Palethorpes' Rail Traffic' by K. Lloyd (Autumn 1981, Vol. 14, No. 4)

'Princes End and Its Railway' by M. Hale (Autumn 1992, Vol. 25, No. 4)

'Princes End and Its Railway - Conclusion' by M. Hale (January 1993, Vol. 26, No. 4)

'Busy Lines at Dudley' by K. Tibbetts (Summer 1993, Vol. 26, No. 3)

'Railway Reminiscences: Dudley Station 1938-41' by K. Tibbetts (Autumn 1993, Vol. 26, No. 4)

This work could not have been completed without considerable help and cooperation from many people who were keen to see a finished result. These include Audie Baker, Roger Carpenter, Ian Falcus, Jack Haddock, Michael Hale, Keith Hodgkins, Harry Jack, Bill Mayo, Robert Selvey, Terry Smitheman and Ted Talbot. Mention should also be made to the staffs at the local libraries used to accumulate information and provide local contacts: Brownhills, Dudley, Pleck, Rushall, Tipton, Walsall, Walsall Wood, Wednesbury, and Pelsall History Centre.

Every effort has been made to ensure that photographs used in this work are credited to the appropriate photographer and/or copyright holder. In some cases the author has not been able to determine the individuals, and apologies are offered to anyone omitted or incorrectly attributed.

Index